E G L I

BEYOND THE
NEW LEFT

Other books by IRVING HOWE

Sherwood Anderson: A CRITICAL BIOGRAPHY
William Faulkner: A CRITICAL STUDY
Politics and the Novel
A World More Attractive
The American Communist Party: A CRITICAL HISTORY
(with Lewis Coser)
Thomas Hardy: A CRITICAL STUDY
Steady Work: ESSAYS IN DEMOCRATIC RADICALISM
The Decline of the New: LITERARY AND CULTURAL ESSAYS

BEYOND THE NEW LEFT

Edited and with an introduction by

Irving Howe

THE McCALL PUBLISHING COMPANY

NEW YORK

CONTENTS

BEYOND THE
NEW LEFT

INTRODUCTION

by Irving Howe

The analysis and critique of the New Left that appears in this book stems, in the main, from the political outlook of democratic socialism. I say in the main, because a few of the authors included here might not care to identify themselves with this or any other political outlook. So it seems best to note that each writer speaks for himself. Here, in this brief introduction, I will avoid repeating what the contributors to this book say, and will confine myself mainly to some historical background.

What *is* the New Left? The phrase has become part of our journalistic currency, but the phenomena to which it points are barely a decade old and remain strikingly diverse in character, scattered in organization, and not always coherent in statement. In any traditional sense, the New Left does not comprise a structured movement. Whenever it has tried to form a national organization, as at the disastrous Conference for a New Politics held in Chicago during the summer of 1967, it has quickly fractured into several hostile groups. As this is being written, Students for a Democratic Society, the major New Left group, is split into three or four embattled factions, with the two main ones using physical violence on one another, as if intent upon reenacting the worst of Stalinism. (Says Mark Rudd, leader of the SDS Weatherman faction, "We sometimes beat them up [the other faction] and they beat us up. What we usually do is beat them up when we find them. . . ." *The New York Times,* 26 September 1969.)

The New Left has become an important force, though only in certain limited segments of American society. It has made no impact on such major institutions as the trade unions or such major social groups as the working class, which is by traditional Marxist expectations the lever of revolution. It has not been able to establish itself as a significant presence in either national or regional politics (e.g., the pitiably small vote received by Eldridge Cleaver and Dick Gregory in the 1968 election, the failure of New Leftists to win even a primary in a stronghold like Berkeley). But the New Left has had a notable effect on campus life; it has exerted an oblique influence on the more extreme black militants; and it has contributed to the growth of a distinctive "youth culture," as well as to the swinging, pop-guerrilla, middle-class culture that has scored commercial successes in our cities.

Some questions about New Left influence are hard to answer. The claim is often made that it has played a major role in mobilizing public sentiment, even if through confrontationist shock tactics, against the Vietnam war. My own judgment is that large sections of both the American population and our political leadership turned to opposing the war mainly out of a realization that it could not be won short of an intolerable escalation. Nevertheless, it seems indisputable that on this score, despite some exaggeration, the New Left deserves credit. It did play a valuable role in stirring dissent against the war, it did serve as a pressure on the conscience of liberals. Yet the paradox that must be noted here is that such credit is of a kind that the New Left can't, in ideological consistency, be very enthusiastic about. For a central New Left dogma has insisted that "the system can't be changed," and that to achieve even limited ends it is necessary to complete a wholesale social transformation, what is loosely called these days "a revolution." (Like many other New Left notions, this one is rarely developed or examined: *Which* limited ends can't be achieved short of revolution? ending the war in Vietnam? the abolition of racial discrimination? reform of the universities?) Insofar as the New Left claims credit for mobilizing popular sentiment in behalf of changing U.S. policy in Vietnam—and I think it has some right to make that claim—it undercuts its "revolutionary" theories and tacitly acknowledges that, despite its intentions and rhetoric, it has played the role of a pressure or reformist group mobilizing sentiment for change within this society. I see nothing dishonorable in playing such a role. I only wish to point to the problems it presents the New Left. And let me also stress that it is not I, or people of my persuasion, who insist that achieving short-range goals within the present society is incompatible with working toward long-range social change.

If, however, we do try to estimate the short-run consequences of New Left activities, we must also look at the other side of the balance. We must ask ourselves, how much sentiment has the New Left helped to mobilize for the far Right? to what extent has it contributed to the victories of Nixon in the country as a whole, Reagan in California, and Stenvig in Minneapolis? Now, there is no completely accurate or "scientific" way of measuring the consequences of any political conduct, not even conduct as abrasive as that of the New Left; but every available source of evidence—from opinion polls to electoral results to the use of common sense—indicates that among large segments of the middle and working classes there has set in a strong, though not yet violent, reaction against New Left methods. My impression is that the more candid New Left spokesmen would not deny this, for believing as they do in "polarization" (that is, in provoking large numbers of people toward the extremes of the political spectrum and thereby dislodging and disabling the liberal center), some of them would actually see the growth of the far Right as a tribute to their own effectiveness. And so it is, though hardly in the way they suppose. For what the New Left, in its feckless hunger for apocalypse, fails to reckon with is the probable lineup of forces in this country if there is to be a "polarization" during the next few years—to say nothing of the probable victor in such a showdown. Soberly estimating the likely consequences of its tactics isn't one of the strong points of the New Left.

Other questions concerning its influence are equally hard to answer. To what extent, for instance, was the recent appearance of that promising political tendency we call the New Politics— the leftist-liberal coalition associated with the campaigns of Senator Eugene McCarthy and the late Senator Robert Kennedy—a consequence of pressures from the New Left? Again, there can't be an assured reply, but I for one would be prepared to say that yes, some credit should go to the New Left. Saying that, however, I would also want to note that most New Left segments, and especially SDS, sneered at and refused to support Senator McCarthy's candidacy when he rallied public sentiment against the war. One New Left spokesman, Tom Hayden, even declared publicly that "a vote for George Wallace would further his objective more than a vote for RFK." (*Village Voice*, 30 May 1968.) Both the morality and the logic of such a view seem too shabby to require an answer.

As writers in Part Two of this book argue, the New Left has made few serious contributions to political thought or cultural experience. Whatever interest the New Left shows in political theory is usually directed toward the work of older writers whose work it appropriates and sometimes twists for its own sake. At the same time the New Left has had a considerable impact on intellectual styles and fashions, reviving radical sentiments in elderly men of letters who found it expedient to restrain themselves during the conservative fifties, providing a rhetoric of excitement for young writers often well-attuned to the demands of the market, and helping to make "radicalism" a hot journalistic property in magazines as various as *Esquire* and *The New York Review of Books*. A series of heroes and gurus from the intellectual world has been raised to fame by the student New Left: Mills, Goodman, Marcuse, and Chomsky at home, and Fanon, Debray, and Guevara abroad. (Goodman, who has a habit of being critical, has recently been dismissed from the role of mentor.) Our intellectual life is especially susceptible to the lures of novelty, and novelty is what some people have supposed the New Left to be providing—especially those whose historical memories extend no further back than a decade or two, or who do not trouble to read books older than themselves.

In its few years of existence, the New Left has already gone through two distinct phases. The first was a phase of populist fraternity, stressing an idealistic desire to make real the egalitarian claims of the American tradition, a non- and even anti-ideological approach to politics, and a strategy of going into local communities in order to help oppressed minorities. Perhaps the major stimulant to this early New Left was the upsurge of the American Negroes in the early 1960s, as they began to struggle for their dignity as men and for their rights as citizens. And perhaps the most dramatic action of the early New Left was the journey hundreds of young people took in the summer of 1963 to live and work in Mississippi, helping Negroes organize themselves for local community and political ends. The main slogan of that moment—appealing but vague—was "participatory democracy." For those of us committed to democratic socialism, this first phase of the New Left was, despite occasional tactical blunders, a profoundly welcome and promising reinvigoration of American political life. How many of the young people who responded to the appeal of nonviolence, fraternity, and an undogmatic radicalism would later remain with the New Left we don't really know. Clearly, many of the founders of the Student Nonviolent Coordinating Committee, black and white youth who believed in both integration and nonviolence, abandoned that group once it fell into the hands of people like Stokely Carmichael and Rap Brown.

The second phase of the New Left signifies a sharp turn: away from fraternal sentiment and back to ill-absorbed dogma, away from the shapelessness of "participatory democracy" and back to the rigidity of vanguard elites, away from the loving spirit of nonviolence and back to a quasi-Leninist fascination with violence. In this second phase the New Left grows in numbers yet makes certain, through its sterile authoritarianism, that it will not be more than a blown-up reincarnation of the radical sects of the past.

What are the causes of this sharp change? The break-up of the Negro-labor-liberal coalition that had sparked the civil rights movement and ensured the victory of John F. Kennedy; the despair, most of it warranted and authentic, over U.S. involvement in Vietnam; the rise of separatist and nationalist sentiment among black youth; an intense disillusionment not only with liberal politics of the moment but with the whole idea of liberalism; and the growing appeal of the "Third-World Revolution" conceived (or misperceived) by the New Left as an odd blend of romantic anarchism and Leninist authoritarianism. In this second phase of the New Left, it sometimes seemed as if the SDS were transforming itself into a society for the resurrection of the god that failed. Notions, dogmas, ideologies, and slogans that an earlier generation of radicals had discarded after painful reflection and experience now came back in crude form. The theory of "social fascism," Stalin's contribution to the victory of Hitlerism, was transformed into a theory of "liberal fascism" by SDS leaders. The idea of a self-appointed "vanguard" that will prod the sluggish masses into rebellion—one of the more dubious contributions of Leninist orthodoxy—was uncritically embraced by affluent middle-class students. Confrontationist tactics, often similar to those Lenin had so caustically denounced in *Left-Wing Communism: An Infantile Disorder*, were used by SDS and other New Left groups with no visible concern for how well or poorly they had worked in the past, or what their likely consequences would be in the future. The vulgar-Marxist notion that "bourgeois democracy" is no more than a mask for the domination of capital and therefore not to be valued by radicals, found strong echoes in the sixties. And perhaps most distressing of all, the liberal values of tolerance and respect for the rights of opponents were sneeringly dismissed in accordance with the formulas of Herbert Marcuse. To be sure, not all New Leftists succumbed to this authoritarian debauch; some, like Greg Calvert, former SDS National Secretary, complained sadly about the "Stalinization of the New Left" and looked back wistfully to its earlier years; but, in the main, the drift was toward the sectarian wastelands, marked by the ideologizing of the Maoists and the adventurism of the Guevarists.

(In this book, the two opening essays, by myself and Michael Harrington, respectively, deal primarily with what I've called the first phase of the New Left, though both contain warnings that there is an authoritarian potential in its populist sentiment. These are followed by my critique of the New Left's "confrontation" methods. The next essay, by Richard Lowenthal, is, I think, the most extensive and profound analysis yet to appear of the second phase of the New Left; it offers a fundamental critique such as I cannot pretend to undertake in a brief introduction. And Paul Goodman's essay tries to establish a certain historical distance from contemporary phenomena, so that the New Left is seen not in exclusively political terms at all but rather as a quasireligious upsurge. The reader will note that these essays, arranged in order of publication, roughly parallel the political development of the New Left.)

It now begins to seem that we are on the verge of still another phase in the development of the New Left. Some elements within it—the Weathermen and the Crazies, for example—seem to be abandoning what they have regarded as orthodox Leninism and to be turning to a mixture of violent adventurism, staged desperation, and even hooliganism, all marked by symptoms of social pathology. Any contrast between the United States today and Russia in the late nineteenth century must of course be made with a maximum of caution, yet it is hard to avoid the impression that the desperado-totalitarian Left, in both the United States and Europe, is a reenactment of the politics of Nechaev, the Russian terrorist of the late nineteenth century. The Weathermen, having given up hope for the proletariat, now see the main revolutionary force in our society as the high school students; their experience may yet lead them to the kindergartens. Nor is it impossible that we may also see in this country the desperate children of the affluent reenacting the terrorism of Russia in the 1880s.

How far some elements—not, it should be said in fairness, the majority—of the New Left have sunk into the pathology of violence can be seen from the following report about a Weatherman gathering, which appeared in the 10 January 1970, issue of *The Guardian*, a New Left weekly. The report summarizes the keynote speech of Bernardine Dohrn, former interorganization secretary of SDS:

> Dohrn characterized violent, militant response in the streets as "armed struggle" against imperialism. . . .
> "We're about being a fighting force alongside the blacks, but a lot of us are still honkies and we're still scared of fighting. We have to get into armed struggle."
> Part of armed struggle, as Dohrn and others laid it down, is terrorism. Political assassination—openly joked

about by some Weathermen—and literally any kind of violence that is considered anti-social were put forward as legitimate forms of armed struggle. . . .

A 20-foot long poster adorned a wall of the ballroom. It was covered with drawings of bullets, each with a name. Along with the understandable targets like Chicago's Mayor Daley, the Weathermen deemed as legitimate enemies to be offed, among others, *The Guardian* (which has criticized Weatherman) and Sharon Tate, one of several victims in the recent mass murder in California. She was eight months pregnant.

"Honkies are going to be afraid of us," Dohrn insisted. She went on to tell the war council about Charlie Manson, accused leader of the gang which allegedly murdered the movie star and several others on their Beverly Hills estate. Manson has been portrayed in the media as a Satanic, magnetic personality who held near-hypnotic sway over several women whom he lent out to friends as favors and brought along for the murder scene. The press also mentioned Manson's supposed fear of blacks—he reportedly moved into rural California to escape the violence of a race war.

Weatherman, the "Bureau" says, digs Manson . . .

"Dig it, first they killed those pigs, then they ate dinner in the same room with them, then they even shoved a fork into a victim's stomach! Wild!" said Bernardine Dohrn.

It will be said that these sentiments are in no way characteristic for the thousands of young people who have been protesting against the Vietnam war. I entirely agree. It will be said that the Weatherman group isn't representative of the New Left. In one sense, that also is true. No other New Left tendency has abandoned itself so completely to corrupting fantasies of blood. But it needs to be added that Miss Dohrn's ravings have a connection —distorted, extreme yet with the representativeness of caricature—to things one can hear and see these days among portions of the New Left. The cult of violence, the celebration of bombs, the arrogant identification of a tiny group of affluent youth with the "destiny of the revolution," the adulation of charismatic

authoritarian leaders, the crude hatred for liberal values: all
these can be found in most New Left tendencies, even if without
the vivid pathology of the Weathermen.

The most interesting theoretical question concerning the rapid
changes within the New Left has to do with the relation between its earlier and later phases. Those of us who write for
journals like *Dissent,* whatever our many shortcomings, can at
least claim some credit for having foreseen (the evidence appears in these pages) the possibility that a politics of populist
vagueness would lead to a politics of authoritarian rigidity. For
this decline I would suggest two causes:
1. *The crisis and virtual collapse of U.S. liberalism.* During
the 1960s, with the possible exception of John F. Kennedy's brief
tenure as President and Eugene McCarthy's effort to win the
Democratic nomination, American liberalism has been in a bad
way. Without pretending to a full explanation, let me at least indicate a few summary reasons for this decline: the exhaustion of
traditional New Deal politics, alliances, and outlooks; the appearance of moral-political issues which bread-and-butter liberalism was not equipped to deal with; the involvement of certain
liberal leaders (e.g., Humphrey) in a war that large numbers of
young people rightly saw as indefensible.
A rough but useful axiom can be suggested about recent
American politics: The New Left has flourished as a result of, or
in direct proportion to, the failures and failings of liberalism.
When the candidacies of Eugene McCarthy and Robert Kennedy seemed to offer a significant alternative, a way of realizing
the hopes of the idealistic young through electoral politics, then
thousands of young radicals and liberals flocked to their campaigns. Both on and off the campus, the New Left began to
wither into a marginal group, limited for the time to nasty and
impotent sniping. But when there seemed no viable alternative,
and both candidates in the 1968 presidential election spoke as
supporters of the Vietnam war, then moods of despair swept
across the campus, and the New Left could transform these
moods into a disillusionment with liberal politics in particular
and the idea of liberalism in general. The way was then open

for the growth of anarcho-authoritarian sentiment: Castroite, Maoist, Guevarist, and still more exotic varieties.

2. *An internal connection between the thought of the early New Left and the thought of the later New Left.* What both shared was an impatience, sometimes a distrust, and more recently a downright contempt for the methods and norms of democracy—the "cumbersomeness" or "sham" of representative elections, the "irrelevance" of undemonstrative majorities, the "manipulation" of the masses by politicians and the media, the "dullness" of ordinary middle-class people, and so on. Under the guidance of such authoritarian thinkers as Herbert Marcuse, the New Left in both its phases, though more so in the later one, revealed a profoundly elitist bias. It might speak about "the people," and sometimes even "the workers," but it found its base of support mainly among the alienated middle-class young.

When the phrase "participatory democracy" first began to be heard, it gained its impact partly as a response to a genuine problem that had been troubling both socialist and nonsocialist thinkers for some time: What could be done to stop the gradual erosion of democratic institutions, in which the formal appearance of participation by the people continued but the real substance declined?

At first the New Left's emphasis on "participatory democracy" signified mainly a desire to reinvigorate democracy, to give it greater meaning and immediacy—though the New Left rarely had any concrete proposals for achieving this end. Too often "participatory democracy" meant in practice a blithe dismissal of parliamentary rules within the discussions of the New Left groups, a practice that may have encouraged collective expressiveness (and interminable meetings) but also proved to be peculiarly open to manipulation by tight little factions and charismatic figures emphasizing their modesty. At best such procedures helped enliven—were relevant to—the politics of small groups, but they could contribute almost nothing to solving the problem of democratic politics in large societies, where the sheer number of citizens and complexity of competing interests require a system of representative institutions.

The stress on "participatory democracy" proved to be especially damaging in the curious way it prepared the ground for authoritarian politics. There was not too great a distance between the contempt shown for the limitations of representative institutions by the early New Left and the contempt shown for the very idea of representative institutions by the later New Left. To dismiss "formal democracy" in behalf of "participatory democracy" was in effect to jettison the values of both—as if, in reality, democratic rights didn't always require a commitment to "forms," that is, rules both fixed and open to change through agreed-upon procedures. By the late sixties one rarely heard much about "participatory democracy" from the New Left. Now the fashionable phrase was "revolution," unspecified as to social character, political possibility, or ultimate goal and too often reduced to a ritual of expressiveness that required neither thought nor moral justification.

Those of us who want to preserve and extend democracy while simultaneously working toward fundamental social change must acknowledge that the coming decade is likely to be a time of trouble, even peril. There are linked dangers from the irrationalities and violence of both polar extremes, which together could destroy our hopes for an American movement at once democratic, militant, and radical. The New Left plays a double role here. It contributes valuable energy to the needed task of protest and insurgency, but also a political-moral confusion, sometimes verging on nihilism, which threatens liberal values and helps provoke a popular backlash.

Much recent behavior of New Left students goes against the grain. Destroying computers, burning buildings, breaking up meetings, shouting down teachers in classrooms, carrying guns —this has nothing to do with the socialist, or radical, tradition. It is a strange mixture of Guevarist fantasia, residual Stalinism, anarchist braggadocio, and homemade tough-guy methods.

Nor are our objections merely tactical. The kind of "revolution" envisaged by all the SDS factions has nothing to do with the large-scale social transformation this country needs. Who, with a reasonable impulse to self-preservation and democratic survival, would care to test out the dispensation of a Tom Hayden or Mark Rudd? Worthy fellows, perhaps; but better powerless.

The perspective I would advance for the immediate future combines a broad coalition of popular forces to work for immediate social improvements along a liberal course, and a regathering of those people, now a tiny minority in this country, who believe in the values of democratic socialism. This signifies:

the premise that we are not and will not soon be in a "revolutionary situation";

the subpremise that if "revolutionary activity" in the next few years comes to more than loud talk, it will have an elitist, desperado, and adventurist character;

the belief that it is in our interest to preserve and improve the present agencies of democratic politics, marred as they may be, requiring changes as they do, and even liable to sudden collapse as they are;

the prognosis that the necessary social and economic reforms can be achieved through a reactivated coalition of liberal-left-labor forces, though one that would be different in stress and internal composition from the New Deal–inspired coalition that has slowly been disintegrating these last several years.

I think that the more sensitive and undogmatic elements in and near the New Left will soon have to face the futility of trying to "go it alone." Their movement has grown and it probably will continue to grow; yet, barring some major self-transformation, it will continue to have the character of a sect isolated in fundamental outlook, language, and psychology from the American people. Nevertheless, it contains precious resources of energy and idealism, and this energy and idealism ought to be thrust into the mainstream of American politics.

One can only hope for a slow regathering of forces among the liberal-labor-left in the United States. A movement that fails to understand the needs and aspirations of the American workers and their unions, or which dismisses them contemptuously in the name of some abstract revolutionary purity, is doomed to failure. A movement that fails to understand the urgency of moral protest animating the young, and stays rigidly within the limits of traditional New Deal and post–New Deal liberalism, is also doomed to failure.

Can we then bring together the strategy of coalition with the passions of insurgency? Can we recognize that in the American system wide and loose electoral blocs, inherently unsatisfactory to ideological purists, are essential, while at the same time the idea of stirring the bottom layers of society to speak out for themselves is also urgent? Such a view of things is inherently complex, and this is a moment when many people are seized by a mania for simplicity; but I think it is a political perspective that, no matter how difficult to realize, is required by the present state of things. Oddly enough, if you were to go back to the founding document of SDS, the now-famous Port Huron statement, you would find a view of politics fairly close to what has been said here. One can only hope that many young people will yet return to it.

PART ONE

Analyses and Critiques

NEW STYLES IN "LEFTISM"

by *Irving Howe*

I propose to describe a political style or outlook before it has become hardened into an ideology or the property of an organization. This outlook is visible along limited portions of the political
scene; for the sake of exposition I will make it seem more precise
and structured that it really is.

There is a new radical mood in limited sectors of American society: on the campus, in sections of the civil rights movement.
The number of people who express this mood is not very large,
but that it should appear at all is cause for encouragement and
satisfaction. Yet there is a segment or fringe among the newly
blossoming young radicals that causes one disturbance—and not
simply because they have ideas different from persons like myself, who neither expect nor desire that younger generations of
radicals should repeat our thoughts or our words. For this disturbing minority I have no simple name: Sometimes it looks like
kamikaze radicalism, sometimes like white Malcolmism, sometimes like black Maoism. But since none of these phrases will
quite do, I have had to fall back upon the loose and not very
accurate term, "New Leftists." Let me therefore stress as strongly
as I can that I am not talking about all or the majority of the
American young and not-so-young who have recently come to regard themselves as radicals.

The essay which appears here is a condensed version of a longer study.

The form I have felt obliged to use here—a composite portrait of the sort of New Leftist who seems to me open to criticism—also creates some difficulties. It may seem to lump together problems, ideas, and moods that should be kept distinct. If some young radicals read this text and feel that much of it does not pertain to them, I will be delighted by such a response.

The society we live in fails to elicit the idealism of the more rebellious and generous young. Even among those who play the game and accept the social masks necessary for gaining success, there is a widespread disenchantment. Certainly there is very little of the joy that comes from a conviction that the values of a society are good, and it is therefore good to live by them. The intelligent young know that if they keep out of trouble, accept academic drudgery, and preserve a respectable "image," they can hope for successful careers, even if not personal gratification. But the price they must pay for this choice is a considerable quantity of inner adaptation to the prevalent norms: There is a limit to the social duplicity that anyone can sustain.

The society not only undercuts the possibilities of constructive participation, it also makes very difficult a coherent and thought-out political opposition. The small minority that does rebel tends to adopt a stance that seems to be political, sometimes even ideological, but often turns out to be little more than an effort to assert a personal style.

Personal style: That seems to me a key. Most of whatever rebellion we have had up to—and even into—the civil rights movement takes the form of a decision on how to live individually within this society, rather than how to change it collectively. A recurrent stress among the young has been upon differentiation of speech, dress, and appearance, by means of which a small elite can signify its special status; or the stress has been upon moral self-regeneration, a kind of Emersonianism with shock treatment. All through the fifties and sixties disaffiliation was a central impulse both as a signal of nausea and a tacit recognition of impotence.

Now, to a notable extent, all this has changed since and through the civil rights movement—*but not changed as much as may seem.* Some of the people involved in that movement show an inclination to make of their radicalism not a politics of common action, which would require the inclusion of saints, sinners, and ordinary folk, but rather a gesture of moral recitude. And the paradox is that they often sincerely regard themselves as committed to politics—but a politics that asserts so unmodulated and total a dismissal of society, while also departing from Marxist expectations of social revolution, that little is left to them but the glory or burden of maintaining a distinct personal style.

By contrast, the radicalism of an earlier generation, despite numerous faults, had at least this advantage: It did not have to start *as if* from scratch, there were available movements, parties, agencies, and patterns of thought through which one could act. The radicals of the thirties certainly had their share of bohemianism, but their politics were not nearly so interwoven with and dependent upon tokens of style as is today's radicalism.

The great value of the present rebelliousness is that it requires a personal decision, not merely as to what one shall do but also as to what one shall be. It requires authenticity, a challenge to the self, or, as some young people like to say, an "existential" decision. And it makes more difficult the moral double-bookkeeping of the thirties, whereby in the name of a sanctified movement or unquestioned ideology, scoundrels and fools could be exalted as "leaders" and detestable conduct exonerated.

This is a real and very impressive strength, but with it there goes a significant weakness: the lack of clear-cut ideas, sometimes even a feeling that it is wrong—or worse, "middle-class"—to think systematically, and as a corollary, the absence of a social channel or agency through which to act. At first it seemed as if the civil rights movement would provide such a channel; and no person of moral awareness can fail to be profoundly moved by the outpouring of idealism and the readiness to face danger which characterizes the vanguard of this movement. Yet at a certain point it turns out that the civil rights movement, through the intensity of its work, seems to dramatize . . . its own insufficiency. Indeed, it acts as a training school for experienced, gifted, courageous people who have learned how to lead, how to sacrifice, how to work, but have no place in which to enlarge upon their gifts.

The more shapeless, the more promiscuously absorptive, the more psychologically and morally slack the society becomes, the more must candidates for rebellion seek extreme postures which will enable them to "act out" their distance from a society that seems intent upon a maliciously benevolent assimilation; extreme postures which will yield security, perhaps a sense of consecration, in loneliness; extreme postures which will safeguard them from the allure of everything they reject. Between the act of rebellion and the society against which it is directed, there remain, however, deeper ties than is commonly recognized. To which we shall return.

These problems are exacerbated by an educational system that often seems inherently schizoid. It appeals to the life of the mind, yet justifies that appeal through crass utilitarianism. It invokes the traditions of freedom, yet processes students to bureaucratic cut. It speaks for the spirit, yet increasingly becomes an appendage of a spirit-squashing system.

New Leftism appears at a moment when the intellectual and academic worlds—and not they alone—are experiencing an intense and largely justifiable revulsion against the immediate American past. Many people are sick unto death of the whole structure of feeling—that mixture of chauvinism, hysteria, and demagogy—which was created during the cold war years. Like children subjected to forced feeding, they regurgitate almost automatically. Their response is an inevitable consequence of over-organizing the propaganda resources of a modern state; the same sort of nausea exists among the young in the Communist world.

Unfortunately, revulsion seldom encourages nuances of thought or precise discriminations of politics. You cannot stand the deceits of official anti-Communism? Then respond with a rejection equally blatant. You have been raised to give credit to every American power move, no matter how reactionary or cynical? Then respond by castigating everything American. You are weary of Sidney Hook's messages in *The New York Times Magazine*? Then respond as if talk about Communist totalitarianism were simply irrelevant or a bogey to frighten infants.

Yet we should be clear in our minds that such a response is not at all the same as a commitment to Communism, even though it may lend itself to obvious exploitation. It is rather a spewing out of distasteful matter—in the course of which other values, such as the possibility of learning from the traumas and tragedies of recent history, may also be spewed out.

Generational clashes are recurrent in our society, perhaps in any society. But the present rupture between the young and their elders seems especially deep. This is a social phenomenon that goes beyond our immediate subject, indeed it cuts through the whole of society; what it signifies is the society's failure to transmit with sufficient force its values to the young, or, perhaps more accurately, that the best of the young take the proclaimed values of their elders with a seriousness which leads them to be appalled by their violation in practice.

In rejecting the older generations, however, the young sometimes betray the conditioning mark of the very American culture they are so quick to denounce. For ours is a culture that celebrates youthfulness as if it were a moral good in its own right. Like the regular Americans they wish so hard not to be, yet, through wishing, so very much are, they believe that the past is mere dust and ashes and that they can start afresh, immaculately.

A generation is missing in the life of American radicalism, the generation that would now be in its late thirties, the generation that did not show up. The result is an inordinate difficulty in communication between the young radicals and those unfortunate enough to have reached—or, God help us, even gone beyond —the age of forty. Here, of course, our failure is very much in evidence too: a failure that should prompt us to speak with modesty, simply as people who have tried, and in their trying perhaps have learned something.

Let me specify a few characteristic attitudes among the New Leftists:

1. *An extreme, sometimes unwarranted, hostility toward liberalism.* They see liberalism only in its current version, institutional, corporate, and debased; but avoiding history, they know very little about the elements of the liberal tradition which should remain valuable for any democratic socialist. And thereby they would cut off the resurgent American radicalism from what

is, or should be, one of its sustaining sources: the tradition that has yielded us a heritage of civil freedoms, disinterested speculation, humane tolerance.

2. *An impatience with the problems that concerned an older generation of radicals.* Here the generational conflict breaks out with strong feelings on both sides, the older people feeling threatened in whatever they have been able to salvage from past experiences, the younger people feeling the need to shake off dogma and create their own terms of action.

There are traditional radical topics which no one, except the historically minded, need trouble with. To be unconcerned with the dispute in the late twenties over the Anglo-Russian Trade Union Committee or the differences between Lenin and Luxembourg on the "national question"—well and good. These are not quite burning problems of the moment. But *some* of the issues hotly debated in the thirties do remain burning problems: In fact, it should be said for the anti-Stalinist Left of the past several decades that it anticipated, in its own somewhat constricted way, a number of the problems (especially, the nature of Stalinism) which have since been widely debated by political scientists, sociologists, indeed, by all people concerned with politics. The nature of Stalinism and of post-Stalinist Communism is not an abstract or esoteric matter; the views one holds concerning these questions determine a large part of one's political conduct: and what is still more important, *they reflect one's fundamental moral values.*

No sensible radical over the age of thirty (something of a cutoff point, I'm told) wants young people merely to rehearse his ideas, or mimic his vocabulary, or look back upon his dusty old articles. On the contrary, what we find disturbing in some of the New Leftists is that, while barely knowing it, they tend to repeat somewhat too casually the tags of the very past they believe themselves to be transcending. But we do insist that in regard to a few crucial issues, above all those regarding totalitarian movements and societies, there should be no ambiguity, no evasiveness.

So that if some New Leftists say that all the older radicals are equally acceptable or equally distasteful or equally inconsequential in their eyes; if they see no significant difference between,

say, Norman Thomas and Paul Sweezy such as would require
them to regard Thomas as a comrade and Sweezy as an oppo-
nent—then the sad truth is that they have not at all left behind
them the old disputes, but on the contrary, are still completely in
their grip, though perhaps without being quite aware of what is
happening to them. The issue of totalitarianism is neither academic nor merely historical; no one can seriously engage in politics without clearly and publicly defining his attitude toward it. I
deliberately say "attitude" rather than "analysis," for while there
can be a great many legitimate differences of analytic stress and
nuance in discussing totalitarian society, morally there should be
only a candid and sustained opposition to it.

3. *A vicarious indulgence in violence, often merely theoretic
and thereby all the more irresponsible.* Not being a pacifist, I believe there may be times when violence is unavoidable; being a
man of the twentieth century, I believe that a recognition of its
necessity must come only after the most prolonged consideration,
as an utterly last resort. To "advise" the Negro movement to
adopt a policy encouraging or sanctioning violence, to sneer at
Martin Luther King for his principled refusal of violence, is to
take upon oneself a heavy responsibility—and if, as usually happens, taken lightly, it becomes sheer irresponsibility.

It is to be insensitive to the fact that the nonviolent strategy
has arisen from Negro experience. It is to ignore the notable
achievements that strategy has already brought. It is to evade
the hard truth expressed by the Reverend Ralph Abernathy:
"The whites have the guns." And it is to dismiss the striking
moral advantage that nonviolence has yielded the Negro movement, as well as the turmoil, anxiety, and pain—perhaps even
fundamental reconsideration—it has caused among whites in the
North and the South.

There are situations in which Negroes will choose to defend
themselves by arms against terrorist assault, as in the Louisiana
towns where they have formed a club of "Elders" which patrols
the streets peaceably but with the clear intent of retaliation in
case of attack. The Negroes there seem to know what they are
doing, and I would not fault them. Yet as a matter of general
policy and upon a nationwide level, the Negro movement has
chosen nonviolence: rightly, wisely, and heroically.

There are "revolutionaries" who deride this choice. They show a greater interest in ideological preconceptions than in the experience and needs of a living movement; and sometimes they are profoundly irresponsible, in that their true interest is not in helping to reach the goals chosen by the American Negroes, but is rather a social conflagration which would satisfy their apocalyptic yearnings even if meanwhile the Negroes were drowned in blood. The immediate consequence of such talk is a withdrawal from the ongoing struggles.

4. *An unconsidered enmity toward something vaguely called the Establishment.* As the term "Establishment" was first used in England, it had the value of describing—which is to say, delimiting—a precise social group; as it has come to be used in the United States, it tends to be an all-purpose put-down. In England it refers to a caste of intellectuals with an Oxbridge education, closely related in values to the ruling class, and setting the cultural standards which largely dominate both the London literary world and the two leading universities.

Is there an Establishment in this, or any cognate, sense in the United States? Perhaps. There may now be in the process of formation, for the first time, such an intellectual caste; but if so, precise discriminations of analysis and clear boundaries of specification would be required as to what it signifies and how it operates. As the term is currently employed, however, it is difficult to know who, besides those merrily using it as a thunderbolt of opprobrium, is *not* in the Establishment. And a reference that includes almost everyone tells us almost nothing.

5. *An equally unreflective belief in "the decline of the West"* —apparently without the knowledge that, more seriously held, this belief has itself been deeply ingrained in Western thought, frequently in the thought of reactionaries opposed to modern rationality, democracy, and sensibility.

The notion is so loose and baggy, it means little. Can it, however, be broken down? If war is a symptom of this decline, then it holds for the East as well. If totalitarianism is a sign, then it is not confined to the West. If economics is a criterion, then we must acknowledge, Marxist predictions aside, that there has been an astonishing recovery in Western Europe. If we turn to culture, then we must recognize that in the West there has just

come to an end one of the greatest periods in human culture—
that period of "modernism" represented by figures like Joyce,
Stravinsky, Picasso. If improving the life of the workers is to
count, then the West can say something in its own behalf. And if
personal freedom matters, then, for all its grave imperfections,
the West remains virtually alone as a place of hope. There remains, not least of all, the matter of racial prejudice, and here no
judgment of the West can be too harsh—so long as we remember that even this blight is by no means confined to the West,
and that the very judgments we make draw upon values nur-
tured by the West.

But is it not really childish to talk about "the West" as if it
were some indivisible whole we must either accept or reject
without amendment? There are innumerable strands in the Western tradition, and our task is to nourish those which encourage
dignity and freedom. But to envisage some global apocalypse
that will end in the destruction of the West is a sad fantasy, a
token of surrender before the struggles of the moment.

6. *A crude, unqualified anti-Americanism, drawing from every
possible source, even if one contradicts another: the aristocratic
bias of Eliot and Ortega, Communist propaganda, the specula-
tions of Tocqueville, the* ressentiment *of postwar Europe, etc.*

7. *An increasing identification with that sector of the "third
world" in which "radical" nationalism and Communist authoritarianism merge.* Consider this remarkable fact: In the past decade there have occurred major changes in the Communist world,
and many of the intellectuals in Russia and Eastern Europe have
reexamined their assumptions, often coming to the conclusion,
masked only by the need for caution, that democratic values are
primary in any serious effort at socialist reconstruction. Yet at
the very same time most of the New Leftists have identified not
with the "revisionists" in Poland or Djilas in Yugoslavia—or even
Tito. They identify with the harder, more violent, more dictatorial segments of the Communist world. And they carry this au-
toritarian bias into their consideration of the "third world,"
where they praise those rulers who choke off whatever weak im-
pulses there may be toward democratic life.

About the problems of the underdeveloped countries, among
the most thorny of our time, it is impossible even to begin to

speak with any fullness here. Nor do I mean to suggest that an attack upon authoritarianism and a defense of democracy exhaust consideration of those problems; on the contrary, it is the merest beginning. But what matters in this context is not so much the problems themselves as the attitudes, reflecting a deeper political-moral bias, which the New Leftists take toward such countries. A few remarks:

a. Between the suppression of democratic rights and the justification or excuse the New Leftists offer for such suppression there is often a very large distance, sometimes a complete lack of connection. Consider Cuba. It may well be true that United States policy became unjustifiably hostile toward the Castro regime at an early point in its history; but how is this supposed to have occasioned, or how is it supposed to justify, the suppression of democratic rights (including, and especially, those of all other left-wing tendencies) in Cuba? The apologists for Castro have an obligation to show what I think cannot be shown: the alleged close causal relation between United States pressure and the destruction of freedom in Cuba. Frequently, behind such rationales there is a tacit assumption that in times of national stress a people can be rallied more effectively by a dictatorship than by a democratic regime. But this notion—it was used to justify the suppression of political freedoms during the early Bolshevik years—is at the very least called into question by the experience of England and the United States during the Second World War. Furthermore, if Castro does indeed have the degree of mass support that his friends claim, one would think that the preservation of democratic liberties in Cuba would have been an enormously powerful symbol of self-confidence; would have won him greater support at home and certainly in other Latin-American countries; and would have significantly disarmed his opponents in the United States.

b. We are all familiar with the "social context" argument: that for democracy to flourish there has first to be a certain level of economic development, a quantity of infrastructure, and a coherent national culture. As usually put forward in academic and certain authoritarian-left circles, it is a crudely deterministic notion which I do not believe to be valid: for one thing, it fails to show how the suppression of even very limited political-social rights contributes, or is *in fact* caused by a wish, to solve these problems. (Who is prepared to maintain that Sukarno's suppression of the Indonesian Socialists and other dissident parties helped solve that country's economic or growth problems?) But for the sake of argument let us accept a version of this theory: Let us grant what is certainly a bit more plausible, that a full or stable democratic society cannot be established in a country ridden by economic primitivism, illiteracy, disease, cultural disunion, etc. The crucial question then becomes: Can at least some measure of democratic rights be won or granted?—say, the right of workers to form unions or the right of dissidents within a single-party state to form factions and express their views? For if a richer socioeconomic development is a prerequisite of democracy, it must also be remembered that such democratic rights, as they enable the emergence of autonomous social groups, are also needed for socioeconomic development.

c. Let us go even further and grant, again for the sake of argument, that in some underdeveloped countries authoritarian regimes may be necessary for a time. But even if this is true, which I do not believe it is, then it must be acknowledged as an unpleasant necessity, a price we are paying for historical crimes and mistakes of the past. In that case, radicals can hardly find their models in, and should certainly not become an uncritical cheering squad for, authoritarian dictators whose presence is supposed to be unavoidable.

The New Leftists, searching for an ideology by which to rationalize their sentiments, can now find exactly what they need in a remarkable book recently translated from the French, *The Wretched of the Earth*. Its author, Frantz Fanon, is a Negro from Martinique who became active in the Algerian revolution. He articulates with notable power the views of those nationalist-revolutionaries in the underdeveloped countries who are contemptuous of their native bourgeois leadership, who see their revolution being pushed beyond national limits and into their own social structure, who do not wish to merge with or become subservient to the Communists yet have no strong objection in principle to Communist methods and values.

Fanon tries to locate a new source of revolutionary energy: the peasants who, he says, "have nothing to lose and everything to gain." He deprecates the working class: In the Western countries it has been bought off, and in the underdeveloped nations, it constitutes a tiny "aristocracy." What emerges is a curious version of Trotsky's theory of permanent revolution, concerning national revolts in the backward countries which, to fulfill themselves, must become social revolutions. But with one major difference: Fanon assigns to the peasants and the urban declassed poor the vanguard role Trotsky had assigned to the workers.

What, however, has really happened in countries like Algeria? The peasantry contributes men and blood for an anticolonial war. Once the war is won, it tends to disperse, relapsing into local interests and seeking individual small-scale ownership of the land. It is too poor, too weak, too diffuse to remain or become the leading social force in a newly liberated country. The bourgeoisie, what there was of it, having been shattered and the working class pushed aside, what remains? Primarily the party of nationalism, led by men who are dedicated, uprooted, semieducated, and ruthless. The party rules, increasingly an independent force perched upon and above the weakened classes.

But Fanon is not taken in by his own propaganda. He recognizes the dangers of a preening dictator and has harsh things to say against the Nkrumah type. He proposes, instead, that "the party should be the direct expression of the masses," and adds, "Only those underdeveloped countries led by revolutionary elites who have come up from the people can today *allow* the entry of the masses upon the scene of history."(Emphasis added.)

Fanon wants the masses to participate, yet throughout his book the single-party state remains an unquestioned assumption. But what if the masses do not wish to "participate"? And what if they are hostile to "the"—always "the"—party? Participation without choice is a burlesque of democracy: indeed, it is an essential element of a totalitarian or authoritarian society, for it means that the masses of people act out a charade of involvement but are denied the reality of decision.

The authoritarians find political tendencies and representative men with whom to identify in the Communist world; so do we. We identify with the people who have died for freedom, like Imre Nagy, or who suffered in prison, like Djilas. We identify with the "revisionists," those political *marranos* who, forced to employ Communist jargon, yet spoke out for a socialism demo-cratic in character and distinct from both Communism and capitalism. As it happens, our friends in the Communist world are not in power; but since when has that mattered to socialists?

In 1957, at the height of the Polish ferment, the young philosopher Leszek Kolakowski wrote a brief article entitled "What Is Socialism?" It consisted of a series of epigrammatic sentences describing what socialism is not (at the moment perhaps the more immediate concern), but tacitly indicating as well what socialism should be. The article was banned by the Gomulka regime but copies reached Western periodicals. Here are a few sentences.

Socialism is not:

A society in which a person who has committed no crime sits at home waiting for the police.

A society in which one person is unhappy because he says what he thinks, and another happy because he does not say what is in his mind.

A society in which a person lives better because he does not think at all.

A state whose neighbors curse geography.

A state which wants all its citizens to have the same opinions in philosophy, foreign policy, economics, literature, and ethics.

A state whose government defines its citizens' rights, but whose citizens do not define the government's rights.

A state in which there is private ownership of the means of production.

A state which considers itself solidly socialist because it has liquidated private ownership of the means of production.

A state which always knows the will of the people before it asks them.

A state in which the philosophers and writers always say the same as the generals and ministers, but always after them.

A state in which the returns of parliamentary elections are always predictable.

A state which does not like to see its citizens read back numbers of newspapers.

These negatives imply a positive, and that positive is a central lesson of contemporary history: the unity of socialism and democracy. To preserve democracy as a political mode without extending it into every crevice of social and economic life is to allow it to become increasingly sterile, formal, ceremonial. To nationalize an economy without enlarging democratic freedoms is to create a new kind of social exploitation. Radicals and liberals may properly and fraternally disagree about many other things; but upon this single axiom concerning the value of democracy, this conviction wrung from the tragedy of our age, politics must rest.

[1965]

THE MYSTICAL MILITANTS

by Michael Harrington

The young radicals of the early sixties were mystical militants, articulating the authentic miseries of the poor even while maintaining some of the attitudes of the middle class. They were also one of the most significant, hopeful developments in recent American life. I do not emphasize their importance as an uncritical compliment. They have already been subjected to quite enough journalistic flattery, and some of the mass media would probably like to package them as they did the beats. Moreover, I have differences with the young radicals and have on occasion been puzzled, exasperated, and even saddened by them. Yet the happy fact remains that the emergence of a personally committed generation seeking basic social change is momentous. They are a minority of their age group, to be sure, but a creative, activist minority who should place their stamp upon the times. Eventually, and it will probably try the anarchist spirit of some of them, they are going to lead adult movements and change this society. Whatever their shortcomings, the New Leftists hold out the hope for a renewal of American social criticism and action.

When I became a radical in 1948 (the last year of the politics of the thirties), it was taken for granted (on the Left) that the Fourth of July was really a front for the four hundred families. In part, this was a heritage of European socialist theory, in part a legacy of the American experience of a depression which had demystified so many clichés. One did not get angry that the powers-that-be lied and cheated and manipulated. That, after all, was their function in life, just as it was the task of the Left to create a society which would not need to corrupt its avowed values.

The young radicals of today, it seems to me, did not start with this inherited cynicism. They came to teen-age during the American celebration of the Eisenhower years and were, for the most part, not really politically conscious until after both Korea and McCarthyism. They seemed to have believed what they were told about freedom, equality, justice, world peace, and the like. They became activists in order to affirm these traditional values with regard to some ethical cause: defending civil liberties against HUAC, picketing for the life of Caryl Chessman, demanding an end to nuclear testing, fighting for civil rights. The shock generated by the society's duplicity in this or that single issue then opened their eyes to larger, and even more systematic, injustices.

It is, I suspect, this unique fifties-sixties experience which gives the New Left its distinctive flavor: a sense of outrage, of having been betrayed by all the father figures, which derives from an original innocence. And it is also the source of the young radicals' insistence on sincerity and community. They begin, not with an image of the future which was received, in one way or another, from Europe and involves theory and history, but from a sense of the immediate contradiction between democratic posturing and the undemocratic reality. They descend from the abolitionists and Wobblies, not from Marx.

This intense, even painful, consciousness of American hypocrisy has led the young radicals to people who do not, or cannot, play the national rhetorical game: the left-outs, the outcasts. And it has involved them in a clash between mysticism and militancy.

In the iconography of the thirties, the proletarian was a figure of incipient power and a puritan sense of duty. The *lumpen* proletarian was despised because he did not belong to a conscious class, because he floated; and he was feared as a potential shock trooper of fascism. By the fifties, much of the old élan had left the labor movement and, with an overwhelming majority of the people satisfied with Eisenhower, there did not seem to be much of a political perspective for insurgency. At this point a cultural rebellion took place among young people. It was expressed among the beats who contracted out of the system; it informed Norman Mailer's vision of the white man who aspired to the cool and the hip that white society provoked in the Negro.

As disestablishmentarians, the young radicals continue this tradition of the fifties. They identify precisely with the *lumpen,* the powerless, the maimed, the poor, the criminal, the junkie. And there is a mystical element in this commitment which has nothing to do with politics. By going into the slum, they are doing penance for the sins of affluence; by sharing the life of those who are so impoverished that they are uncorrupted, values are affirmed. It is honest and moral and antihypocritical to be on the margin of society *whether the community organization works or not.* Indeed, there is a fear of "success," a suspicion that it would mean the integration of the oppressed into the corruption of the oppressors.

But, on the other hand, the New Leftists are not fifties beats. They are angry militants who see the poor as a new force in America, perhaps even as a substitute for the proletariat that failed. So they insist that the Mississippi and Alabama sharecroppers can choose for themselves. But from this point of view, it does make quite a bit of difference whether the community-organizing campaign works or not.

An analogy from the thirties might illuminate the political hope that is here asserted by the young radicals. In 1932 or 1933, many polite Americans believed that if you gave a worker a bathtub, he would put coal in it. And the skilled AFL members thought it preposterous that mass production machine operators could form *their own* union. On paper, the right to organize was proclaimed by the Wagner Act. In fact, it took at least five tumultuous years of picketing, striking, and sitting-in before the CIO turned the brave words into something of a reality. Similarly in 1964, America declared war on poverty; and most of the well-bred citizenry did not intend by that to have field hands and janitors speaking up for themselves; and the young radicals, who have this knack of taking America's promises seriously, sought a surge from below to give meaning to the phrasemaking on high. But, as I think the New Left realizes, this analogy is faulty in part. The mass production workers were, just as radical theory had said, forced by the conditions of their existence (thousands of men assembled at one miserable place with common problems and interests) into a solidarity which became the basis of union organization. The poor are not grouped into incipient communities. A slum street fragments and atomizes people; the two largest groups of the poor, the young and the old, have little to do with one another; and even if they could get together, the poor are still a minority of the society. Therefore it is going to take even more creativity to help the outcasts into their own than it did to build industrial unionism.

For a number of reasons the New Leftists shied away, until quite recently, from thinking through the problems posed by their own militancy. For one thing, they are indeed "American" in the empirical, activist, antitheoretical sense of the word. For another, they rejected the scholasticism of some of the traditional Left formulae (as well as the genuine profundity of the Left's intellectual heritage) and they were imbued with the spirit of the civil rights movement of the early sixties where the willingness to go to jail was more important than political abstractions. Recently there have been signs that the young radicals are moving into a phase of discussion and debate. And this is necessary if the conflict of mysticism and militancy is to be resolved. For if the poor are seen as Dostoevskian peasants whose beauty is their suffering, then politics and the inevitable alliances with others are a contamination; but if they are to be a social force, then coalition is a necessity.

The New Leftists regard the welfare state, rather than the economic royalists, as the incarnation of the status quo. This is an almost inevitable result of trying to look at America with the eyes of the poor. It is very right—and it is a dangerous half-truth.

The welfare state developed in the thirties was created by, and for, the "middle third" of American society: the liberal middle class and the organized workers. The poor were, and still are, those who were left behind in the depression because of bad geographical, occupational, or political luck: migrants, farm workers, full-time laborers at poverty jobs, racial and ethnic minorities which came into the economic mainstream at the time of the computer rather than of the assembly line. In addition, the poor include all those who have suffered from a *relative deterioration* in various social insurance and income maintenance programs (social security, unemployment compensation, etc.).

The *visible* enemies of the poor are not the captains of industry but the landlords, shopkeepers and, often enough, the agents of the welfare state. For the welfare state is, of course, ill-financed and bureaucratic, and this distorts the good intentions of many of the fine people who work for it and reinforces the vices of the bad. So for the poor the welfare state means a humiliating dependence and fear and requires a constant, cunning battle against authority. The young radicals attempt to articulate these fierce resentments that they discovered in the slums, and the experience does not leave them in a mood for sociological nicety. The welfare state is, they say, a fraud. And the liberals, who actually boast of having created this monster in the name of humane values, are therefore the worst hypocrites.

In formulating this attitude, it is not simply that the New Leftists overlook some history, which youth always does, but that they ignore some *relevant* history. The welfare state did not come out of the thirties as a result of a liberal plot to manipulate the dispossessed. It was created over the violent resistance of most men of property and wealth, and its creation required a major upheaval on the part of the workers, from the bottom up. Business did not begin its conversion to welfare statism until the World War II discovery that a federal agency staffed by corporation executives was not exactly a class enemy of the rich; and its final conversion to "tax cut" Keynesianism waited upon the persuasiveness of Lyndon B. Johnson. There was, and is, a very real element of buying off the restless natives in business acceptance of welfarism.

The relevance of this history is that the current welfare state consensus is not quite so homogeneous as the President and some New Leftists sometimes think. For the apparent agreement conceals the latent conflict between the sophisticated conservatives on the one hand, and the liberal-labor-civil rights forces on the other. One can rightly accuse the liberal welfarists of having been too nostalgically proud of *their* upheaval to understand the terrible urgency of more change now as seen from the bottom of society. But it is something else again to *equate* all present supporters of the welfare state with one another.

And here I think I come to my most serious criticism of the New Left: that they sometimes expect the poor to act out the moral values of the middle-class radical who has come to the slum.

I find, for instance, a genuine poignancy in Tom Hayden's realization that a coalition of the outcasts will not really be able to change the society and that radicalism can only give itself up to, and become part of, "the energy kept restless and active under the clamps of paralyzed imperial society. Radicalism then would go beyond the concepts of optimism and pessimism as guides to work, finding itself working despite odds. Its realism and sanity would be grounded in nothing more than the ability to face whatever comes."

This attitude is a logical deduction from the theory that all the welfare staters, from Henry Ford to Walter Reuther, if you will, are the same kind of manipulative bureaucrats. For if everybody but the poor and outcast are "they," then "we" must inevitably lose, for by definition "we" are not strong enough to transform a fraud and scandal supported by sixty or seventy percent of the society.

The conscious and committed radical can find his solace in such a vision; most of the poor cannot. Indeed, one of the things that has made the poor so inarticulate, so unorganized, so hopeless, is precisely the conviction that they can't win. Are they now to be told stoically to treasure their misery, which, though permanent, is at least not corrupted by the hypocrisy of affluence? That will be cold comfort. And it will not move them to action, but rather reinforce them in their passivity.

The danger is that the poor will thus be assigned roles as abstractions in the morality plays of the disenchanted middle class. To fight this possibility, the New Leftists must come up with a strategy which offers real hope to the other America. And this means making a more sophisticated analysis of the coalition which supports the welfare state.

For the liberal wing of this consensus certainly did not start with the intention to build a manipulative bureaucracy, and it maintains values which *could* provide a basis for transforming the present structure. If the social-change movements of the previous generation must be shaken up by the poor, they must be shaken up in order to be made allies. To do this requires an intensification of the efforts to organize the slums and ghettos and backwoods as an independent political force. But if there is to be honest hope, that organization must be thought of as the catalyst of a new political majority in the United States, and not as a doomed last stand of noble savages.

[1966]

"CONFRONTATION POLITICS" IS A DANGEROUS GAME

by Irving Howe

A new term has entered the American language—"confrontation politics," the equivalent in public life of Russian roulette in private life. Some who play this new political game are authentic desperadoes, mostly young Negro militants; others are white middle-class students acting—or acting out—a fantasy-wish of revolution.

For the black desperadoes, confrontation politics can bring large risks: prison, violence, death. For the white students, the risks until recently were small; but after the ghastliness of Chicago and the growing popular obsession with "law and order," they will surely increase. For the country as a whole, the problem is perplexing. At a time of social disorder, when gross injustices continue to plague us, there arise combative minorities charged with moral idealism and apocalyptic emotion, which have developed tactics of protest going beyond the usual democratic methods yet short of the usual insurrectionary ones.

Like other New Left notions, confrontation politics has not been well articulated as a theory. It is a kind of politics that grows up through improvisation, and it has been improvised as a way of getting around the sense of futility which has usually beset American radicalism. It has been choreographed as an out-of-door explosion, a sort of real-life theater.

The purpose is to prod and incite a dormant, insensitive society into recognizing its moral failures. No longer committed, as were the Marxists, to the idea that the proletariat would be the crucial lever for the transformation of history, the young semi-anarchists who practice confrontation see themselves as a minority probably doomed to remain one for a long time. They have no expectation of creating new electoral majorities and small expectation of persuading large numbers of people; for they see the mass of Americans as brainwashed by "the media" (the very media which give them vast amounts of publicity). Their politics is a politics of desperation, at best moral shock and at worst nihilist irritation. They assign to themselves the task of sacrifice and assault, as a self-chosen vanguard which must destroy the complacence of "corporate liberalism."

What makes this task seem especially urgent is the feeling that in Vietnam the United States is conducting an immoral war which the ordinary democratic process is too slow and cumbersome to cope with.

One source of confrontation politics, seldom acknowledged, is the strategy worked out by the civil rights movement in the South during the fifties. Under strong pacifist guidance at that point, the civil rights movement "confronted" Southern institutions through direct action—that is, through demonstrations, parades, lunch-counter sit-ins. Conceived as a way to force the South into recognizing that Negroes would no longer be dormant, these actions involved a degree of "obstruction" (Jim Crow arrangements in stores were upset) and a kind of "confrontation" (nonviolent minorities exposed themselves to beatings by police and mobs.)

The success of such actions depended on the following conditions:

The demonstrators were demanding rights which had already been recognized, both in law and moral consensus, by the nation as a whole. Despite failures by the federal government to enforce antidiscrimination laws, the demonstrators could count on at least some practical help from the Kennedy and Johnson administrations, as well as large amounts of support from many Northerners. And while the Southern police often remained brutal, it was no longer possible for municipal and state governments in the South to destroy Negro protest through sheer terror.

The demonstrations came at a time when there were growing differences of response among Southern whites. A majority may still have remained convinced that Jim Crow was a practical convenience, but a growing minority seems to have felt it was morally indefensible. Even if that minority did not always act with courage, it did begin to break the monolithic front which the white South had put up for decades. Doubt and guilt pierced the hard shell of white superiority.

The unconditional nonviolence practiced by Dr. King and his friends was a principle that sections of the middle-class South had to respect—indeed, to respect almost as much as white Northerners came to admire. The sight of men willing to turn the other cheek is one that must move, or at least disturb, people who retain even the flimsiest connections with Christianity. Tactically, it bewildered the Southern police, who would have been delighted to trade one hundred blows for one, but didn't know how to cope with men going limp under beatings.

While the Southern demonstrators sometimes broke local ordinances, their actions were justifiable by democratic standards. For they had long been deprived of the right to vote and thereby participate in changing policies through peaceful means —which meant they now had a certain sanction for resorting to partly coercive but completely nonviolent forms of direct action. Furthermore, they were struggling for the enforcement of national laws superseding local ordinances, many of which were deliberately contrived to circumvent federal legislation and were commonly felt to be of dubious constitutionality. Indeed, one reason for breaking local ordinances was to challenge their constitutionality.

The power of Southern protest derived partly from its alliance with major forces in the North: liberals, unionists, churches, and academicians, all pressing for civil rights legislation. One reason the Selma march proved to be so valuable was that it came just at the moment when it could most dramatically induce popular support for the Voting Rights Act. By contrast, demonstrations leading only to other demonstrations, or demonstrations lacking clearly defined goals (e.g., "justice"), or demonstrations with hopelessly unrealizable goals (e.g., a "black republic" in the

South) will result in a dissipation of energies. The civil rights marches during the fifties and early sixties, however, were directed toward concrete local aims and in support of proposed national legislation.

Now, all of these favorable circumstances were special to the South, and it would be naïve to suppose they can now be duplicated on a national scale. When certain kinds of demonstrations are held by anti-Vietnam protestors—especially if they are feckless enough to include Vietcong banners—it can hardly be said that they act in behalf of moral-political opinions shared by a large majority of the people but thwarted by a sectional minority; or that they have been significantly deprived of their right to organize and protest; or that they act out of a principled devotion to nonviolence.

These are not new problems, either in the development of radical movements or the history of democratic states. There are historical precedents, and something can be learned from glancing at them.

Shortly after the Russian Revolution there appeared tendencies within the Communist movement, opposed by Lenin and Trotsky, which led to a strategy of constant assault: endless demonstrations, unremitting "offensives," indeed a precursor of confrontation politics. Some ultraleft German Communists even gave this strategy a name, the "theory of electrification." Through reckless self-sacrifice, the party would "electrify" the masses into revolution. Predictably, this led to disasters in Germany and elsewhere during the early twenties—brave but suicidal coups by Communist combat groups which failed to gain the support of the workers. About the theory of electrification Trotsky remarked with asperity that the probable consequence was that the electrifiers would burn themselves.

In the immediate pre-Hitler period, there was an even more senseless turn toward a kind of confrontation politics. The Communists came up with the insane notion of "social fascism," according to which the Social Democrats, and not the Nazis, were the main danger in Germany. (Today, it is "the liberals" who are the main danger. . . .) The Communists kept staging endless demonstrations which, in Trotsky's phrase, "succeeded only in irritating all classes without winning over any." They antagonized the middle classes; they wore out the patience of the workers; they exhausted their own cadres. They made loud noises about "taking power" but never came within reach of power. Inevitably there appeared a force calling for the restoration of "law and order," behind which a large segment of the population united, actively or passively. It would be an exaggeration to say that the Communist tactics caused the rise of Hitlerism, but no exaggeration at all to say that they helped the Nazis come to power.

Taken simply as a syndrome of going into the streets (what has been called the "Theory of Permanent Demonstrations"), the politics of confrontation would not be a very serious matter. Demonstrations can be useful; demonstrations can be self-defeating. Opposition to the Vietnam war was surely rallied and increased through demonstrations; but some of them, by allowing themselves to be linked with the Vietcong and overtaken by anti-American hatreds not at all essential to the cause of peace, had a counterproductive effect, stiffening the hostility felt by millions of Americans toward dissent. About such matters we can only make estimates based partly on our sense of what this country is like. There is, finally, no science for measuring the consequences of going into the streets.

Far more serious is the political outlook which inspires confrontationist acts. As developed by Herbert Marcuse, the current New Left guru, this political outlook advances the following propositions: We live in an advanced stage of capitalism, a mass society providing bread, circuses, and technology, which has tamed the forces of opposition and thereby undercut hopes for "transcendence." There is no great likelihood, in Marcuse's view, that we will soon witness an end to a social oppression sustained by material plenty but yielding no spiritual gratification. Efforts at reform tend to be superficial, and many of the values of liberalism—tolerance, free speech, electoral activity—are depreciated as devices for adjusting people to the status quo.

Revolution thus being declared all but impossible and reform all but ineffectual, Marcuse's doctrines justify those radicals who turn away from both traditional Leninism and social democracy, in order to launch a series of adventures or "raids," perhaps to usurp, perhaps to unsettle established power, but clearly without much concern for democratic processes. The claim here is that the society can be shaken into change, if shaken at all, only through attacks by marginal groups: the outraged poor, alienated hippies, rebellious students.

Whatever one may think about the analytical portions of Marcuse's thought, his political conclusions offer a simultaneous rationalization for withdrawal and wildness, copping-out and turning-on. Precisely insofar as numbers of students have come under Marcuse's influence, the picture of society he draws seems less and less valid. Men are not slipping into apathy and somnolence, at least not yet; they are disturbed, restless, worried. In the last decade the United States has not become stultified, immobile, and indifferent. The *cul-de-sac* of historical stagnation posited by Marcuse is indeed a nightmare haunting every sensitive man, but one must be able to distinguish between the fears of the dark and the facts of day.

Still, if you hold a version of Marcuse's ideas and believe liberalism is exhausted or corrupt or inseparable from "racist imperialism"; if you further conclude that no major social classes within society can be expected significantly to transform it; you then have no serious alternative to either a Salinger-like withdrawal or the political equivalent of guerrilla raids. By this last phrase I don't mean literally shooting it out—though there are a few free-lance lunatics advocating as much—but rather a series of actions, dramatic, desperate, and provocative, which keep the society in a state of constant turmoil and the university in a state of constant chaos.

This strategy, in my view, can lead only to disaster and a backlash of terrifying proportions. The signs of it are everywhere about us.

A tacit premise behind confrontation politics is that the university largely resembles the surrounding society, or is even identical in nature with it. The result is to damage academic life and distort political action.

Within the university the New Left students engage with more or less liberal faculties, and behind these engagements there is often the assumption that, finally, the university will behave like a middle-class parent. When sometimes it does not, there follow among students considerable shock and rage. At Columbia the students who seized buildings and declared "communes" were engaged in a quasi-revolutionary action—or so some of them said. But when the Columbia administration (quite stupidly, I think) retaliated with the police force which New Left theory says is inevitable but which New Left feelings are often not really prepared for, the students cried foul. They invoked the traditional view of the university as a cloister of intellect from which police should be barred.

At this point they were caught in a dilemma. If they believed it proper to transform the campus into a training ground for revolutionary action, they could hardly complain when the powers-that-be retaliated with force. If they genuinely believed (as I, for one, believe) that the campus should be a center of learning from which the police are barred, then they could hardly treat the university as if it were *no more than* a microcosm of capitalist society. True, they might argue with much cogency that many universities have been contaminated and should be returned to their true purposes of scholarship and teaching; but to say that would be to accept—O dreadful prospect!—a view of the university close to that of liberalism.

The analogy between university and society breaks down in a still more serious way. One reason the tactics of the Students for a Democratic Society have worked on certain campuses is that implicitly they count on that mixture of affection and irritation many faculty people feel toward "the students." In good measure the politics of confrontation as practiced on the campus depends on a benevolent or indecisive response from the liberal professors whom the New Left treats with such contempt. But once such tactics are transferred to the society at large, the result is going to be very different. The professors, who count for a good deal on the campus, count for fairly little in the society; and the society itself is not nearly so pacific or indulgent as are most professors. One needs a talent for self-delusion to say that in the United States liberalism—for all its many faults and failures—represents the main danger to humane aspirations.

No; this society retains large potentials of hatred and violence, its capacities for tolerating what it regards as disruption have a visible limit, and its response to confrontation tactics could well be a crushing display of force which would harm many people who have nothing to do with the New Left. I say none of this by way of approval, only by way of describing hard facts which those of us who believe in radical politics must take into account.

If anything should give the New Left pause, it is the fact that according to the polls, a clear majority of the American people approved of Mayor Daley's treatment of the Chicago demonstrators. I don't mean it should give them pause in their opposition to the Vietnam war, an opposition I share; but it should stir them into rethinking the value of confrontation methods.

Now, when arguments of this kind are put forward in debates with the New Left, one of the usual replies goes like this: "You liberals, you Social Democrats are always trying to hamstring protest by raising the specter of backlash. But where is the backlash? Is it perhaps just a bogey with which you're trying to frighten us? And if we pay attention to it, how can we ever mount an effective protest?"

The backlash is everywhere. Some of us, raised on memories of earlier decades, carry a mental picture of reactionary mobs and American Legionnaires assaulting radicals in the street: That was true in the twenties and thirties; it may yet prove true in the next few years. But just as everything else in modern society becomes bureaucratized, so has backlash. Instead of swarming mobs, there are now trained police. The white workers of Italian or Polish or Slavic origin who have managed to save up enough money to buy themselves little homes in the suburbs aren't likely to organize mobs to invade the black ghettos—at least not yet; but they are inclined, many of them, to vote for George Wallace in the name of law and order. That some twenty per cent of the American electorate could even consider voting for Wallace—surely that's a sufficient sign of backlash.

Is the answer, then, for dissidents to crawl into holes and keep silent? Of course not. But in order to protest the Vietnam war it isn't necessary to rouse all the prejudices millions of Americans hold, and it isn't even necessary to outrage their sincere patriotic sentiments. In order to fight for Negro rights, it isn't necessary to talk blood or to call white men "honkies" and policemen "pigs." That's a way of blowing off steam, and the resulting profit goes to George Wallace.

One aim of confrontation politics is the "polarization" of society. In plain English, this means that by constant assault the activists hope to drive a segment of the liberals into radicalism; thereupon the "mushy middle" of the country will be broken up; and we can then look forward to an apocalypse, with two extremes hardened and ready for a final conflict.

When they invoke this vision the confrontationists are drawing upon political emotions that have been very powerful in the twentieth century—emotions concerning "the seizure of power," a political Second Coming. Having shared these emotions and still being susceptible to them, I can appreciate their force. But I must nevertheless ask: What, in the present circumstances, would be the likely outcome of such a polarization in the United States?

Were anything of the sort to happen, millions of ordinary Americans—for whom student protest-drugs-hippiedom-black rioting forms a stream of detested association—would also be activated. Lower-class white ethnic groups would be stirred up. *Lumpen* elements would be emboldened. Both respectable and marginal classes would turn to demagogues promising order in the streets.

Despite its talk about "the power elite" and the idiotic notion it sometimes proposes that we live under "liberal fascism," the New Left clings to an excessively optimistic view of American society. Its spokesmen have neither memory nor awareness of what fascism—the real thing, *fascist* fascism—would be like. They fail to recognize that there are sleeping dogs it would be just as well to let lie. And they are shockingly indifferent to the likelihood that the first victim of a new reaction in America would be the universities in which they now find shelter.

Only in terms of a theory of polarization can one explain the peculiar intensity with which New Left students kept trying to break up the meetings of Hubert Humphrey, while virtually ignoring those of Richard Nixon. (I am against breaking up any-one's meetings.) They were acting on the premise that liberalism is their main enemy, and some of them have even said that they would find attractive an alliance between far Left and far Right.

Such notions tacitly continue the old Stalinist tradition of "the worse, the better" and "*Nach Hitler, uns.*" Yet all of recent history enforces the lesson that misery cannot be the seedbed of progress or chaos of freedom. Polarization helps, not the Left, but the Right; not those with grievances, but those with guns. In any case, is the prospect of polarization an attractive one? How many of us would like to face a choice between an America symbolized by George Wallace and an America symbolized by Tom Hayden? Morally, because he is against racism, Hayden is superior; but politically, neither has much respect for democracy. I for one would fear for my safety almost as much with one as with the other. Wallace might have me pistol-whipped as a Communist, and Hayden have me sent to a labor camp as a Social Democrat. Hayden would be more accurate politically, but what sort of consolation would that be?

For a while confrontation politics seems to work. Caught off-balance, the enemy panics. College administrators aren't sure how to cope with students who seize buildings. But in time, for better or worse, they are going to figure out a way of dealing with this problem.

There is some truth in the claim—it constitutes a damning criticism of our society—that provocative demonstrations spilling over into violence have a way of gaining attention, certainly from TV, which programmatic and disciplined protest does not. But it is a truth easily overstated. The ghetto riots in Detroit and Watts have not brought notable improvements to their communities; they have not led to those increased federal appropriations which are the only serious way of starting to clear the slums. At best they have enabled these communities, at enormous cost to themselves, to gain a slightly larger share of the funds already available. And as the California election of Ronald Reagan showed, the violence helped set off an electoral trend which can only signify a tight-fisted and mean-spirited policy toward the blacks.

Concerning this, let me quote from a discussion between Bayard Rustin, the Negro leader, and myself in the November 1968 *Dissent:*

> *Howe:* I keep encountering the argument in regard to riots: "We know in principle it's not a good thing. But

when you have a society that is not susceptible to pressure or moral appeals, the only way you can get them to pay attention is through raising hell."

Rustin: There are two tragedies here. One is that to some extent they're right. You don't get concessions until there's been trouble. . . . The second tragedy is that although we receive minor concessions from the establishment, once the rioting reaches a certain point there will be repression against the entire Negro community.

Howe: Raising the ante indefinitely isn't going to work. . . .

Rustin: Right. To repress one-tenth of the population will require an assault on the civil liberties of everyone. And in such an atmosphere, no genuine progress in the redistribution of wealth can take place. . . . There's another factor. Sooner or later the unity of the Negroes, small as it is, in making demands on the whole society will be splintered, because the Negro community gets into a debate—are you or are you not for violence?—instead of uniting around a fight for political and economic objectives

The advocates of confrontation seem undisturbed by the fact that they are setting precedents which could lead to a major crisis for democracy. If it is permissible for opponents of the war to burn government records, why may not neo-Fascists do the same thing a few years later? If it is permissible for left-wing students to seize buildings in behalf of virtuous ends, why may not their action become a precedent for doing the same thing in behalf of detestable ends? At the very least, such problems must be discussed.

Some will say that violence and illegality are already rampant in the society, and that they are merely responding to their official use. This has a measure of truth. But I would reply that democratic procedures, incomplete as they may still be, have been established only after decades of struggle, and that it would be feckless to dismiss them as mere sham. Those of us who see the need for radical change have the most interest in preserving democracy.

A few years ago Staughton Lynd wrote about an antiwar demonstration in Washington: "It was unbearably moving to watch the sea of banners move out . . . toward the Capitol. . . . Still more poignant was the perception that as the crowd moved toward the seat of government . . . our forward movement was irresistibly strong . . . nothing could have stopped that crowd from taking possession of its government. Perhaps next time we should keep going, occupying for a time the rooms from which orders issue."

One must ask Staughton Lynd: Under whose mandate were the marchers to occupy the government? And if they did "perhaps next time" arrogate to themselves the privilege of a coup d'etat, even a symbolic one lasting five minutes, how will they keep other crowds, other causes—equally sincere, equally "moving"—from doing the same "perhaps the time after next"?

The politics of confrontation bears an inherent drift toward antidemocratic elitism. Electoral processes are declared irrelevant, majorities mere formalities. Once such notions are indulged, the choice is either to sink back into apathy with pot or to plunge into a desperate elitism which dismisses the people as boobs and assigns the "tasks of history" to a self-appointed vanguard. And in the current atmosphere, it isn't hard to drift from elitism to talk of violence. Mostly, so far, it is talk.

But there are troubling signs. In the summer of 1968 the office of Stanford University's president was set afire, an event that followed in time a season of student sit-ins. I see no reason to connect these two, and would never have dreamed of doing so had I not read the following in a New Left paper, *The Midpeninsula Observer:*

"Most leftists in this area seem to feel that the fire was politically motivated, and a split of opinion has developed with regard to the tactical efficacy of the act. Some believe that the fire was an effective attack on state power and that it was a logical extension of the leftist activity that has been going on at and around Stanford. Others think that the fire itself was a mistake . . . since it is not clearly connected with a political movement and since most of the people who might be educated by such an act are gone for the summer."

Significant here is not the speculation that the fire was politically motivated but the argument offered by those leftists opposed to setting fires. They seem to have a seasonal theory of the revolutionary uses of arson. In the winter, apparently, when more people can be "educated" by such an act, these critics would find arson more acceptable. The whole thing, I must say, reminds one of Dostoevski's *The Possessed*—as also of George Orwell's caustic remark that a certain kind of infantile Leftism is "playing with fire on the part of people who don't even know that fire is hot."

Or here, to cite another instance, is a 25 August 1968 report by Robert Maynard in *The Washington Post* about a feud between SNCC and the Black Panthers. At a meeting between leaders of the two groups, writes Maynard, there was a sharp dispute which "resulted in Panthers drawing guns on James Forman," the SNCC leader. Another SNCC leader, Julius Lester, is quoted by Maynard as having written: "The shoot-out was averted, fortunately, but there was no doubt . . . that whatever merger or alliance may have existed was finished."

As a sign of the fraternal spirit induced by Black Power, this isn't much more convincing than the civil war in Nigeria. No doubt, much of this gun-drawing is a kind of playacting; but playacting can lead to acting.

Nor is the rhetoric of violence likely to diminish soon. The New Left will continue to talk blithely about revolution, but the police will do most of the shooting. Might it not, therefore, be in order to plead with the young confrontationists that if the ethic of democracy seems to them hollow or irrelevant, they at least think in terms of common prudence? And perhaps that they take off an hour to read Lenin's *Left-Wing Communism: An Infantile Disorder* in which the great revolutionist explains why compromise and even retreat are sometimes necessary?

One defense sometimes offered for confrontation politics is that, effective or not, it provides a dramatic way of releasing emotions. Of all the arguments, this seems to me the least tolerable. It means that in behalf of self-indulgence one is ready to bring down on oneself and others the forces of repression, of which the first victims would surely be the Negroes about whom the New Left declares itself so deeply concerned. This is a form of middle-class frivolity; a politics of the kindergarten. About such carryings-on (Yippies' trippies) I would cite a remarkable statement recently made by the English writer, David Caute, himself a New Left sympathizer, after his return from Czechoslovakia:

"These observations reveal to me a certain perversity in my own attitude. Nostalgia for student riots, clashes with the police, and totally exposed thighs suggest a false romanticism, an irritable desire to inflict on an ostensibly sane society a form of chaos which, as a way of life, is superficial and nihilistic. The manner in which the young Czechs are conducting themselves is really a model of civic control and enlightenment, whereas we have become alcoholic on sensation and violence."

Far more serious are those who advance the view that, as a matter of conscience and regardless of consequences, they must break a given law. If a man finds the Vietnam war a moral crime and says he cannot serve in the Army even though the result be his imprisonment, then I think he merits respect and, often, admiration. He is ready to accept punishment for his behavior, ready to pay the price of his convictions. His violation of the law is undertaken in behalf of a higher principle and out of respect for law in general; he hopes to stir the conscience of society or, failing that, to live according to his own. Such a version of civil disobedience, Spiro Agnew notwithstanding, is a legitimate act when seriously undertaken in a democratic society.

What is not legitimate is to use tactics that look like civil disobedience but are meant to further "revolutionary" ends (e.g., blocking draft boards), since these can only lead to displays of impotence and are likely to harm those who genuinely care about civil disobedience. Nor is it legitimate to resort to civil disobedience, or a tactic easily confused with it, every Monday and Thursday morning. Acts of conscience violating the law can be taken seriously only if they are concerned with the most fundamental moral issues. And there is also, I think, an obligation to obey many laws one dislikes, in order to preserve the possibility for peacefully changing them.

This is a bad moment in American politics. The Vietnam war is a scandal and a disaster; social obligations pile up shamefully in the cities; radical measures are called for; the exploited cannot remain silent. Militant protest is therefore needed. Yet we must try to make certain that the methods we use to fight against injustice do not give the opponents of liberty an occasion for destroying both the struggle for justice and the procedures of liberty. That would be to invite disaster through a celebration of mindlessness.

[1968]

UNREASON AND REVOLUTION

by Richard Lowenthal

This is a tentative exploration of what I believe to be a major phenomenon of our time—the rise of a new type of revolutionary movement. Hitherto, we have been familiar with two broad classes of revolutions and revolutionary movements. First, there are the movements which may be understood as resulting when the normal growth, the spontaneous evolution of a society, meets an obstacle in the form of rigid political institutions that are increasingly felt as oppressive. In such cases, sooner or later an acute political crisis occurs in which the obstacle is swept away by revolutionary action. That is, broadly speaking, the formula fitting the great democratic revolutions of modern Western history; it may also be applied to a number of the national movements for independence from colonial rule that have occurred in our time.

In the last fifty years we have learned, to our cost, to distinguish a second type of revolution and revolutionary movements—those which I, for want of a better name, would still describe as "totalitarian revolutions." It seems to be characteristic of them that they do not occur because of the clash between a growing, dynamic society and a static political framework tending to shackle its growth, but because of some elements of stagnation, some major lopsidedness of development *within* the society itself, leading to a deadlock which a dynamic state is then called upon to resolve by the massive use of political force. This appeal from a deadlock in society to the "savior state" has been the background to the rise of German National Socialism as a mass movement and to the long-lasting reign of violence which its victorious regime inflicted on the prostrate body of society. But the overcoming of social stagnation in the midst of change and of lopsided development has also been underlying the rise of Communist regimes in a number of underdeveloped countries—the only ones that have come to power by the victory of indigenous revolutionary movements—and has given them the opportunity for their repeated, forcible transformations of the social structure.

Now it seems to me that in recent years we have begun to be confronted by yet another kind of revolutionary movement. These new movements, both within our Western world and in the so-called underdeveloped countries, use much of the familiar language of Communist ideology, and actually have taken over much of the substance of the Marxist-Leninist critique of Western capitalism and imperialism as well as the Marxist utopia of a society without classes or domination. Nevertheless they are radically different from the Communist movements that had been created in the image of Lenin's Bolshevik party—different in their forms of organization, their strategies of political action, and indeed in the rank order of values that gives operative meaning to their vision of the goal. In fact, one of the preconditions for the rise of these new movements has been the increasingly obvious disintegration of the Marxist-Leninist doctrinal synthesis; they grow out of an ideological soil that has been fertilized by its decomposition. But some of the products of this decay appear to be as virulently destructive as any Leninist movements have been in the past—without, so far, offering any tangible prospect of comparable constructive achievements.

A preliminary survey of these new movements may perhaps best start by marking them off with two negative statements. On one side, they are not the democratic expressions of stable, productive sectors of the societies in which they arise; in other words, they do not originate as class movements, as interest groups, or coalitions of interest groups. On the other hand, they are not disciplined parties of the Communist type, organized from the top downward as instruments of a single will, with a systematic, strategic concept of what they want and how to get there given in advance. On the contrary, it is typical for them that action often precedes thought. Despite the verbal echoes of the Marxist pathos of rationality that may still be heard from the ideological spokesmen of the Western New Left, in practice the urge for violent action increasingly outruns consideration of any precise short-term objectives and of the rational, tactical, and organizational means for achieving them. It is the style of action and the utopian goal that define the movement, while all other ideas and organizational forms remain very much in flux. The goal itself, though it remains a powerful motivating force, never takes the form of a political program with precise institutional content. That, on the contrary, is increasingly rejected: The tendency is to say that the new institutions, if any, will have to emerge from the process of struggle and from the destruction of the old order.

While the New Left in the West thus replaces Communist programs, strategies, and organizational forms by a faith in utopia and a cult of violent action, a number of revolutionary movements in the underdeveloped world show a parallel trend—away from the elaborations of Communist doctrine and the organizational discipline based on ideological authority, and toward the primacy of violent action over social analysis and of military over political and ideological leadership. We may observe this tendency in the practice first of Castro's Cuban revolution and then of the guerrilla actions started in other Latin-American countries under the influence of the Cuban model; and we find its ideological justification sketched out by Che Guevara and elaborated by Régis Debray. A parallel, if delayed, breakthrough of immediate utopianism and immediate violence seems to have occurred in the transformation of Chinese Communism in the course of the last decade, beginning with the Great Leap Foward and the creation of the People's Communes and culminating in the recent Cultural Revolution. Finally, analogous processes seem to be at work in some of those revolutionary nationalist movements which, without ever having become formally Communist, are developing as passionately an anti-Western, antimodernistic, and antirational outlook as the last-named products of the disintegration of world Communism.

This, then, is our theme. Why do those phenomena arise in

various parts of the world at this time? What are the intellectual
roots of their beliefs and the social roots of their strength? And
what are their significance and possible prospects?

Let us begin with a subject we know fairly well—the role of
Marxism and Leninism in the development of revolutionary
ideas. If we cast our minds back to the 1840s when Marxism was
born, and if we recall Engels' proud phrase about the development of socialism from a utopia into a science, it is evident to us
today that the real difference between Marx and many of his so
cialist precursors was not that Karl Marx was no utopian: His
goals were just as utopian, just as rooted in a profound need to
discover a road to salvation on earth, as theirs had been. The difference was that Marx turned his back on *romantic* and *immediate* utopianism in favor of a historical and forward-looking version. The birth of utopian socialism in the early nineteenth
century had been part of the romantic revolt of the newborn European intelligentsia against the beginning of industrialization
and the transformation of human relations by an increasingly
specialized division of labor and an increasingly pervasive cash
nexus. The new turn which Marx gave to those ideas was that he
rejected the romantic element in them, the resistance to modernization based on an idealization of the past, and proclaimed instead that, thanks to the logic of history, utopia would be
achieved by ruthlessly carrying through the painful process of
industrialization to the end. To quote Raymond Aron, Marx put
forward the thesis that the only way to achieve the goals of
Rousseau was to follow the precepts of Saint-Simon.

This was a highly original idea at the time, one might even
say a rather absurd idea. But it also proved an extremely powerful idea: for it enabled Marx to forge a link between the belief
in utopia and the belief in the logic of history. As a result, he
was able to inspire a movement that combined the religious fer-
vor of utopianism with a historical and rational element. Utopia,
and the violent revolution that was to precede it, were not to be
achieved by mere enthusiasm and an act of will. They depended
on well-defined economic and social conditions; but the laws of

history guaranteed that these conditions would be achieved in the fullness of time. Moreover, one effect of this analysis was to inspire the followers of Marx with a conviction of the vital importance of material progress; for together with the growth of the organization and consciousness of the working class, the rise of productivity was the most important of the conditions that must mature before mankind could enter the realm of freedom. Increasing productivity would eventually lead to abundance, and only abundance would permit the creation of a social order without classes or domination. Thus the utopian goal and the violent overthrow of the old order were not the objectives of immediate action: Their possibility was mediated by the laws of the historical process, by reason as manifested in history—their achievement by a rational strategy based on the insight into that process.

In a sense, the disintegration of this rationalist and historic concept of the road to revolution and utopia may be said to have started with Lenin—as well as with the early "revisionists" at the opposite pole. For while the latter sought to retain the evolutionary optimism of Marx yet to eliminate the revolutionary and utopian perspective, Lenin was the first pupil of Marx deliberately to separate the task of "organizing the revolution" from some of its economic and social preconditions as formulated by the teacher. He argued, under the impact of World War I, that it was the duty of the Socialist party to seize power in backward Russia without waiting for the maturing of the economic conditions for a socialist society. He had even earlier "emancipated" this party from dependence on the actual support of the working class by giving it a highly centralistic, instrumental structure. Implicitly, Lenin had thus attempted to replace the missing "objective" preconditions of socialism by the creation of his new vanguard party as an instrument for the seizure of power and for the subsequent transformation of the immature society, and to that extent had begun to turn Marxism upside down. But even while doing so, Lenin still clung to the Marxist analysis in believing that *some* objective conditions were needed for the victory of the revolution—not indeed the condition of economic abundance, of objective maturity for socialism, but certainly the condition of a profound and acute crisis of capitalist society, and of a mass mood of bitter discontent enabling the revolutionary party to gain a mass following. Only once the crisis had reached that stage, he taught to the end, only once the revolutionary party had won a strategically decisive following among the masses— only then could the violent seizure of power take place. As a result, the role of the party never consisted for Lenin *primarily* in the organization of violence. Violence might play a crucial part in its action at the critical moment, but the primary task of the party was to win over the masses *before* that moment by a policy based on a correct analysis of the crisis of society.

Some of the strategic changes introduced by Mao Tse-tung in transferring revolutionary Marxism to Asian soil and deliberately "adapting" it to Asian conditions may still be interpreted as mere developments along the road shown by Lenin. Striving to conquer power in a country where economic and social conditions were incomparably more backward—and correspondingly more remote from "objective" maturity for socialism in the Marxist sense—than in the Russia of 1917, Mao became the first pupil of Lenin to make use of the structural flexibility of the centralized vanguard party by seeking the necessary mass support among the peasants rather than the urban working class, and that for many years. He thus completed the effective emancipation of a "Marxist" party from working-class support that had been implied as a potentiality in Lenin's separation of the seizure of power from conditions of economic maturity and of the party organization from working-class democracy. Moreover, Mao recognized at an early stage that the role of armed force in the struggle for power was likely to be far more continuous and decisive in China than it had been in Russia—that here, power would "grow out of the barrel of a gun." But this greatly expanded role of violence in Mao's revolutionary strategy was still tied to objective political and social conditions in two important ways.

In the first place, it was in Mao's own view only made possible by the special conditions of a semicolonial country, in which neither a single native government nor a single colonial power enjoyed an effective monopoly of armed force. That, at least, was Mao's view at the time of his own struggle for power, though after his victory he came to persuade himself that similar "protracted war" strategies would prove appropriate for *all* the colonial and underdeveloped coutries of the world.[1]

In the second place, Mao never ceased to insist that the success of the strategy of armed struggle depended not only on developing the correct military tactics for guerrilla warfare, but on winning and retaining the support of the peasant population in the regions concerned, by correct policies and effective forms of political and economic organization. Only a policy based on a realistic analysis of the conditions and needs of the people in the area, and a type of organization that maintained communication with them, could enable the guerrillas "to live among the population like a fish in water," preventing their isolation by the militarily superior enemy and assuring them of intelligence, of supplies, and of a reservoir for new recruitment. This insistence on maintaining mass support by policies based on a study of the concrete social situation constitutes the indispensable corollary to the Maoist emphasis on armed struggle and its link with the Marxist-Leninist tradition: It is the foundation for Mao's dictum that while power grows out of the barrel of a gun, the party must command the gun. For, though the party no longer represents (as with Marx) the actual evolving consciousness of a working class increasingly aware of its true historical interests, it still represents (as with Lenin) the leaders' "scientific," analytical consciousness of the total social situation, its contradictions and tendencies, and hence of the objective possibilities for action which any successful political strategy must take into account. To that extent, Mao's concept of the leading role of the party preserves, like Lenin's concept, the Marxian idea of a rational strategy based on perception of the rational laws of history.

Yet there is in Mao's emphasis on the decisive role of armed struggle also the germ of a different, more basically "voluntaristic" approach to social reality. This is to be found in his view that the use of violent action by itself may be one of the most effective means for changing the relation of forces between revo-

---

[1] Mao's original view of the special conditions permitting protracted guerrilla warfare in China is contained in his 1928 resolution "Why Can China's Red Political Power Exist," printed in *Selected Works*, vol. 1 (London, 1954); see particularly p. 65. The later view generalizing this method is expressed in the editorial note 7 to this document, p. 304.

lution and reaction, because the right technique of armed struggle may enable an initially much inferior, revolutionary force to whittle down step by step the initial superiority of its enemy—to tire him out by exhaustion, cause splits in his ranks, and finally wear down his will to fight. In a sense, the art of ensuring the survival and regeneration of inferior forces resisting a stronger and better-armed enemy is, of course, the essence of *all* guerrilla tactics, and the hope that this will enable the guerrillas to outlast the enemy's determination has always been their rationale. But the fulfillment of that hope depends clearly not on the dedication and skill of the guerrillas alone, but on a number of independent factors—such as the enemy's fighting commitments outside the theater of guerrilla warfare, the importance of that theater in relation to his general policy objectives, and the cohesion of his political system as reflected in the support for the antiguerrilla campaign and the loyalty of his troops.

In the Chinese case, the evidence does not show that the Communists were effectively wearing down the Kuomintang regime (or even substantially increasing its divisions) before the attack of Japan, nor that they had any chance to defeat the Japanese occupants (who regarded control of China as vital to their purposes), until their will to fight was broken by defeat on other fronts. Similarly, nobody has ever suggested that the Yugoslav Communists could have evicted the armies of Hitler Germany independent of the outcome of World War II. Conversely, guerrilla "wars of liberation" in Vietnam and Algeria could achieve political victory by military means because neither area was truly vital for the French republic; and Mao's own final civil war defeated a nationalist regime whose political and moral cohesion had been gravely undermined by the disastrous effects of the long-lasting Japanese invasion.

Mao's original doctrine of protracted warfare, so far from neglecting the crucial importance of these "objective conditions," took them into account by laying down what conditions must be fulfilled for passing from guerrilla tactics proper to the stage of decisive battles, and thus implying that these conditions cannot be created at will but must be patiently waited for. (There have been echoes of that realistic approach even in fairly recent Chinese advice to the Vietnamese Communists.) Yet, on the other hand, the attempts of the victorious Chinese Communists to recommend the Maoist strategy of armed struggle as a model for colonial revolutions in general (which became prevalent since about 1959, in the context of their ideological rivalry with the Soviet Communists) have increasingly treated the revolutionary faith and tactical military skill of the guerrillas as universal and sufficient prescriptions for victory in "wars of liberation" that would achieve their magic effects *independent* of the objective conditions in any particular case.

This growing tendency to separate the use of armed revolutionary force from any analysis of political and social conditions, implicit in the transformation of Maoist doctrine under the impact of the ideological rivalry with Russia for leadership of the revolutionary movements of the underdeveloped world, has become quite explicit with the leaders of the Cuban revolution and its would-be imitators in Latin America—with Fidel Castro, Che Guevara, and Régis Debray.

Long before Fidel Castro ever dreamed of calling himself a Marxist-Leninist, and presumably before he read any serious Marxist literature, he acted on the assumption that armed minority action would by itself be sufficient to *create* a revolutionary situation. After this prescription had proved successful in Cuba, Guevara spelled out this new doctrine in so many words as early as 1960. Guevara, of course, did have a background of Marxist knowledge, and in 1960 he still made the validity of the new strategy dependent on one objective condition: the existence of a —presumably unpopular—dictatorial regime. Armed minority uprisings, he then suggested, would not be effective against a government which enjoyed some degree of democratic legitimacy. However, this qualification was dropped by the *Fidelistas* a few years later, when the democratic government of Venezuela became the main target of their effort to export the strategy— and to some extent the leading personnel—of guerrilla insurrection.[2] Since then it has become an official dogma of

---

[2] In 1960, Guevara wrote: "Where a government has come to power by popular vote, of whatever kind, whether falsified or not, and preserves at

"Castroism" that a small but determined and well-led *foco* of professional guerrillas is in principle sufficient to shake the stability of *any* political system in Latin America, and thus to create eventually, by its own action alone, the conditions for the seizure of power.

The consequences of this separation of armed violence from any analysis of social and political preconditions, and hence from any rational political strategy, have been most fully developed in Régis Debray's book *Revolution in the Revolution*. The political significance of this statement of the new doctrine lies in the fact that it represents more than its author's individual opinion. It was written on the basis of long conversations with Castro and other Cuban leaders, who had made the diaries and other documents of their struggle for power accessible to the author, and it was published for mass circulation and used as training material by the ruling party in Cuba.[3] Hence it must be regarded as an authorized summary of Castro's and Guevara's own views of the "Cuban model" for the conquest of power. Now Debray has become the first to state plainly that it is positively harmful for the chances of armed struggle if it arises from the defense of the interests of a particular productive group; for such a struggle by people who are tied to their place of production— like the miners in Bolivia or the peasants of the most impoverished region of Colombia—tends to take the form of "armed self-defense" also in military tactics. People who lead normal working lives, however poor and oppressed, have something

---

least the appearance of constitutional legality, guerrilla warfare cannot be started because the possibilities of peaceful struggle have not yet been exhausted." *La guerra de guerrillas* (Havana, 1960), p. 13. But in September 1963 he wrote that *all* Latin-American regimes were oligarchic dictatorships, and that the struggle could be successfully intensified by forcing them to drop their legalistic mask. "Guerra de guerrillas: un método," in *Cuba socialista*, no. 25 (1963).

[3] For Debray's privileged sources, see the preface to the Cuban edition by its publisher, Roberto Fernandez Retamar, *Revolución en la revolución*, p. 5. For its use as official training material, see Raoul Castro's attack on the pro-Soviet "microfaction" (which had complained about it) in *Granma*, 30 January 1968. I am indebted to Dr. Wolfgang Berner's study: *Der Evangelist des Castroismus-Guevarismus: Régis Debray und seine Guerilla-Doktrin* (1969).

to lose—their working place, their houses with their families— which they want to defend; hence they are militarily too vulnerable and are bound to be defeated in the end by the government's regular forces. In order to have a chance of success, the revolutionary struggle must be conducted by perfectly rootless, and therefore perfectly mobile, professional guerrillas alone!

In the context of this complete dissociation of the "revolution" from any concrete social basis, it is only logical that Debray goes so far as to give his own, arbitrary new meaning to the familiar Marxist terms of "bourgeois" and "proletarian." According to him, only the uprooted guerrilla is the true "proletarian," because he has chosen a life of extreme deprivation and constant danger; he has nothing more to lose but his life, and is willing to sacrifice that. Conversely, the industrial worker in the towns of Latin America is in the eyes of Debray a "bourgeois," simply because he has a regular job and values it. Now any writer is, of course, free to choose and define his own terminology. But an ideologist who uses the terms of "bourgeois" and "proletarian" in this purely moralistic and emotional way, and defines his "proletarian" as a figure wholly divorced from the productive process, has evidently completely abandoned the method of social analysis which Karl Marx inaugurated by *his* use of those terms in the *Communist Manifesto.*

Finally, the cutting of all ties between the revolutionary movement and any defined social basis leads Debray with equal logic to a reversal of the relation between military and political leadership and to a new view of the role and formation of the revolutionary party. He argues that it is futile to concentrate first on creating a Marxist-Leninist party which would then organize a guerrilla movement in due course, because the party could only develop in the towns and its leaders might then be afraid to leave the towns. Instead, the only promising way in Latin America will be to begin by recruiting a band of armed volunteers who will form a guerrilla focus. The volunteers may have little or no previous political experience; they should be attracted on no narrower basis than their willingness to risk their lives in fighting Yankee imperialism and its ruling native stooges. As their ideas become more clearly defined due to the experience of the common struggle, a party will eventually arise—usually only after victory—with the proven guerrilla leaders at its head. Thus military leadership precedes political leadership both in time and as a source of authority.

It is no longer the party that commands the gun—it is the gun that creates the party.

So far I have discussed the progressive dissociation of the revolutionary struggle *for* power from "objective conditions"—first from the maturity of the productive forces and of the consciousness of a large, organized working class for a socialist society, then from any objectively given crisis of society and any defined social basis—along the road leading from Marx via Lenin and Mao to Castro.

If we now turn to the problems of a Communist regime *in* power, we notice in some countries a progressive dissociation of the effort to achieve the utopian goal from the objective conditions of economic development. This is a fairly recent phenomenon. For while Lenin was the first to sanction the seizure of power independent of the conditions of economic maturity, it would never have occurred to Lenin (or, for that matter, to Stalin or any other Russian party leader) to suggest that the criteria of the higher stage of the classless society—work according to ability and distribution according to needs—could become reality before a state of economic abundance had been reached. Stalin was emphatic that the basic task in "building socialism" was to create, at high pressure, those economic preconditions which had been lacking at the moment of political victory. Pending the achievement of economic abundance, the link between individual contribution and individual reward—distribution of scarce goods not according to needs but according to performance— was an indispensable incentive to rapid economic progress. Yet in recent years, conscious attempts to cut this link and to introduce the distributive principles of the "higher stage" of Communism in conditions of poverty and want have been made both in China and in Cuba.

In China, this occurred first at the time of the Great Leap Forward in 1958, when the creation of the People's Communes was accompanied by a major effort to introduce specifically "Communist" relationships, with distribution approaching complete equality, as the share of equal "free supplies" in kind in the members' income rose quickly at the expense of the still unequal cash wages. Thus, the peasants were expected to work less and less for material incentives and more and more from enthusiasm for the common good. In fact, this armylike system of equal supplies in kind was for a time described as "distribution according to needs," even though on the basis of the existing poverty the "needs" were assessed by the authorities, and not by the individuals themselves as Marx had envisaged on a basis of abundance. This attempt was severely criticized by the Soviets at the time, and the Chinese themselves soon backtracked under the impact of its disastrous economic consequences. Yet in the course of the Cultural Revolution, they have largely returned to the same basic view that the use of material incentives and income differentiation, which Lenin and Stalin had regarded as necessary tools of economic development, was really a "revisionist" concession to the capitalist spirit. Mao's decisive argument seems to be that, in the light of Russian experience, a desperate effort must be made to educate the new Communist man here and now, without waiting for the achievement of economic abundance, because otherwise he may never be created at all. The remolding of the people to create the new, collectively motivated man should be given priority over the immediate need for increasing productivity by material incentives, because the latter tend to create not the "new socialist man," but the familiar type of economic man—which to Mao means "capitalist man." [4]

To an increasing extent, the same principles have lately come to be applied in Cuba as well. The use of youthful "volunteer" labor to work under discipline in the rural *campamento* recalls both the earlier Chinese communes and the more recent mass transfer of Chinese students to work in the countryside. It has lately been supplemented by a general ban on overtime payments, based on the same principle that, in the interest of socialist education, the needed increases in output must be achieved by appealing only to collective solidarity and enthusiasm, not to ambition and avarice. In other words, here, too, the connection

---

[4] See my discussion of "Mao's Revolution" in *Encounter*, April 1967.

between the achievement of utopia and the stage of economic development is being denied in action: The goal is dissociated from the objective conditions stipulated by Marx.

Finally, just as the dissociation of the revolutionary struggle for power from an analysis of objective social conditions leads ultimately to the replacement of the primacy of the party and the political leadership by the primacy of the guerrilla *foco* and the military leadership, so the dissociation of the attempt to build a Communist utopia from the effort to achieve its economic preconditions leads to a change in the basic legitimation for ruling a country engaged in that attempt. It issues in a transfer of the claim to legitimate leadership from the exponents of the "scientific" road to socialism and Communism to the exponents of heroic determination, from the technicians skilled in adopting the ideology to economic needs by interpretation to the technicians skilled in enforcing ideological conformity by violence. This is a development that has not, so far, been fully consummated, but is recognizable as an increasingly powerful tendency in both China and Cuba.

In Cuba, the old Communist party had a much clearer economic program as well as a much more effective centralistic discipline than the ideologically heterogeneous crowd of Castro's original followers, and up to a point Castro was eager to learn from them as well as to use their disciplined apparatus. But ultimately it was the charismatic prestige of the successful insurrection rather than the bureaucratic merits of long-term party-building, the military prowess of Castro and a few men around him rather than the ideological certainty of the old Communists that legitimated the new leadership. The resulting regime is probably as much a pseudomorphosis—a similar shape without similar substance—of a Communist party dictatorship as many Latin-American "democracies" have been of true parliamentary or presidential democracies. The Marxist-Leninist party is supposed to rule and its offices are everywhere, but its central organs hardly ever meet. Actual power is exercised by the revolutionary *caudillo*, using his personal impact on television on one side and the armed force of the militia on the other.

In China, the virtual destruction of the Communist party machine as well as of much of the state administration in the course of the Cultural Revolution seems to have started a similar shift of the basis of legitimacy. For Mao turned on the bureaucracy of party and government with its growing preference for routine and economic rationality in the name of the heroic traditions of the Long March and in an effort to train the young generation in the spirit of its veterans. He found it much easier to revive the utopian spirit of the heroic period in the army than in the party or in economic life, and since 1964 increasingly called on all other organizations to "learn from the army." Having undermined the discipline of all other organizations by proclaiming the "right to rebel" in the Cultural Revolution, while leaving only army discipline intact, he has now proceeded to reorganize the shattered party from the top with an unprecedentedly high share of military men in the leadership, on the principle of sworn personal loyalty to him and to the head of the Military Council which is his designated successor.

There seems to be a significant parallel here with developments in some of those revolutionary nationalist single-party regimes, particularly in the Arab world, in which the official ideological doctrine was poorly developed from the beginning, and in which military prestige has therefore sooner or later proved superior to party legitimacy. The case of Nasser's Egypt may be regarded as too obvious to be really significant in our context, because there the military *junta* was first, and the successive attempts to create a state party have only confirmed its character as at best an auxiliary to charismatic rule by a military leader. But it seems symptomatic that the Algerian *FLN*, which originated as a fighting guerrilla organization under political nationalist leadership, proved unable to provide stable one-party rule until a full-time military commander took political control by force barely bothering to have himself confirmed by the legitimate party organs afterwards. The transformation of the *Ba'ath* party, which started with a more elaborate nationalist-socialist ideology than either the Algerians or the Nasserites, yet has degenerated into little more than a congeries of rival officers' clans in both Syria and Iraq, the two countries in which it officially governs, seems even more eloquent testimony to the strength of a general tendency. It may be at least worth inquiring whether this parallel tendency to a decline in the role of political leadership and ideological guidance, and to a reversion of legitimacy to the military hero (or would-be hero), to the charismatic specialist in the techniques of violence, in a number of underdeveloped countries under both Communist and national-revolutionary regimes is not due to the impact of similar causes.

The dissociation of revolutionary passion and action from the Marxist belief in the rationality of history is not confined to the particular examples I have analyzed. On the contrary, it appears to be a universal process, in which movements and regimes that remain strongly influenced by a Marxist outlook are ceasing to be revolutionary, while those that remain revolutionary renounce essential parts of the Marxist analysis.

Thus we observe that the Communist party regime in the Soviet Union—as it comes increasingly to regard the development of its productive capacity as the only decisive factor for its advance towards the "higher stage" of Communism and as its principal contribution to the victory of its cause on a world scale—is becoming less concerned with either forcibly imposing "revolutions from above" on its own people or actively fostering revolutionary movements elsewhere.[5] It has retained the belief that the final, world-wide achievement of Communism is guaranteed by the laws of history—but it interprets those laws in an increasingly revisionist spirit as working mainly through the logic of economic development, so that the eventual attainment of utopia will not require further revolutionary action on its part. Even more explicitly, Communist parties in some advanced Western countries, particularly those with a strong following in a modern, industrial working class, are proposing revisionist strategies for the socialist transformation of their countries by peaceful, democratic methods, based on the expectation that the inherent trends of modern industrial societies will enable them to join the gov-

---

[5] For a fuller analysis of this development, see my "Has the Revolution a Future?" *Encounter*, January–February 1965.

ernments and carry out their program with majority support, and preferably without violence.

Conversely, those New Left movements in the same countries, recruited chiefly from students and other adolescents divorced from production, that are preoccupied with the need for violent action and the revolutionary overthrow of the social order, have come increasingly to reject the Marxist belief in the rationality of history and the link between the progress of industrialization, the growth of the working class, and the utopian goal. Instead, they are looking for support to the peoples of the underdeveloped "countryside of the world" whose revolutionary ardor has not yet been dampened by material comfort, and for guidance to Mao and Castro who promise to solve the economic problems of their poor countries through an upsurge of collective effort called forth by an appeal to solidarity rather than to egoistic self-interest. Nor is their choice difficult to understand in view of the fact that the working class in the industrially advanced countries has become less and less revolutionary, and that the successful industrialization of Russia has evidently not created a society without classes and domination, but a bureaucratic class society still ruled by a harsh party dictatorship after fifty years.

To return to the remark of Raymond Aron's that I quoted earlier, it has become obvious that the world has not come the least bit closer to the goals of Rousseau after following the precepts of Saint-Simon for more than a century. Hence those who will not abandon utopianism have at long last decided to try and approach those goals directly. The intellectual importance of Herbert Marcuse for the development of the Western New Left is that he has classically formulated this disappointment of the Marxist utopian who feels betrayed by the logic of history. The author of *Reason and Revolution* still puts his trust in that Goddess; to the author of *One-Dimensional Man*, the Devil is the Prince of the Modern World. But once the assurance is gone that justice will triumph when the millennium comes in the fullness of time, the only alternative left to the believer is to try and bring it about by storming the heavens here and now. We are faced with a regression to a more primitive kind of secular religion—as different from that of Marx as was the faith of the Bohemian

Taborites and the Muenster Anabaptists from the mainstream of Western Christianity.

As the term "regression" implies, the breakdown of the rationalist and historical constructs by which Marx had "mediated" the revolutionary struggle for utopia, and the consequent return to immediate utopianism and immediate violence links the contemporary New Left to an earlier type of revolutionary tradition. It is a tradition which, in contrast to Marx, directly expressed the romantic resistance to the growth of mechanized industry and to the destruction of "natural" communities by the process of modernization, and exalted the values of "life," community feeling, and spontaneous, violent action in opposition to "calculating" reason. There are, in fact, two distinct but frequently entangled strands of this romantic-revolutionary tradition, which we may provisionally designate by the names of two friends who were together involved in the Dresden insurrection of 1849: Mikhail Bakunin and Richard Wagner.

It is hardly accidental that Bakunin has lately been rediscovered by sections of the New Left in a number of countries. What seems to attract them is not just his anarchist vision, the goal of a stateless society of free associations of producers (which others have developed more fully both before and after him), but his passionate opposition to the bureaucratic rationality of the rising industrial age; his readiness to assign priority to the "creative passion for destruction" over any program for what was to come afterward; his hatred and contempt for liberalism, reform, and all representative institutions, not only in Russia but everywhere; his belief that a cumulation of uncoordinated, spontaneous acts of local violence could bring down both the Czarist regime and the ruling economic and social system (alternating with fantasies of a supercentralistic, conspirative organization which were never put into practice), and his tendency to rely on the uprooted peasant (the "bandit") as the true revolutionary, and on the backward regions on the eastern and southern periphery of Europe—on Russia, Spain, southern Italy—for the ultimate revolutionary assault on the modern core that was already corrupted by capitalism and bureaucracy. Yet Bakunin's Pan-

Slavism, his hatred of Germans and Jews, and his abiding hostility to liberalism (which he did not disdain to use as arguments in the *"Confession"* he sent to the Czar from prison in the hope of being reprieved) constitute a bond with other ideologies of antimodern violence directed not to the goal of egalitarian anarchy, but to that of the dictatorship of an elite in the name of nationalism. Richard Wagner, who was to become one of the intellectual ancestors of Nazism, already dreamed—and spoke and wrote—of the destruction of the bankers' rule by a popular emperor and of the replacement of Westernized, liberal pseudoculture by a truly national German folk culture at the time of his youthful friendship with Bakunin.[6] The kinship between the more violent and irrational forms of anarchism and fascist tendencies has since been repeatedly demonstrated in other countries and later generations.

Thus Georges Sorel, whose special contribution to the syndicalist movement has been to give it an irrationalist turn and to exalt the role of violence as the test of social vitality, came for a time to support the extreme right-wing *Action Française* and influenced the elitism of Pareto and Mussolini. Again, if one asks to what historical model Fidel Castro's early intellectual background, his style of governing Cuba by harangues, and his reliance on a mixture of nationalist and socialist appeals bear the most striking resemblance, the picture that comes to mind is not that of any victorious Communist leader, but of Gabriele D'Annunzio, his "Republic of Fiume," and his highly original witches' brew of nationalist passion, anarchist ideals, and plebiscitary techniques of government (though Castro, no doubt, has shown less poetical and more political ability than his illustrious predecessor). And D'Annunzio's movement, by its ideological prestige and its practical failure, helped to recruit many of the cadres for Italian Fascism.

Finally, the semianarchist violence of Benito Mussolini's antimilitarist agitation during the Libyan war of 1911, when he was at the height of his New Left period as editor of the Social-

---

[6] For Wagner's views at the time, see the chapter on Wagner in Hans Kohn, *The Mind of Germany* (1960), particularly pp. 196–197. For the Dresden episode in Bakunin's life, see E. H. Carr, *Michael Bakunin* (1937), pp. 186–194.

ist party daily, fed on the same emotional and partly on the same ideological sources which enabled him in 1914–15 to break with the Socialist workers' movement as a violent advocate of a "revolutionary" war for nationalist objectives on the side of the Entente, and later to become the founder of Fascism and lead it to victory through terror. I might also mention as belonging to the same spiritual family those German ideologues of the 1920s —the period preceding the victory of National Socialism—who were then known as "National Bolsheviks" or "*Linke Leute von Rechts.*" They sought to combine an anticapitalist social radicalism (which in their case was much more genuine than with the Nazi party) with an anti-Western but often explicitly pro-Russian nationalism and with a cult of heroic violence based on the memory of the "frontline experience"—of the true community of those who had been ready to die (and to kill) for the fatherland.

In short, those ardent believers in salvation on earth by political revolution who rejected the historical and rationalist "mediation" of their goal in favor of irrational passion and immediate violence have always tended to rely on romantic ideologies using varying mixtures of arguments of the Bakunist and the nationalist-fascist type. It is typical that in the later writings of Marcuse, his earlier Hegelian-Marxist rationalism is getting increasingly overlaid by the elitist anti-Western cultural pessimism of Martin Heidegger—his first teacher.

The revival of both strands of the romantic ideological tradition in the irrational revolt of the Western New Left indicates a revival of the basic emotional attitude underlying them both. The rebels reject the modern industrial world in both its Western-capitalist and Soviet-Communist forms—the crude materialism of its values, the pervasive bureaucratism of its organization, the purely instrumental character of its rationality. Indeed, their despair is a reaction to the discovery that the process of "rationalization" in the instrumental sense, which Max Weber recognized as a universal law of the modern world, does not assure the triumph of "Reason" in the sense of the achievement of utopia. It is the same rejection of the industrial order that also constitutes the fundamental link between the Western New Left and some of the revolutionary movements of the poor nations. To the new romantics, Mao Tse-tung and Castro embody the promise of a spontaneous community without conflict, hence without need for rational rules and institutions—just as to Frantz Fanon, Sorel has revealed the liberating dignity of irrational violence.

But this means that in some of the revolutionary movements of the excolonial and semicolonial peoples, we are now facing a "revolt against the West" in a new and different sense. The classical nationalist movements for colonial liberation and for the independent development of the underdeveloped countries have always been, and many of them still are, characterized by ambivalence toward the West. They have been fighting for political independence from the Western powers, for economic independence from Western capital, to some extent also for the chance to preserve their cultural identity, to keep their own soul. But they have also wished to learn from the West in order to imitate it successfully in the techniques of production and power, to catch up with it in science and material development. For the classical movements of national liberation from colonialism or semicolonialism, one essential goal has been to make their country as rich and powerful as its former Western masters, though this goal could only be achieved by a struggle for independence which often required prolonged conflicts with the Western powers. This was an ambivalent attitude in that it was *not* inspired by a total rejection of Western models and values, but in part by a desire to emulate Western achievements even though the road there led through a struggle against Western domination.

The new attitude which we encounter in Mao's cultural revolution, in Castro's Cuba, and potentially in other movements influenced by them (whether formally Communist or not) *is* a total rejection of some Western values. It is a determination to stay poor-but-honest rather than imitate the West in promoting the development of economic man (as the Soviets have done), to accept some of the consequences of nondevelopment (though not all) rather than assimilate to Western civilization. Indeed, we observe for the first time since the decline of the early nativistic movements in those countries, for the first time in movements that claim to be not traditionalist but modern, nationalist, and revolutionary, a fundamental resistance not just to Western power and Western capital, but to the pull of Western civilization that had hitherto been inseparable from any effort at the modernization of non-Western countries.

This in turn throws further light also on the revolt of part of the young generation in the West; for that revolt, too, is directed against important aspects of Western civilization.

This is often denied by well-meaning liberals who, in trying to understand the young rebels, argue that the latter "really" share our liberal values—that they merely take them more seriously than their hypocritical elders and want to *act* on principles which the establishment merely *talks* about. If that were all, we should be faced with a political and social movement of a familiar type, for that is indeed the classical role of revolutionary (and also of reformist) movements within a growing civilization —to regenerate the traditional values of that civilization by giving them a new institutional content corresponding to changed social conditions. Thus the basic Western idea of the rights of the human person has been reinterpreted in course of time from referring to "the rights of each according to his station" to meaning "equal political rights for all," and more recently to imply the rights of each to equal opportunity and social security. But this, it seems to me, no longer applies to many of either the politically active or the passive and nonpolitical young rebels of our time.

For while it is true that they generally accept the familiar values of love and individual freedom, of truth and social justice, merely seeking to turn these values into an indictment of the older generation, it is also true that they have increasingly come to reject the values of material and in part even of intellectual achievement and of the effort and discipline needed to accomplish it, including the discipline of reason—values which are equally essential parts of the cultural heritage of the West. The same is apparent in their rejection of any time perspective in the name of a cult of immediacy; for the sense of measured time and the gearing of action to foresight have been basic for all Western civilization from the age when Western church towers were first endowed with clocks to the latest achievements of science and industry. In other words, we are witnessing a major failure to transmit an important part of our basic values to a significant part of the young generation.

Indeed it seems to me that the rebellion of the young which is taking place in all advanced Western countries, and which is assuming both politically revolutionary forms and the form of a passive nonpolitical refusal to grow into roles within the industrial society and submit to its pressures, is not primarily a political phenomenon. It is, above all, a sign of a crisis in our civilization.

For there are, I believe, two basic tests for the vitality of a civilization. One is the ability to transmit to the young generation its essential values even while adapting their concrete, practical meaning to changing conditions. The other is its capacity to attract and assimilate outsiders, "barbarians," who come within range of its material influence—and not only subject them and disrupt their traditional forms of life.

As recently as the last generation, this vitality of Western civilization was subjected to extremely serious strain, for the destructive outbreak of Nazism constituted a radical, nihilistic revolt against that civilization from within. Yet following its military defeat, the reassimilation of Germany by the West has been extremely successful, and even the Soviet Union, for all the rigidity of its political structure and all the seriousness of its continuing conflicts with the Western powers, shows unmistakable signs of a progressive *cultural* "convergence" with the West. Now for the first time, the West is faced simultaneously with growing evidence of a crisis both in its capacity to assimilate its "external proletariat" (in the sense given to this term in Toynbee's *Study of History*), the poor, underdeveloped, non-Western peoples, and in its ability to transmit its heritage to its own youth.

This diagnosis is confirmed by the fact that the quasi-religious character of some of the new movements is manifested not only in their commitment to chiliastic goals, but in their cult of savior-leaders and in their search for a new code of conduct. Thus the asceticism and heroic self-sacrifice of Che Guevara have permitted the growth of a legend around him that combines Christ-like features with those of a militant secular leader. The official cult of Mao Tse-tung no longer describes him as a mere creative continuator of the Marxist-Leninist revolutionary tradition, not even merely as the unique architect of the political rebirth of the Chinese nation and state: He is presented as the author of a totally new system of thought and action—a system that will enable all those to work miracles who believe in Mao and live by his new rules. Many of the "Quotations from Chairman Mao" in the little *Red Book,* from which hundreds of millions of Chinese are taught to recite several times a day, stand in competition not with any Western or Soviet political document, but with the *Analects* of Confucius and the Bible.

Yet while the new movements are largely united in their rejection of the Western way of life (or, at any rate, of major aspects of it), they diverge widely in seeking to define their alternatives. Castro and Mao reject Western materialism, and, at least Mao, also Western individualism. But both believe in the need for collective effort and discipline which are rejected by large parts of the Western New Left as well as by the nonpolitical Western hippies, dropouts, and drug-takers. Conversely, many of the would-be revolutionaries of the New Left retain an anarchist type of individualism; but "petty bourgeois anarchism" remains a term of abuse in Cuba and China as much as in Russia, while the prophets of a nonpolitical drug culture clearly believe that community can only be established by escaping from individuality.

There is thus no unity of values among the new movements except in their common target of attack—their negation of the modern industrial society. Beyond that the New Left's admiration for Castro and Mao is based on a romantic misunderstanding that sees those hard-striving, hard-driving taskmasters of their peoples as the Noble Savages of our time.

This, then, is the tentative conclusion at which we have arrived. The new type of revolutionary movements, both on the outer fringes of our Western-centered world and in the advanced Western countries, as well as some phenomena within the latter that are not "revolutionary" in the conventional, political sense of the term, can best be understood as symptoms of a crisis of Western civilization. It is this which explains their increasing turning away from the Marxist type of analysis and strategy: for Marxism, in its origin, its values, and its commitment to rationality, is indissolubly linked to its Western heritage.

I am conscious that while that conclusion may help us to grasp the historical significance, intellectual background, and spiritual character of the new movements, it does not answer the further questions about their concrete social roots, the reasons for their appearance at this time, and their prospects of political success. Nor can I even attempt to deal seriously with those questions in the framework of the present essay. All that is possible here is to sketch out some of the directions in which the answers may be looked for.

The main point I should like to make here is that the crisis in our civilization has followed an unprecedented acceleration both of the external expansion of its influence and of the pace of its internal change.

Externally, Western expansion over the last two centuries has effectively disrupted the traditional societies created by other civilizations all over the globe. The political reflux of that expansion, the extrusion of Western dominance from the former colonial areas in the last few decades, has not reversed its disruptive effects and has left the new nations with problems of "modernization" which in most cases are proving far more difficult than anticipated.

As I have already suggested, the goal of modernization was at first generally conceived as implying at least a partial imitation of the West, even if often by different institutional means—for instance, industrialization not by free enterprise but by state planning, or political mobilization by single-party rule rather than by multi-party competition. But it now looks as if in countries where "development" in this sense proves particularly difficult—owing to the pressure of population, or to the extreme shortage of cadres with modern training, or simply to the strength of traditionalist cultural resistance, or to any combination of those factors—important aspects of the goal itself are coming to be doubted. Total rejection of the Western model is proclaimed in the accents of revolt in order to avoid the confession of failure and the disappointment of the expectations aroused. As the West can always be blamed for having started the whole agonizing process by its intrusion, and for either having refused to help the development of the latecomers or at any rate having failed to give enough aid to be effective, the rejection of the unattainable model is accompanied by a deepening of resentment against its possessors.

Internally, the acceleration of change in technology, and with it, in social structures and habits of living, has in the last few decades created intense moral uncertainty in many Western countries. That moral uncertainty of a generation of parents who on many issues are no longer sure what is right or wrong is probably at the root of their failure to transmit their values effectively, and of the consequent revolt among the young. What appears today as a widespread rebellion of youth against authority is, I suspect, largely born of frustration caused by the absence of authority—in the sense of a lack not of severity, but of convinced and therefore convincing models of conduct. For a growing civilization to survive in a climate of unending social change, as is the fate of ours, the central problem is to combine a belief in the absolute validity of its fundamental values with flexibility in the practical rules derived from them. As the pace of change accelerates, the difficulty of solving this problem increases, and the tendency towards a polarization of attitudes between a combination of firm belief with impractical rigidity on one side and of pragmatic flexibility with fundamental relativism on the other becomes stronger.

In the Western industrial societies of today, this basic problem of preserving a continuity of values in the flux of changing conditions and rules appears in a variety of concrete shapes. Probably the most important of those is the loss of a sense of common purpose in the midst of enormous, accelerating material progress. While that progress has not abolished scarcity and made effort and discipline superfluous (as the new utopians believe), it has indeed created an unprecedented degree of relative affluence, solved the crucial problem of steadiness of employment, and permitted improvements in the standards of living, leisure, and social security on so broad a front as to deprive traditional class conflicts of their revolutionary potential.

Yet this tremendous progress has been achieved at the price of a concentration on individual material advantage and been accompanied by the loss of a sense of common purpose, as first the traditional certainties of religious faith and then the substitutes offered by national loyalties were undermined. The moral sensitivity of the young is shocked by the contrast between the intense effort devoted by their elders to the pursuit of minor individual advantages or to expenditure for national military power on one side, and their lack of concern for the suffering of the marginal poor inside and the undernourished majority of mankind outside the industrial world on the other. The young are all the more assured of the righteousness of their criticism because they have experienced the moral uncertainty of their elders from an early age. As a result, many of them perceive an acute moral conflict between the ideals they have been taught and the competitive conformism into which they are expected to grow—a conflict all the more insoluble because the society which they reject as "empty" is technically well-functioning and is apparently accepted without question by the large majority of adults. Now where intolerable moral conflict is not confined to individuals but expresses a crisis of civilization, the response has always been an upsurge of utopian beliefs—a collective escape into the dream of a perfect society where every conflict would be solved in advance. The difference this time is that we are dealing with a utopianism inspired not by hope, but by despair. That is the ultimate reason for its lack of a time perspective, its irrationality, and its violence.

As for the social locus of the revolt, just as a turn toward total rejection of the Western model is most likely to occur among those non-Western nations which experience the most discouraging difficulties in their effort at modernization, so a radical denial of the need for material effort and discipline appears to prove most attractive to those strata of Western youth that have remained longest and furthest removed from the productive process—be it as students from upper- and middle-class families or as undereducated members of minority groups who find themselves virtually unemployable through no fault of their own.

Indulgence in pipe dreams about the effortless abundance possible in the "postindustrial society" is most natural for those who have either been preserved from any contact with the productive sources of our relative affluence by the economic security of their parents, or have been barred from both those sources and their benefits by the underprivileged position of theirs. Karl Marx once pointed out that while the (nonproductive) proletariat of ancient Rome lived on society, modern capitalist society lived on its (industrial) proletariat. But the "internal proletariat" that is coming to be as disaffected from Western civilization as some parts of its "external proletariat" does not consist of the industrial workers for whom Marx reserved the term. It is a "proletariat" in the ancient Roman sense, divorced from production but convinced that society owes it a living, and willing only to supplement the publicly supplied bread by providing its own circuses. For today as in Rome, the only forms of separate collective action open to a group that cannot withdraw its productive contribution, because it makes none, are highly emotional and violent. The neo-Bakuninism of the New Left appears to be the ideological expression of this transfer of the revolutionary mission from the industrial working class to the neo-Roman proletariat of our time. As its purely destructive forms of action repel all productive sectors of society but attract its marginal and semicriminal elements, the danger of its degeneration into a movement of the *Lumpenproletariat* becomes manifest.

There remains the question of the political prospects of these new movements. In terms of "power politics," I do not rate their chances of success very high; that is indeed implied in what I have described as their lack of rationality. Because of Maoist irrationality, China seems to have made very little progress in the last decade, except on the narrowest sector of nuclear weapons; and it will not become an effective model of development so long as it remains Maoist in this sense. Nor has the model of Castroism, and the strategy of small guerrilla bands starting operations regardless of social and political conditions, gained much influence in Latin America or shown much promise of doing so in the foreseeable future—unless widespread failures of development give them a chance. Finally, today's campus rebels are not, like the student movements of Czarist Russia or Weimar Germany or British India, the forerunners of a political revolution. They do not operate in stagnant or politically oppressed societies and are not the articulate expression of the inarticulate mood of large masses of people. Moreover, for all the traits of kinship we have mentioned, the New Left students are not fascist—and Bakuninists have never and nowhere taken power: Indeed, they would not know what to do with it.

Nevertheless, the danger to Western society from these new movements is serious. It is not the danger of a "Third World bloc" abroad or "revolution" at home; it is the prospect of destruction, decay, and barbarization. The real threat is not that Mao will be able to overrun Asia or that Castro will revolutionize Latin America. It is that overpopulation and hunger, indigenous governmental incompetence, and Western self-satisfied indifference will cause the festering sores of despair, political instability, and violence to spread. Again, the real menace within the West is not that young extremists will "take over"; they cannot even take over the universities. But they can paralyze and, in some cases, destroy them by first destroying the climate of tolerance and rational discourse which is the breath of academic life. They can deprive our societies of an important part of the well-trained and loyal elites needed for the steady renewal of administration and economic management, of research and education. And they can create a backlash of police brutality and right-wing extremism which will in effect help them to obstruct the working of democracy and the constructive solution of urgent problems.

I do not, of course, know any simple answer to these problems, any magic prescription for coping with them. All I should like to state in conclusion is that, in dealing with the danger constituted by the new type of revolutionary movements, it is wrong —even more wrong than it was with the old type of Communist movements—to be obsessed with "the enemy" as if he were a devil suddenly appearing out of nowhere, a *diabolus ex machina*. The forces of destruction have, of course, to be resisted; civilization cannot be defended by surrendering to violence. But this is only the minor part of the task. Above all, civilization must be defended by upholding and renewing its standards in action, by combining a faith in its values with the determination to apply them constructively in a changing world—and therefore to make sacrifices for them—inside and outside the West. Only if we can restore hope by doing that will the West survive. Otherwise it will succumb to barbarization—and that means (as the whole of history is there to teach us) succumbing not to some particular barbarian ideology, movement, or tribe, but to its own failure.

[1969]

THE NEW REFORMATION

by Paul Goodman

For a long time modern societies have been operating as if religion were a minor and moribund part of the scheme of things. But this is unlikely. Men do not do without a system of "meanings" that everybody believes and puts his hope in even if, or especially if, he doesn't know anything about it; what Freud called a "shared psychosis," meaningful because shared, and with the power that resides in deep fantasy and longing. In advanced countries, indeed, it is science and technology themselves that have gradually, and finally triumphantly, become the system of mass faith, not disputed by various political ideologies and nationalisms that have also had religious uses.

Now this basic faith is threatened. Dissident young people are saying that science is antilife, it is a Calvinist obsession, it has been a weapon of white Europe to subjugate colored races, and scientific technology has manifestly become diabolical. Along with science, the young discredit the professions in general, and the whole notion of "disciplines" and academic learning. If these views take hold, it adds up to a crisis of belief, and the effects are incalculable. Every status and institution would be affected. Present political troubles could become endless religious wars. Here again, as in politics and morals, the worldwide youth disturbance may indicate a turning point in history, and we must listen to it carefully.

In 1967 I gave a course on "Professionalism" at the New

School for Social Research in New York, attended by about twenty-five graduate students from all departments. My bias was the traditional one: Professionals are autonomous individuals beholden to the nature of things and the judgment of their peers, and bound by an explicit or implicit oath to benefit their clients and the community. To teach this, I invited seasoned professionals whom I esteemed—a physician, engineer, journalist, architect, etc. These explained to the students the obstacles that increasingly stood in the way of honest practice, and their own life experience in circumventing them.

To my surprise, the class unanimously rejected them. Heatedly and rudely they called my guests liars, finks, mystifiers, or deluded. They showed that every professional was co-opted and corrupted by the System, all decisions were made top-down by the power structure and bureaucracy, professional peer-groups were conspiracies to make more money. All this was importantly true and had, of course, been said by the visitors. Why had the students not heard? As we explored further, we came to the deeper truth, that they did not believe in the existence of real professions at all; professions were concepts of repressive society and "linear thinking." I asked them to envisage any social order they pleased—Mao's, Castro's, some anarchist utopia—and wouldn't there be engineers who knew about materials and stresses and strains? Wouldn't people get sick and need to be treated? Wouldn't there be problems of communication? No, they insisted; it was important only to be human, and all else would follow.

Suddenly I realized that they did not really believe that there was a nature of things. Somehow all functions could be reduced to interpersonal relations and power. There was no knowledge, but only the sociology of knowledge. They had so well learned that physical and sociological research is subsidized and conducted for the benefit of the ruling class that they did not believe there was such a thing as simple truth. To be required to learn something was a trap by which the young were put down and co-opted. Then I knew that I could not get through to them. I had imagined that the worldwide student protest had to do with changing political and moral institutions, to which I was sympathetic, but I now saw that we had to do with a religious crisis of the magnitude of the Reformation in the fifteen-hundreds, when not only all institutions but all learning had been corrupted by the Whore of Babylon.

The irony was that I myself had said ten years ago, in *Growing Up Absurd*, that these young were growing up without a world for them, and therefore they were "alienated," estranged from nature and other people. But I had then been thinking of juvenile delinquents and a few beats; and a few years later I had been heartened by the Movement in Mississippi, the Free Speech protest in Berkeley, the Port Huron statement of SDS, the resistance to the Vietnam war, all of which made human sense and were not absurd at all. But the alienating circumstances had proved too strong after all; here were absurd graduate students, most of them political "activists."

Alienation is a Lutheran concept: "God has turned His face away, things have no meaning, I am estranged in the world." By the time of Hegel the term was applied to the general condition of rational man, with his "objective" sciences and institutions divorced from his "subjectivity," which was therefore irrational and impulsive. In his revision of Hegel, Marx explained this as the effect of man's losing his essential nature as a cooperative producer, because centuries of exploitation, culminating in capitalism, had fragmented the community and robbed the workman of the means of production. Comte and Durkheim pointed to the weakening of social solidarity and the contradiction between law and morality, so that people lost their bearings—this was anomie, an acute form of alienation that could lead to suicide or aimless riot. By the end of the nineteenth century, alienation came to be used as the term for insanity, derangement of perceived reality, and psychiatrists were called alienists.

Contemporary conditions of life have certainly deprived people, and especially young people, of a meaningful world in which they can act and find themselves. Many writers and the dissenting students themselves have spelled it out. For instance, in both schools and corporations, people cannot pursue their own interests or exercise initiative. Administrators are hypocrites who sell people out for the smooth operation of the system. The budget for war has grotesquely distorted reasonable social priorities. Worst of all, the authorities who make the decisions are incompetent to cope with modern times: We are in danger of extinction, the biosphere is being destroyed, two-thirds of mankind are starving. Let me here go on to some other factors that demand a religious response.

There is a lapse of faith in science. Science has not produced the general happiness that people expected, and now it has fallen under the sway of greed and power; whatever its beneficent past, people fear that its further progress will do more harm than good. And rationality itself is discredited. Probably it is more significant than we like to think that intelligent young people dabble in astrology, witchcraft, psychedelic dreams, and whatever else is despised by science; in some sense they are not kidding. They need to control their fate, but they hate scientific explanations.

Every one of these young grew up since Hiroshima. They do not talk about atom bombs—not nearly so much as we who campaigned against the shelters and fall-out—but the bombs explode in their dreams, as Otto Butz found in his study of collegians at San Francisco State, and now George Dennison, in *The Lives of Children,* shows that it was the same with small slum children whom he taught at the First Street School in New York. Again and again students have told me that they take it for granted they will not survive the next ten years. This is not an attitude with which to prepare for a career or to bring up a family.

Whether or not the bombs go off, human beings are becoming useless. Old people are shunted out of sight at an increasingly earlier age, young people are kept on ice till an increasingly later age. Small farmers and other technologically unemployed are dispossessed or left to rot. Large numbers are put away as incompetent or deviant. Racial minorities that cannot shape up are treated as a nuisance. Together, these groups are a large majority of the population. Since labor will not be needed much longer, there is vague talk of a future society of "leisure," but there is no thought of a kind of community in which all human beings would be necessary and valued.

The institutions, technology, and communications have infected even the "biological core," so that people's sexual desires are no longer genuine. This was powerfully argued by Wilhelm Reich a generation ago and it is now repeated by Herbert Mar-

cuse. When I spoke for it in the nineteen-forties, I was condemned by the radicals, for example, C. Wright Mills, as a "bed-
room revisionist."

A special aspect of biological corruption is the spreading
ugliness, filth, and tension of the environment in which the
young grow up. If Wordsworth was right—I think he was—that
children must grow up in an environment of beauty and simple
affections in order to become trusting, open, and magnanimous
citizens, then the offspring of our ghettos, suburbs, and compli-
cated homes have been disadvantaged, no matter how much
money there is. This lack cannot be remedied by art in the curriculum, nor by vest-pocket playgrounds, nor by banning bill-
boards from bigger highways. Cleaning the river might help, but
that will be the day.

If we start from the premise that the young are in a religious
crisis, that they doubt there is really a nature of things, and they
are sure there is not a world for themselves, many details of their
present behavior become clearer. Alienation is a powerful motivation, of unrest, fantasy, and reckless action. It leads, as we
shall see, to religious innovation, new sacraments to give life
meaning. But it is a poor basis for politics, including revolutionary politics.

It is said that the young dissidents never offer a constructive
program. And apart from the special cases of Czechoslovakia
and Poland, where they confront an unusually outdated system,
this is largely true. In France, China, Germany, Egypt, England,
the United States, and so on, most of the issues of protest have
been immediate gut issues, and the tactics have been mainly disruptive, without coherent proposals for a better society. But this
makes for bad politics. Unless one has a program, there is no
way to persuade the other citizens, who do not have one's gut
complaints, to come along. Instead one confronts them hostilely
and they are turned off, even when they might be sympathetic.
But the confrontation is inept too, for the alienated young cannot take other people seriously as having needs of their own; a
spectacular instance was the inability of the French youth to
communicate with the French working class, in May 1968. In
Gandhian theory, the confronter aims at future community with
the confronted; he will not let him continue a course that is bad

for *him,* and so he appeals to his deeper reason. But instead of this *Satyagraha,* soul force, we have seen plenty of hate. The confronted are *not* taken as human beings, but as pigs, etc. But how can the young people think of a future community when they themselves have no present world, no profession or other job in it, and no trust in other human beings? Instead, some young radicals seem to entertain the disastrous illusion that other people can be compelled by fear. This can lead only to crushing reaction.

All the "political" activity makes sense, however, if it is understood that it is not aimed at social reconstruction at all, but is a way of desperately affirming that they are alive and want a place in the sun. "I am a revolutionary," said Cohn-Bendit, leader of the French students in 1968, "because it is the best way of living." And young Americans pathetically and truly say that there is no other way to be taken seriously. Then it is not necessary to have a program; the right method is to act, against any vulnerable point and wherever one can rally support. The purpose is not politics, but to have a movement and form a community. This is exactly what Saul Alinsky prescribed to rally outcast blacks.

And such conflictful action has indeed caused social changes. In France it was conceded by the Gaullists that "nothing would ever be the same." In the United States, the changes in social attitude during the last ten years are unthinkable without the youth action, with regard to war, the military-industrial, corporate organization and administration, the police, the blacks. When the actors have been in touch with the underlying causes of things, issues have deepened and the Movement has grown. But for the alienated, again, action easily slips into activism, and conflict is often spite and stubbornness. There is excitement and notoriety, much human suffering, and the world no better off. (*New Left Notes* runs a column wryly called, "We Made the News Today, Oh Boy!") Instead of deepening awareness and a sharpening political conflict, there occurs the polarization of mere exasperation. It often seems that the aim is just to have a shambles. Impatiently the ante of tactics is raised beyond what the "issue" warrants, and support melts away. Out on a limb, the leaders become desperate and fanatical, intolerant of criticism, dictatorial. The Movement falls to pieces.

Yet it is noteworthy that when older people like myself are critical of the wrongheaded activism, we nevertheless almost invariably concede that the young are *morally* justified. For what is the use of patience and reason when meantime millions are being killed and starved, and when bombs and nerve gas are being stockpiled? Against the entrenched power responsible for these things, it might be better to do something idiotic now than something perhaps more practical in the long run. I don't know which is less demoralizing.

Maybe the truth is revealed in the following conversation I had with a young hippie at a college in Massachusetts. He was dressed like an (American) Indian—buckskin fringes and a headband, red paint on his face. All his life, he said, he had tried to escape the encompassing evil of our society that was trying to destroy his soul. "But if you're always escaping," I said, "and never attentively study it, how can you make a wise judgment about society or act effectively to change it?" "You see, you don't dig!" he cried. "It's just ideas like 'wise' and 'acting effectively' that we can't stand." He was right. He was in the religious dilemma of Faith vs. Works. Where I sat, Works had some reality; but in the reign of the Devil, as he felt it, all Works are corrupted, they are part of the System; only Faith can avail. But he didn't have Faith either.

Inevitably, the alienated seem to be inconsistent in how they take the present world. Hippies attack technology and are scornful of rationality, but they buy up electronic equipment and motorcycles, and with them the whole infrastructure. Activists say that civil liberties are bourgeois and they shout down their opponents; but they clamor in court for their civil liberties. Those who say that the university is an agent of the powers that be, do not mean thereby to reassert the ideal role of the university, but to use the university for their own propaganda. Yet if I point out these apparent inconsistencies, it does not arouse shame or guilt. How is this? It is simply that they do not really understand that technology, civil law, and the university are *human* institutions, for which they too are responsible; they take them as brute-given, just what's there, to be manipulated as convenient. But convenient for whom? The trouble with this attitude is that these institutions, works of spirit in history, are how Man has made himself and is. If they treat them as mere things, rather than being vigilant for them, they themselves become nothing. And nothing comes from nothing.

In general, their lack of a sense of history is bewildering. It is impossible to convey to them that the deeds were done by human beings, that John Hampden confronted the king and wouldn't pay the war tax just like us, or that Beethoven too, just like a rock 'n' roll band, made up his music as he went along, from odds and ends, with energy, spontaneity, and passion—how else do they think he made music? And they no longer remember their own history. A few years ago there was a commonly accepted story of mankind, beginning with the beats, going on to the Chessman case, the HUAC bust, the Freedom Rides, and climaxing in the Berkeley Victory—"The first human event in forty thousand years," Mike Rossman, one of the innumerable spokesmen, told me. But this year I find that nothing antedates Chicago '68. Elder statesmen, like Sidney Lens and especially Staughton Lynd, have been trying with heroic effort to recall the American antecedents of present radical and libertarian slogans and tactics, but it doesn't rub off. I am often hectored to my face with formulations that I myself put in their mouths, that have become part of the oral tradition, two years old, author prehistoric. Most significant of all, it has been whispered to me—but I can't check up, because I don't speak the language—that among the junior-high-school students, aged twelve and thirteen, that's really where it's at! Quite different from what goes on in the colleges that I visit.

What I do notice, however, is that dozens of Underground newspapers have a noisy style. Though each one is doing his thing, there is not much idiosyncrasy in the spontaneous variety. The political radicals are, as if mesmerized, repeating the power plays, factionalism, random abuse, and tactical lies that aborted the Movement in the thirties. And I have learned, to my disgust, that a major reason why the young don't trust people over thirty is that they don't understand them and are too conceited to try.

Having grown up in a world too meaningless to learn anything, they know very little and are quick to resent it.

This is an unpleasant picture. Even so, the alienated young have no vital alternative except to confront the Evil, and to try to make a new way of life out of their own innards and suffering. As they are doing. It is irrelevant to point out that the System is not the monolith that they think and that the majority of people are not corrupt, just browbeaten and confused. What is relevant is that they cannot see this, because they do not have an operable world for themselves. In such a case, the only advice I would dare to give them is that which Krishna gave Arjuna: to confront with nonattachment, to be brave and firm without hatred. (I don't here want to discuss the question of "violence"; the hatred and disdain are far more important.) Also, when they are seeking a new way of life, for example when they are making a "journey inward," as Ronald Laing calls it, I find that I urge them occasionally to write a letter home.

As a citizen and father I have a right to try to prevent a shambles and to diminish the number of wrecked lives. But it is improper for us elders to keep saying, as we do, that their activity is "counterproductive." It's our business to do something more productive.

Religiously, the young have been inventive, much more than the God-is-dead theologians. They have hit on new sacraments, physical actions to get them out of their estrangement and (momentarily) break through into meaning. The terribly loud music is used sacramentally. The claim for the hallucinogenic drugs is almost never the paradisal pleasure of opium culture nor the escape from distress of heroin, but tuning in to the cosmos and communing with one another. They seem to have had flashes of success in bringing ritual participation back into theater, which for a hundred years playwrights and directors have tried to do in vain. And whatever the political purposes and results of activism, there is no doubt that shared danger for the sake of righteousness is used sacramentally as baptism of fire. Fearful moments of provocation and the poignant release of the bust bring unconscious contents to the surface, create a bond of solidarity, are "commitment."

But the most powerful magic, working in all these sacraments, is the close presence of other human beings, without competition or one-upping. The original sin is to be on an ego trip that isolates; and angry political factionalism has now also become a bad thing. What a drastic comment on the dehumanization and fragmentation of modern times that salvation can be attained simply by the "warmth of assembled animal bodies," as Kafka called it, describing his mice. At the 1967 Easter Be-In in New York's Central Park, when about ten thousand were crowded on the Sheep Meadow, a young man with a quite radiant face said to me, "Gee, human beings are legal!"—it was sufficient, to be safe, to be exempted from continual harassment by officious rules and Law and Order.

The extraordinary rock festivals at Bethel and on the Isle of Wight are evidently pilgrimages. Joan Baez, one of the hierophants, ecstatically described Bethel to me, and the gist of it was that people were nice to one another. A small group passing a joint of marijuana often behaves like a Quaker meeting waiting for the spirit, and the cigarette may be a placebo. Group therapy and sensitivity training, with Mecca at Esalen, have the same purpose. And I think this is the sense of the sexuality, which is certainly not hedonistic, nor mystical in the genre of D. H. Lawrence; nor does it have much to do with personal love—that is too threatening for these anxious youths. But it is human touch, without conquest or domination, and it obviates self-consciousness and embarrassed speech.

Around the rather pure faith there has inevitably collected a mess of eclectic liturgy and paraphernalia. Mandalas, beggars in saffron, (American) Indian beads, lectures in Zen. Obviously the exotic is desirable because it is not what they have grown up with. And it is true that fundamental facts of life are more acceptable if they come in fancy dress, e.g., it is good to breathe from the diaphragm and one can learn this by humming "OM," as Allen Ginsberg did for seven hours at Grant Park in Chicago. But college chaplains are also pretty busy, and they are now more likely to see the adventurous and off-beat than, as used to be the case, the staid and square. Flowers and strobe lights are indigenous talismans.

It is hard to describe this (or any) religiosity without lapsing into condescending humor. Yet it is genuine and it will, I am convinced, survive and develop—I don't know into what. In the end it is religion that constitutes the strength of this generation, and not, as I used to think, their morality, political will, and common sense. Except for a few, like the young people of the Resistance, I am not impressed by their moral courage or even honesty. For all their eccentricity they are singularly lacking in personality. They do not have enough world to have much character. And they are not especially attractive as animals. But they keep pouring out a kind of metaphysical vitality.

Let me try to account for it. On the one hand, these young have an unusual amount of available psychic energy. They were brought up on antibiotics that minimized depressing chronic childhood diseases, and with post-Freudian freedom to act out early drives. Up to age six or seven, television nourished them with masses of strange images and sometimes true information —McLuhan makes a lot of sense for the kindergarten years. Long schooling would tend to make them stupid, but it has been compensated by providing the vast isolated cities of youth that the high schools and colleges essentially are, where they can incubate their own thoughts. They are sexually precocious and not inhibited by taboos. They are superficially knowledgeable. On the other hand, all this psychic energy has had little practical use. The social environment is dehumanized. It discourages romantic love and lasting friendship. They are desperately bored because the world does not promise any fulfillment. Their knowledge gives no intellectual or poetic satisfaction. In this impasse, we can expect a ferment of new religion. As in Greek plays, impasse produces gods from the machine. For a long time we did not hear of the symptoms of adolescent religious conversion, once as common in the United States as in all other places and ages. Now it seems to be recurring as a mass phenomenon.

Without doubt the religious young are in touch with something historical, but I don't think they understand what it is. Let me quote from an editorial in *New Seminary News*, the newsletter of dissident seminarians of the Pacific School of Religion in Berkeley; "What we confront (willingly or not we are thrust into it) is a time of disintegration of a dying civilization and the emergence of a new one." This seems to envisage something like the instant decline of the Roman Empire and they, presumably, are like the Christians about to build, rapidly, another era. But there are no signs that this is the actual situation. It would mean, for instance, that our scientific technology, civil law, professions, universities, and so forth, are about to vanish from the earth and be replaced by something entirely different. This is a fantasy of alienated minds. Nobody behaves as if civilization would vanish, and nobody acts as if there were a new dispensation. Nobody is waiting patiently in the catacombs, and the faithful have not withdrawn into the desert. Neither the yippies nor the New Seminarians nor any other exalted group have produced anything that is the least bit miraculous. Our civilization may well destroy itself with its atom bombs or something else, but then we do not care what will emerge, if anything.

But the actual situation *is* very like 1510, when Luther went to Rome, the eve of the Reformation. There is everywhere protest, revaluation, attack on the Establishment. The protest is international. There is a generation gap. (Luther himself was all of 34 when he posted his 95 theses in 1517, but Melanchthon was 20, Bucer 26, Münzer 28, Jonas 24; the Movement consisted of undergraduates and junior faculty.) And the thrust of protest is not to give up science, technology, and civil institutions, but to purge them, humanize them, decentralize them, change the priorities, and stop the drain of wealth.

These were, of course, exactly the demands of the 4 March 1969 nationwide teach-in on science, initiated by the dissenting professors of the Massachusetts Institute of Technology. This and the waves of other teach-ins, ads and demonstrations have been the voices not of the alienated, of people who have no world, but of protestants, people deep in the world who will soon refuse to continue under the present auspices because they are not viable. It is populism permeated by moral and professional unease. What the young have done is to make it finally religious, to force the grown-ups to recognize that they too are threatened with meaninglessness.

The analogy to the Reformation is even closer if we notice that the bloated universities, and the expanded school systems under them, constitute the biggest collection of monks since the time of Henry VIII. And most of this mandarinism is hocus-pocus, a mass superstition. In my opinion, much of the student dissent in the colleges and especially the high schools has little to do with the excellent political and social demands that are made, but is boredom and resentment because of the phoniness of the whole academic enterprise.

Viewed as incidents of a Reformation, as attempts to purge themselves and recover a lost integrity, the various movements of the alienated young are easily recognizable as characteristic Protestant sects, intensely self-conscious. The dissenting seminarians of the Pacific School of Religion do not intend to go off to primitive love feasts in a new heaven and new earth, but to form their own Free University; that is, they are Congregationalists. The shaggy hippies are not nature children as they claim, but self-conscious Adamites trying to naturalize Sausalito and the East Village. Heads are Pentecostals or Children of Light. Those who spindle IBM cards and throw the dean down the stairs are Iconoclasts. Those who want Student Power, a say in the rules and curriculum, mean to deny infant baptism; they want to make up their own minds, like Henry Dunster, the first president of Harvard. Radicals who live among the poor and try to organize them are certainly intent on social change, but they are also trying to find themselves again. The support of the black revolt by white middle-class students is desperately like Anabaptism, but God grant that we can do better than the Peasants' War. These analogies are not fanciful; when authority is discredited, there is a pattern in the return of the repressed. A better scholar could make a longer list; but the reason I here spell it out is that, perhaps, some young person will suddenly remember that history was about something.

Naturally, traditional churches are themselves in transition. On college campuses and in bohemian neighborhoods, existentialist Protestants and Jews and updating Catholics have gone along with the political and social activism and, what is probably more important, they have changed their own moral, esthetic, and personal tone. On many campuses, the chaplains provide the only official forum for discussions of sex, drugs, and burning draft cards. Yet it seems to me that, in their zeal for relevance, they are badly failing in their chief duty to the religious young: to be professors of theology. They cannot really perform pastoral services, like giving consolation or advice, since the young believe they have the sacraments to do this for themselves. Chaplains say that the young are uninterested in dogma and untractable on this level, but I think this is simply a projection of their own distaste for the conventional theology that has gone dead for them. The young are hotly metaphysical—but, alas, boringly so, because they don't know much, have no language to express their intuitions, and repeat every old fallacy. If the chaplains would stop looking in the conventional places where God is dead, and would explore the actualities where perhaps He is alive, they might learn something and have something to teach.

[1969]

PART TWO

Figures and Themes

INTRODUCTION

Having offered a series of general analyses of the New Left, we now turn to some of the topics that have figured most prominently in its responses to contemporary politics. The opening essay, by David Spitz, is a detailed examination of a notion that has achieved a disturbing popularity on the American campus, mostly through the writings of Herbert Marcuse: The notion that the liberal virtue of tolerance has become, in present-day society, a form of repression and a device for avoiding basic social change. Marcuse's thought, perhaps the most influential in the New Left, is subjected to a wide-ranging critique by Allen Graubard, both on philosophical and political grounds.

The remaining essays touch upon, and criticize, key elements in New Left thought and feeling. Two of its international heroes, Frantz Fanon and Régis Debray, are sharply examined by Lewis Coser, who notes in them a characteristic blend of utopian sentiment and authoritarian method. In a lengthy study Henry Pachter turns to another subject that has occupied much attention on the New Left: The effort of "revisionist" historians to provide a new picture of the conflict between East and West during the cold-war years.

Other essays in this part of the book deal with a wide range of topics—from problems of university life (Robert Brustein) to the politics of the Black Panthers (Theodore Draper), from the snobbism sometimes displayed toward workers by the New Left (Brendan Sexton) to the cultural styles of New Left youth (Erazim V. Kohák). Certain topics that ideally should appear in the following pages, do not: a discussion of imperialism, a political critique of Che Guevara. There will, we hope, be other occasions. Meanwhile, here is abundant material for a democratic Left critique of the New Left.

PURE TOLERANCE:

A Critique of Criticisms

by *David Spitz*

Ever since men climbed down from the trees and found it necessary to establish ground rules, they have fought over what those
rules shall be. They have fought longest, and perhaps most bit-
terly, over the most fundamental rule of all—the rule by which
the ground rules themselves shall be determined. For he who
controls the ground rules is in a position to control the game.

That the rule of tolerance is this fundamental rule is revealed
by the fact that dictatorships exclude it and democratic states
make it central to their enterprise. Only in democratic states are
governments established and changed in response to the free
play of conflicting opinions.

This—the securing of responsible government—is not, of
course, the only reason for supporting tolerance. Those who defend it also contend that tolerance makes for diversity, which is
essential to progress and the development of individuality, and
thus to the common good. They also believe that tolerance, at
least in a pluralist society, is the only principle under which diverse groups can live together without resorting either to mutual
slaughter or to an authoritarian regime that will impose one
group's creed on others.

The argument for intolerance, in contrast, is generally put forward by men who mean to have their way but fear that free dis-

cussion will "mislead" other men—either because those others are less wise or virtuous than they or because conditions are such as to favor the false doctrine.

Now, the classic case for tolerance has been set forth in John Stuart Mill's celebrated essay *On Liberty*. Ever since Mill published that essay in 1859, the critics of tolerance have been diligently at work refuting him. It needs to be said, if unkindly, that one obvious reason for this is that later critics have recognized the difficulties that earlier critics have had with him. It is a mark of no mean significance that this process still continues; indeed, it has become the foundation of a flourishing industry.

As a part-time member of this guild (though one essentially in sympathy with Mill), I can do no other than commend it to the newcomers. I ask only that they first familiarize themselves with already existing products. Then they might spare their readers, if not themselves, the labor of reencountering ancient formulations under the guise of a new suit of phrases; and in doing so they might also learn to distinguish reputable from shoddy merchandise. For it needs also to be said that much of what is produced by this industry today is neither novel nor imaginative nor important. That is the judgment I propose in regard to *A Critique of Pure Tolerance,* co-authored by Herbert Marcuse, Barrington Moore, Jr., and Robert Paul Wolff (Boston: Beacon Press, 1965).

What distinguishes the three essays that constitute this book is *not* an awareness, and hence transcendence, of these elementary considerations. It is rather the marshaling and ocasionally the revision of old arguments to attack Mill from what might (for the moment) be called radical perspectives. Traditionally, Mill has been identified with the Left and his critics with the Right. This ideological cleavage by no means accounts for all of Mill's critics; some of them—Dorothy Fosdick, J. C. Rees, and Isaiah Berlin, for example—have dealt with Mill and his arguments in terms divorced from such partisanship. But it accounts for a good many of them, including, I venture to think, the three critics who here attack Mill's plea for complete freedom of thought and expression on the ground, so they say, that it prevents, or at the very least militates against, the supremacy of "correct" ideas, that is, "their" ideas. And because they profess to be of the radical Left, Mill stands condemned (in their eyes) as a protagonist of the "wrong" ideas, as a purveyor of a political philosophy that safeguards the *status quo.*

The keynote of their argument—on which, despite other differences, they are agreed—is contained in this introductory sentence: "For each of us the prevailing theory and practice of tolerance turned out on examination to be in varying degrees hypocritical masks to cover appalling political realities." And here I must begin with a confession of inadequacy: I have tried, but I am unable to make sense of this statement. What, apart from its strident terminology, does it mean? Is the theory referred to one that accounts for the practice or one that articulates an ideal to which that practice should conform? If it accounts for the practice, then the theory is not a mask but a revelation of the realities. If it articulates an ideal, then the theory stands not as a description of what is but as a prescriptive norm, and hence as a criterion of judgment by which those realities are to be judged. If it is replied that theory here means what people say, then we are simply confronted by the usual dichotomy between rhetoric and performance, between espoused or intended conduct and actual behavior. But a theory is never this; it is always an attempt to describe the true reality—our function, Klee somewhere said, is "not to reveal the visible but to make visible the real"—or to prescribe the proper conduct. Then, if we omit the word "theory" and look only at the word "practice," all that the statement seems to mean is that people do not behave very nicely, which is hardly a piercing insight.

In what sense, then, can the theory or practice of tolerance be termed hypocritical? Presumably in the sense that the theory is at odds with, and a rationalization of, the practice. But this means only that the theory (as explanation rather than as prescription) is deficient, that in fact it is not a theory at all but an ideology.

What, finally, is meant by the phrase "prevailing theory"? Is it Mill's theory of liberty, or what the writers call the doctrine of "pure tolerance"? If so, there is obviously a considerable gap not only between Mill's teaching and current (e.g., American) practice, but also, I think, between that teaching and whatever may be said to be the dominant legal and political view (or views) of liberty. Is it some other theory, a doctrine more in keeping with what our three writers are pleased to call the realities of an industrial democracy? If so, this is not identified. What they attack, then, is not *the* prevailing doctrine of liberty, and not always, as will become clear, Mill's doctrine, but doctrines and conditions imputed to Mill and which, in their view, constitute the hallmark of a sorry liberalism.

Let us consider the contentions of our three critics.

Take, first, the argument of Robert Paul Wolff. I am not altogether sure whether he misunderstands Mill or intends his readers to misunderstand Mill, but to the extent that I may read him correctly he depicts Mill at one point as an exponent of psychological egoism and at another as an advocate of individual liberty free of all social restraints. Neither of these characterizations accurately describes Mill. He also asserts that Mill defended the freedoms of thought and of action so long as these did not harm others. But Mill clearly and explicitly distinguished his defense of freedom of thought, which he made an absolute, from freedom of action, which was conditioned by its consequences. Wolff makes the important point that tolerance should not be confused with neutrality or condescension but should be recognized as a positive good; however, though Wolff does not mention it, this is also central to Mill's thought.

What is of interest, then, is not Wolff's critique of Mill—which is, strictly speaking, essentially irrelevant—but the fact that his essay, though it is entitled "Beyond Tolerance," deals less with tolerance than with the conditions that make it ineffective. Wolff believes that tolerance is a doctrine that has emerged from and is only appropriate to a particular stage of historical development, namely, the stage of democratic pluralism. But—and this is what he is most concerned to show—democratic pluralism is no longer adequate to the so-called stage of modernity in which we now find ourselves, and for two reasons primarily: It discriminates against certain disadvantaged social groups or interests— those that are outside the Establishment, that lack "legitimate representation," and that are not consequently given a place or a

voice in society—and it discriminates against certain social policies, most directly those that look to the promotion of the common good rather than to the satisfaction of diverse particular interests or claims. As a result, democratic pluralism in its concrete
application—though not, Wolff adds, in its theory—supports
inequality, maintains the *status quo*, blocks social change. What
is required, Wolff concludes, is a new philosophy of community,
of the common good, one that goes "beyond pluralism and beyond tolerance."

Now it is curious that one who, like Wolff, relates ideas in
near-deterministic fashion to particular stages of historical development—and I must bypass here the familiar and age-old controversy over this asserted but still unproved thesis—should ignore the fact that earlier theories of tolerance, those of Locke
and Milton, for example, and perhaps even of Socrates in the
Apology before them, were not merely arguments for a *qualified*
tolerance, but were in a very real sense also arguments consistent
with a kind of homogeneous, or largely homogeneous, society.
To go beyond pluralism is presumably to plead for a new type of
homogeneity, and hence for a new kind of orthodoxy; for from
what individuals or groups, and for what purpose, will new and
diverse ideas then emerge?

What makes Mill distinctive, and vitally important, is that
while he recognized and even pleaded for a sense of national
cohesion and for the pursuit of the public interest, he insisted
along with this that it was necessary to respect and to build
upon a certain heterogeneity, that progress required *both* the
promotion of the common good and furtherance of individual
and group differences. Consequently, in line with his utilitarian
philosophy, he argued for the absolute toleration of ideas and for
the maximum toleration of variety in practices. He sought a
unity that would contain rather than eliminate diversity. In these
terms, to argue against pluralism and for the idea of a common
good, as if these were opposing and mutually exclusive principles, is to argue for a self-defeating proposition; for it may well
be—and I am convinced it is—that democratic pluralism, properly understood and properly institutionalized, is precisely what
defines or constitutes the core of the common good.

It is noteworthy that Wolff nowhere defines or articulates the nature of his common good; nor does he set out a program for its realization. Were he to attempt to do so, he might find, as many another writer has found, that in a multigroup society the common good requires not the rejection of pluralism but the determination of the appropriate kinds and degrees of pluralism compatible with a political goal. Otherwise there can emerge only a deadening, even if new, conformity. However this may be, if it is true, as Wolff admits, that the fault is not in the theory of pluralism, or of tolerance, but in the shortcomings of its practice, why does he attack the theory of pure tolerance? Why does he not focus instead on the conditions—whether of structure, institutions, attitudes, or all of these combined—that hinder its attainment and impair or delimit its free exercise, and on measures calculated to redress those deficiencies? For it is not Mill and his theory of liberty but the arrangements and practices of modern industrial society that are clearly the issues at stake.

Barrington Moore's essay, "Tolerance and the Scientific Outlook," is a more sophisticated and relevant effort. In part, this is because Moore is aware of many of the foregoing considerations and avoids certain elementary confusions. In part, it is because Moore restates and builds upon a number of Mill's arguments—though he does not, curiously, acknowledge this indebtedness. In part, finally, it is because Moore advances an interesting argument of his own.

With respect to Mill, the most important of Moore's restatements is the proposition that the intellectual's task is not to agitate or fight for a particular doctrine or ideal "but to find and speak the truth, whatever the political consequences may be." The latter part of this proposition is, of course, standard Millian doctrine, as may be evidenced by Mill's familiar plea (in his essay "On Civilization"), that the very cornerstone and object of education "is to call forth the greatest possible quantity of intellectual *power*, and to inspire the intense *love of truth;* and this without a particle of regard to the results to which the exercise of that power may lead. . . ." But the first part of Moore's statement does not, alas, confront the obvious question: What if one's discovery of the truth is at the same time the discovery of a correct doctrine or ideal? Does one's commitment to the truth not require one then to advocate, even agitate for, that doctrine? Does the intellectual not then become a partisan *malgré lui?* If I am to infer Moore's answer from the content of this essay, it is clearly positive. But Moore does not explicitly say so; nor does he pursue the implications of that conclusion. Mill, of course, essayed both roles, precisely because he saw no necessary incompatibility between them.

Moore properly maintains that historical disputes can often be settled by an appeal to the evidence. But does it follow that "tolerance for different 'interpretations' based on different *Weltanschauungen* merely befuddles the issue"? Or that "a scientific attitude toward human society [does not] necessarily induce a conservative tolerance of the existing order"? Clearly, what constitutes relevant evidence is itself a matter of interpretation; and the issue is not whether tolerance or a scientific attitude implies acceptance (or, for that matter, rejection) of a particular interpretation or social order—it does not—but whether it implies acceptance of one's right to entertain and advance *ideas* that defend (or reject) a particular interpretation or social order. When Moore says, as he does, that tolerance of conflicting interpretations befuddles the issue, does he mean to suggest that the natural consequences of a serious examination of alternative doctrines will always, or mostly, lead to the adoption of the wrong doctrine? This, I think, can only be affirmed by repudiating the value of reason itself, which Moore does not and of course will not do. But if reason itself is not at fault, the rational examination of alternatives cannot lead to befuddlement. What makes for confusion, instead, is the intrusion of unreason, of prejudices or interests or the operation of weighted conditions that militate against the free play of intellect. But then Moore's indictment should turn not on the principle of tolerance but (as with Wolff) on the social conditions in which tolerance is practiced —conditions that deny reason its day in court or that perpetuate the deficiencies of reasoners. All of which would seem to be confirmed by Moore himself when he says that "every idea, including the most dangerous and apparently absurd ones, deserves to have its credentials examined."

This, however, is not the message that Moore is most anxious to communicate. He is concerned rather to argue three things: (a) that the secular and rational (i.e., scientific) outlook, by which he means neither "technicist science" nor "academic humanism" but a conception of science that embraces "whatever is established by sound reasoning and evidence," is adequate both for understanding and evaluating human affairs; (b) that this outlook is able, in principle, to yield clear-cut answers to important questions, including the question of "when to be tolerant and when tolerance becomes intellectual cowardice and evasion", and (c) finally, and most importantly, that in the present historical moment it may well behoove us to abandon the "nauseating hypocrisy" of "liberal rhetoric," to refuse to work under the prevailing system, and to consider "the conditions under which the resort to violence is justified in the name of freedom."

This is a hard teaching, but not for that reason to be avoided. We must first ask, however, whether it is also true. And here, it seems to me, the answer is by no means as simple as Moore takes it to be.

Consider Moore's claim—(a) and (b)—that objective knowledge and objective evaluation of human institutions are possible, thereby yielding correct and unambiguous answers, independent of individual whims and preferences. If Moore really admires Morris R. Cohen, whom he cites approvingly, he should have borne in mind Cohen's important distinction between the meaning of what is asserted in verified scientific theory and the degree of certainty of its verification. This certainty is always a matter of degree; it is never absolute; for what is verified is the theorems, not the postulates, of the theory. This is why Cohen, like Mill, believed that scientific *method* encourages toleration even as it enables us to differentiate beliefs and opinions that have been confirmed from those which have not.

Now Moore avows his commitment to scientific method. He recognizes that as a method it is a procedure for the testing of ideas, from which it follows that no conclusion, including the contents and very conception of science itself, is permanently above and beyond criticism and, possibly, fundamental change. How, then, can he confuse the principle of tolerance, which at one point he explicitly equates with this scientific procedure, with the acceptance of a particular doctrine or system of order, or assert the possibility not merely of objective knowledge but of objective evaluation, of correct answers to human problems? This is not to deny the relevance and utility of scientific method in the evaluation and solution of such problems; it is only to suggest that the most scientific evaluation, along with its alleged clear-cut answers, is still but tentative rather than absolute, relative to our assumptions and values, and always subject to revision.

Moore, however, confident of his "truths," seems prepared to reject the prevailing system and to adopt a revolutionary attitude. So long as three conditions are met—that the prevailing regime is unnecessarily repressive, that a revolutionary situation is in fact ripening, and that through a rough calculus of revolutionary violence one can reasonably believe that the costs in human suffering inherent in the continuation of the *status quo* outweigh those to be incurred in the revolution and its aftermath—the resort to violence, Moore holds, is justified in the name of freedom.

It is not easy for one who views the prevailing regime (or regimes) with considerable unhappiness, and who would consequently welcome certain fundamental changes in the social order, to cavil at Moore's revolutionary posture. Clearly, unless one is prepared to say that under no circumstances may men rebel, that men must remain always at the base of even the most burdensome pyramids of unjust power, there are moments in history when the resort to violence is fully warranted. That many contemporary nations, including the United States, celebrate their own past revolutions is only the more obvious of many instances in point. Thus, as an abstract statement of conditions that require and justify violence to overturn an indecent social order, Moore's argument merits respect. (Though it should not go unnoted that he here goes counter to his own earlier contention that the intellectual is not to be a partisan in the cause of this, or any other, ideal.)

Nevertheless, if we apply his (very far from precise) conditions to the modern industrial societies of the Western world, his argument becomes less than conclusive. For one thing, it is not at all clear that Western industrial societies are so oppressive that violent overthrow of the entire system is justified. For another, it is questionable that the cultural and human drabness to which Moore presumably objects is, in fact, amenable to correction through political action. For still another, the applicability of his second and third conditions is more than problematical. Nor do his conditions take into account certain useful and perhaps necessary distinctions: those, for example, between a class and a national revolution, or between a revolution initiated to seize power and a revolution, like the National Socialist Revolution, imposed after power has been effectively seized. Finally, his argument either neglects or gives insufficient weight to certain risks attendant upon all revolutionary efforts. Of these inconvenient but ever-present risks, I have space here to note only two.

One is the corrupting effect of the revolution itself, which often degrades and alters the characters and principles of the revolutionaries themselves, so that men who emerge at the top after a successful revolution are rarely the same men (even if they retain the same names and carry the same bodies) as those who made the revolution, with all that this implies in the way of altered ends, new hatreds and antagonisms, and new repressions. To be sure, some consequences of a successful revolution may be praiseworthy, e.g., the institution of certain reforms designed to eliminate or abate injustices and discontents. But other consequences are more than likely to be catastrophic. Of these the most immediately probable is the suppression of freedom of speech and political opposition. For it is not uncommon that governments which have survived revolutionary attempts, or which have come to power through revolution, seek with grim determination to eliminate the possibility of further revolutionary efforts. This, certainly, would seem to be one of the more evident lessons of revolutionary movements that have come to power since, say, the Second World War. Thus the appeal to revolution often invites the destruction of the very principle that makes the revolution possible—the principle of tolerance.

The second dangerous risk is the high improbability of success. Paul Kecskemeti has called attention to the striking fact that, despite all the revolutionary talk of the past century, if we except the Iberian peninsula, there have been no serious attempts at internal revolution in peacetime Europe since 1848–49; and if we consider the abortive Hungarian Revolution of 1956 (which took place after Kecskemeti wrote), the point is underscored that in the modern industrial state, with its specialized technology and advanced systems of weaponry, and with the support of powerful external armies and governments, civil revolt is in the ordinary course of events most unlikely to succeed. In fact, the normal complement of apathy, contentment, and especially fear—not of sporadic outbreaks but of wholesale violence and disorder—makes it more than unlikely that the masses will venture to disrupt the prevailing system of order by revolutionary means. It is, then, one thing to call for a revolutionary attitude, quite another to call for and expect revolutionary action. (I speak, let it be emphasized again, not of primitive or developing societies, but only of modern industrial societies; for it is only to such states that our authors apply their arguments.)

Once again, therefore, we are back to the central confusion inherent in this criticism: that which equates the principle of tolerance with the restrictive practices of states avowedly committed to that principle. The criticism actually testifies only to the limitations of those practices, and thus leaves untouched—at least at this level of argument—Mill's plea for freedom of thought and expression.

We come now to the most extreme and convoluted, yet in some ways the most intriguing, of our three indictments of pure tolerance: Herbert Marcuse's essay "Repressive Tolerance." It may seem outrageous to suggest that this very title is a contradiction in terms, as are also other phrases employed by Marcuse, for example "totalitarian democracy" and "the democratic educational dictatorship of free men"; but I shall make this suggestion nonetheless. I am aware that Marcuse, as a neo-Hegelian (also a neo-Marxist and neo-Freudian), prides himself on his dialectical thinking. But the dialectic—or, as Marcuse likes to say, the negation of the negation—aims to produce not a conjunction of two opposites but a synthesis which is different from either of them. And expressions like "repressive tolerance," "totalitarian democracy," and "democratic dictatorship," because they mismate rather than synthesize opposites, are self-contradictory and therefore meaningless. They should be banished from the literature. It is necessary to say this at the outset because Marcuse has dwelt harshly and at length on the inadequacies, even the Orwellian evils, of ordinary language, yet has also condemned philosophers who employ linguistic analysis in an effort to avoid the pitfalls of meaninglessness. Why, then, does he himself foster rather than transcend obscurity?

I will have occasion to return to this problem. Let me first, however, try to state the essentials of Marcuse's argument. Briefly, for it is a reiteration and extension of his argument in *One-Dimensional Man*, it comes to this: We—and by "we" Marcuse means the peoples of *all* modern industrial societies, whether "democratic" or otherwise—live today in a totalitarian system. It is totalitarian because, with the concentration of economic and political power and the use of technology as an instrument of domination, and under the rule of monopolistic media, "a mentality is created for which right and wrong, true and false are predefined wherever they affect the vital interests of the society." Rational persuasion is thus all but precluded. In such a situation tolerance "is administered to manipulated and indoctrinated individuals who parrot, as their own, the opinion of their masters." It is a tolerance abstractly "pure" but concretely "partisan," for "it actually protects the already established machinery of discrimination." It is thus repressive rather than true tolerance. For tolerance to be real, it must discriminate instead against falsehood and evil; it must cancel the liberal creed of free and equal discussion; it must preclude harmful ideas and harmful behavior. It must in fact encourage subversion of the existing order, even if this requires "apparently undemocratic means."

Marcuse articulates these "apparently undemocratic means" as follows:

> They would include the withdrawal of toleration of speech and assembly from groups and movements which promote aggressive policies, armament, chauvinism, discrimination on the grounds of race and religion, or which oppose the extension of public services, social security, medical care, etc. Moreover, the restoration of freedom of thought may necessitate new and rigid restrictions on teachings and practices in the educational institutions

which, by their very methods and concepts, serve to enclose the mind within the established universe of discourse and behavior—thereby precluding a priori a rational evaluation of the alternatives.

All this, Marcuse admits, is censorship, "even precensorship," but warranted because the distinction between liberating and repressive teachings and practices "is not a matter of value-preference but of rational criteria"; and these, Marcuse insists, are empirical in nature, turning on the real possibilities of attaining human freedom in a particular stage of civilization. To the question: Who is to draw these distinctions and make these decisions?—the answer (and here Marcuse mistakenly believes he is following Mill) is: Everyone in the maturity of his faculties as a human being, that is, "everyone who has learned to think rationally and autonomously." To be sure, such men will constitute a minority, but since all systems—even "democratic democracies"—are in fact controlled by a few, the only questions are whether they are the correct few and whether they act in the interests of the many, in short, whether they are qualified to exercise Marcuse's "democratic educational dictatorship of free men." Such free men are not to be identified with any social class; they are rather "fighting minorities and isolated groups . . . hopelessly dispersed throughout the society." To liberate these few, and through them the society as a whole, it is necessary "officially" to practice intolerance—both in speech and in action—against movements from the Right and to be tolerant only of movements from the Left. Through such "repressive tolerance" alone, Marcuse concludes, we can hope to realize the objective of "true tolerance."

Of the many things that might be said by way of analysis of or in reply to this argument, I shall limit myself here to three points: (1) Marcuse confuses the meaning of freedom with its conditions and consequences and hence misunderstands tolerance. (2) Marcuse's argument is essentially, though in reverse, the argument of Dostoevski's Grand Inquisitor, of the Right. (3) Marcuse's solution is contradicted and rendered impossible of attainment by his own analysis.

(1) Freedom is not, as Marcuse variously affirms it to be,

"self-determination, autonomy" or "a specific historical process."
It is rather, as Hobbes properly said, the absence of chains.
Since in the real world men who are unrestrained come into col-
lision with one another, societies have always and everywhere
confronted—and each in its own way resolved—the problem of
determining which liberties are worth protecting, for whom,
under what conditions, and to what degree, and, as a necessary
consequence, which restraints must be imposed. Freedom then
becomes an ordered system of liberties and restraints. Men may
differ as to the right order of priorities with respect to such
liberties, but some order of priorities there must be. Thus, in
democratic states a high value is given to freedom of political
opposition; in dictatorships it is not. But to assure and protect this
freedom, restraints must be imposed on those men (and
practices) who would interfere with it. This is one, though not the
only, function of law; but it is not, of course, merely a matter of
law, for it involves a complex set of attitudes and appropriate
behavior in other realms of social life as well.

Now Marcuse may deplore the particular freedoms granted in
a specific society. He may properly object that a formal or legal
freedom is in fact negated by informal or social pressures. But
freedom as a principle is always a matter of specific liberties and
concomitant restraints. It is not self-determination, though a
measure of self-determination may be achieved through a particular combination of liberties and restraints. Nor is it a specific
historical process, though the specific combination of liberties
and restraints may be conditioned by and reflect the values of a
particular historical period. Nor, again, is freedom limited to rational and autonomous men. While Mill clearly preferred a society made up of such men, he was realistic enough to recognize
that this could not be a necessary condition of freedom. Thus,
while he would not apply his principle of liberty to children and
immature peoples, i.e., those not capable of improvement by free
and equal discussion, he would and did apply it to all mature
(not necessarily "autonomous") men, and not simply to Marcuse's elites. Nor, finally, is freedom vindicated only by "good"
results, or rightfully "confined by truth." Freedom is in part a
value in itself, in part an instrument of individual development,
in part a necessary means of social change. That men and socie-

ties might make the "wrong" or "false" choices is clearly possible, but this too is an essential aspect of freedom. Otherwise a select group of allegedly wise men will make these choices for them, and this, by whatever name it may be called, is not freedom.

From all of which it follows that tolerance is not the freedom to express only the right ideas, but the freedom to express even stupid or loathsome ideas. The results may improve or depress the lot of men or societies, but the results are distinct from the principle of tolerance itself. And those who argue for tolerance, even absolute tolerance of ideas, do so because they believe that reason and experience are not calculated to lead men to the wrong decisions. Marcuse's rejection of pure tolerance is in these terms either a distrust of reason itself or a belief that the conditions under which reason operates today are such as to vitiate the process of reason, and probably both. But to the extent that it is the second, his attack is properly directed to those conditions and not to the principle of tolerance. Clearly, the "tolerance" he espouses is intolerance, and so it should be called, lest we abandon all semblance of meaning in our ordinary use of terms.

(2) Those who believe not merely that there is an objective truth but that, by some mystery of incarnation, it has been given to them to know it, have rarely been willing to respect the claim to such knowledge by others. For such True Believers, allowing others to disseminate what is believed to be true, but what in fact is false, is to make possible the adoption of error. For error, seductively presented, may prevail over truth even in free and equal discussion. How much more likely is it to prevail when the conditions are not free and equal, when those who propound the error (because it gratifies their passions or promotes their conceived interests) also control the sources of information and media of communication, and where the objects of the debate are neither rational nor autonomous but "conditioned" men! In such circumstances to trust to an abstract but spurious toleration is to yield the cause. For truth to prevail, the "right" men must impose it—either by altering the conditions or by directing otherwise irrational men, and generally both. In this way men will be governed by truth, and thus, even though forced, they will also be free.

This, it is clear, is the argument of Socrates in the *Republic*. It is the argument of Rousseau in the *Social Contract*. It is the argument of the Grand Inquisitor, both of the Roman Catholic Church and of Stalin's Russia. It is the traditional argument of the Right, of all who would usurp the gates of heaven and in the name of a higher morality insist as with Gerhart Niemeyer, upon "a firm official stand for what is known as right, true, and good." And it is, in all essentials, the argument of Marcuse. But it is not the argument of John Stuart Mill.

For Mill, as for all democrats committed to the liberal idea of freedom, to believe in Man is not to dispel one's doubts about men. Men are fallible and cannot presume to know the whole truth. Room must therefore be left for the rectification of error and the discovery of additional knowledge. This requires tolerance, the free exploration and articulation of ideas. It may well be that there are deficiencies in the intellectual marketplace, but the remedy is not to mistake Marcuse's authority for truth; it is rather to correct those deficiencies. To substitute one allegedly right authority for another, to compel or manipulate men to do what Marcuse (or anyone else) is convinced it is proper for them to do, is not to force them to be free. It is simply to subject them to Marcuse's (or another's) will. This, by any name, is coercion. It ill accords with the purposes of one who professes to respect humanity.

(3) Finally, and briefly, Marcuse's argument collapses because the reality he portrays renders unattainable, and is in turn contradicted by, the proposals he recommends. If it is true that we live "in a democracy with totalitarian organization" and that this "coordinated society" rests on "firm foundations," how is it humanly possible to change it? Surely not by election, for the "conditioned" masses will simply acquiesce in the opinions of their masters. Surely not by education, for the rulers control both the educators and their media of communication. Surely not by revolution, for who will revolt but "hopelessly dispersed" minorities? It may well be, as Marcuse thinks, that in such a situation the alienated man is the "essential" rather than the sick man, and that rebellious men merit applause rather than condemnation. But such men, however viewed, cannot overturn a firmly established order. Then to whom, and for what purpose, does

Marcuse speak? Is his message really more than a tocsin of futility, a summons to surrender?

If on the other hand, we are to take seriously his plea for fundamental social and political change, for the establishment of "real" tolerance (or, as he says, "official" intolerance), it can only mean that the society is less than totalitarian, that its foundations are not altogether firm, that there are chinks in the monopolistic concentration of power.

Marcuse cannot have it both ways: Either his analysis is correct and his recommendations are unrealizable, or his recommendations are meaningful and appropriate, in which case his analysis cannot stand.

It would be less than just to conclude these remarks without noting the deep anguish and high moral commitment that animate all three of our critics. They are disturbed, and properly so, by the injustices that disfigure modern societies. They are distressed by the realization that these injustices are maintained by an indifferent, because unseeing, or acquiescent public opinion. Consequently they probe to the roots in an effort to uncover the sources and the interests that mold that opinion. And they have found, as every sensitive observer of human societies has always found, that within our cities there are still two cities—the city of the rich and the city of the poor, with all that this implies in inequalities of power, of access to privileges, and of opportunities. One need not accept everything that A. J. Liebling has written in *The Press*, or that C. Wright Mills has written in *The Power Elite*, to recognize that freedom of speech, for example, has a different meaning for those wealthy enough to buy a newspaper company or to purchase time on radio or television, than it has for the masses of individuals who may wish to express their thoughts but have no effective access to the various media of communication. Nor does it require undue imagination to note that men cannot choose what they do not know exists, or will not choose what they have been taught to believe is evil. For these and other reasons, it is less than convincing to argue that the principle of equality accurately characterizes the world of public opinion, or that the free play of ideas does in fact afford people a full range of alternatives.

In underscoring these objectionable features of contemporary life and in urging their correction, our three critics manifest a concern for Man rather than for rich or powerful or prestigious men. Further, in their readiness to foster even revolutionary social and political change in an effort to elevate Man from what he presently is to what he ought to be, to what he *can* be, they identify themselves with an abiding radical tradition. They are legitimately of the Left.

But a wise radicalism seeks to overturn not all things, only unjust and harmful things; and not everything that men have thought and done in the course of human history demands repudiation. There have been achievements, too, and of these not the least noble has been the slow and painful liberation of the human mind. Whatever the merits or demerits of liberalism as a political and economic doctrine, in the realm of the intellect it should command our supreme allegiance: for it has freed reason from the chains of dogma and superstition; it has broken the back of orthodoxy; it has given us a method by which we may continue to correct our errors and improve our understanding. And whatever the merits or demerits of a particular social system in observing, or failing to observe, the principle of liberalism in the intellectual sphere, it is necessary—and I believe that even under circumstances that most humanly approximate the ideal, it will remain necessary—always to distinguish the fact of public opinion, what may be called the will of the people, from the motives and influences that elicit it. Democracies rest on the volume, not on the quality, of that will; and though no one would contend that it is better to have a stupid or misguided will, what distinguishes democratic from nondemocratic governments is that the former rest upon that will even though oligarchic or plutocratic influences may have been powerful in creating it, while the latter reject that will, or at most seek to mold it in support of their policies; it is not, as in democratic states, an initiating and controlling will. To render that will a purer or wiser will is surely a proper concern of democratic (whether liberal or radical) theorists, but this means that they must look not to the removal of that will, or of the process that alone gives it the opportunity to be formed after a consideration of alternatives, but to the correction of those conditions that limit or block the introduction of new and conflicting ideas. In any case, the fact of will and not its purity or disinterestedness remains the foundation of the democratic state.

Those who, therefore, in the name of a social revolution, would destroy not merely the conditions that still constrain reason but the principle of tolerance that alone gives reason its chance to prevail, defy the grim lessons of history. What, then, can one say of those who, like Marcuse, seek to reverse history by substituting for even the imperfect democracies of our day an intellectual and political authoritarianism that would allegedly act *for* the people, on the ground that a government that really acts in the interests of the people is better (and more democratic) than a goverment *by* the people that may, through ignorance or irrationality, act contrary to those best interests? Such men are neither radical nor liberal but, let us use the cruel word, reactionary. This is why, despite all the legitimate criticisms that might be (and in the course of the past century have been) made of Mill's philosophy, or of his political and economic teachings, or even of the subsidiary doctrines and incidental observations in his essay *On Liberty,* the central argument of that essay remains fundamentally unimpaired.

Not Mill's theory of pure tolerance but the repressive intolerance of our critics is, then, to be condemned.

[1966]

FANON AND DEBRAY:

Theorists of the Third World

by Lewis Coser

Three figures associated with the Third World—Che Guevara, Frantz Fanon, and Régis Debray—have become intellectual heroes of the New Left. Guevara has left no significant literary remains, since he taught by example mainly; the other two have produced writings worthy of attention.

1. THE MYTH OF PEASANT REVOLT

Only rarely does a book immediately convey a sense that it will rank among the influential works of the time. Frantz Fanon's *The Wretched of the Earth* is just such a book. It is badly written, badly organized, and chaotic. The author's reasoning is often shoddy and obviously defective. But all this is finally unimportant. This is not a work of analysis. Its incantatory prose appeals not to the intellect but to the passions. Its author wished to create a modern myth, and he must be ranked among the very few great mythopoeists of our age even by those who, like myself, think he has created an evil myth.

"Myths," wrote Georges Sorel, "are not descriptions of things, but expressions of a determination to act. . . . A myth cannot be refuted, since it is, at bottom, identical with the conviction of a group, being the expression of these convictions in the language of movement." "One must not try to analyze such complexes of pictures," he added, "as one would break down a thing into its elements; one must take them as a whole, as historical forces, and . . . must above all refrain from comparing actual accomplishments with the images of them that had been generally accepted before the action." It is such a myth that Frantz Fanon has created and I venture to think that it will have an enduring influence in the world of politics and ideas, perhaps more so than Sorel's own myth of the General Strike.

Frantz Fanon was born in 1925, on the island of Martinique in the French West Indies. He studied medicine in France and specialized in psychiatry. During the Algerian revolt against French domination, Fanon was assigned to an Algerian hospital and soon threw in his lot with the revolutionists to become one of their major ideological spokesmen. Out of this experience came two books, *The Year V of the Algerian Revolution* and the present volume, first published in France in 1961. Fanon died of cancer, at the age of thirty-six, soon after the book appeared.

The Wretched of the Earth could be read as yet another indictment of the evils of colonialism, but so to understand it would bypass its real importance. Fanon wishes to do a great deal more. He wishes to show how the native, degraded by his conquerors, can reconquer himself. The book is, above all, an apologia for violence. The violence of the conquest, he argues, has dehumanized the native and only counterviolence can make him whole again. ". . . Violence is a cleansing force. It frees the native from his inferiority complex and from his despair and inaction; it makes him fearless and restores his self-respect. . . . For the native, life can spring up again out of the rotting corpse of the settler." Violence is the only effective individual and social therapy; it helps overcome a schism of the soul which has been caused by colonialist contempt, and it wields together a body social which had been rent by the colonial system. "Violence unifies the people."

In Sorel's hands the myth of violence had a somewhat bloodless character. Sorel was, to be sure, a man given to apocalyptic visions, yet upon inspection his heroic violence turns out to be more literary than real, more a figure of speech than a concretely envisioned event. This safely settled petty-bourgeois moralist dreamed of heroic virtues, but fantasies of a real bloodbath seem to have been utterly alien to him. Matters stand very differently with Fanon. He was a marginal man, torn from his moorings, most of his adult life working in the world of French medical professionals without being of that world. Scarred and humiliated, stripped of his previous identity, he searched for redeeming wholeness through a cataclysmic destruction. To him, the call to violence, the belief in its redeeming quality, is no rhetorical device; he means it. He believed in the cleansing quality of the knife, the gun, the bomb. Only these, he thought, can make colonial man whole again. During the Mau-Mau revolt, it was required, he writes, "that each member of the group should strike a blow at the victim. Each one was thus personally responsible for the death of that victim. To work means to work for the death of the settler. This assumed responsibility for violence allows both strayed and outlawed members of the group to come back again and to find their place once more, to become integrated. Violence is thus seen as comparable to a royal pardon. The colonized man finds his freedom in and through violence. This rule of conduct enlightens the agent because it indicates to him the means and the end."

Anticolonial violence is to Fanon the only way to bring about a total transformation in the former colonies. It leads to a comprehensive transvaluation of values. "Without any period of transition, there is a total, complete, and absolute substitution." All decolonization creates a *tabula rasa* at the outset, and this is the precondition for all further advances. Decolonization does not mean the substitution of one kind of regime for another; it signifies total rebirth and it can only be the work of new men, men reborn through acts of violence.

Fanon is at his most original when he attempts to locate potential revolutionary actors within the structure of colonial societies. Here he departs most markedly from classical Marxist theory. Very little, he argues, can be expected of the embryonic working class. The workers enjoy a comparatively privileged position. They may be the most faithful followers of the nationalist parties, but when the chips are down, they realize that they have much to lose when the colonial regime is overthrown. By virtue of the privileged position they hold in the colonial system, they constitute a "bourgeois" faction of the colonized people. Pampered, and sheltered from the worst slights and the worst misery, they can easily be bought off. So much for the traditional proletarian vanguard of the Marxist textbooks.

Nor is there reason to believe that the national bourgeoisie can play a role. It has none of the characteristics of its Western counterpart. "It is not engaged in production, nor in invention, nor building, nor labor; it is completely canalized into activities of the intermediary type. Its innermost vocation seems to be to keep in the running and to be part of the racket." Fanon treats this national bourgeoisie with a withering contempt that is only matched by his contempt for the assimilationist and partly Westernized intelligentsia. If the working class can be bought off and the national bourgeoisie is "good for nothing," where, then, can the true agents of total transformation be found? Here Fanon, true to an age-old millenarian tradition which, by the way, strongly informed the thought of the young Marx, answers: Only those who are totally disinherited, those who have nothing to lose in the old system can be the architects of the new. The biblical "the last shall be first and the first last" runs like a refrain through the book.

The last in colonial society are the peasants and they are hence the true agents of the revolution. ". . . The peasants alone are revolutionary, for they have nothing to lose and everything to gain. The starving peasant, outside the class system, is the first among the exploited to discover that only violence pays. For him there is no compromise, no possible coming to terms." The anticolonial revolution must hence be a peasant revolution. Yet this revolution, in order to succeed, must of necessity spread from the countryside into the towns. A peasant *maquis* can hardly be expected to take the cities. Here the mass of ex-peasants, settled in the huts and shantytowns around the fringe of the city, assumes a major strategic role. The city *Lumpenproletariat* is the predestined ally of the rural masses. "The *Lumpenproletariat*, that horde of starving men, uprooted from their tribe and from their clan, constitutes one of the most spontaneous and the most radically revolutionary forces of colonized people." They have not yet found "a bone to gnaw in the colonial system." They are physically near the city but spiritually very far from it. Their very presence is "the sign of the irrevocable decay, the gangrene ever present at the heart of colonial domination. So the pimps, the hooligans, the unemployed, and the petty criminals, urged on from behind, throw themselves into the struggle for liberation like stout working men. These classless idlers will by militant and decisive action discover the path that leads to nationhood." Truly, the last will be the first.

Fanon plays many variations upon the theme of the revolt of the wretched, the eruption of colonial society, bringing to the fore the new heroic man created in and through revolutionary violence. But what after the morrow of victory? Will the heroic days of struggle not be followed by the dullness of quotidian routine? This is a persistent danger of which Fanon is acutely aware. "During the struggle for liberation the leader awakened the people and promised them a forward march, heroic and unmitigated. Today, he uses every means to put them to sleep, and three or four times a year asks them to remember the colonial period and to look back on the long way they have come since then. . . . After independence, the party sinks into an extraordinary lethargy . . . the local party leaders are given administrative posts, and the party becomes an administration, and the militants disappear in the crowd and take the empty title of citizen. . . ." When the revolution grows cold, its leaders tend to develop into cold and calculating monsters. Once it freezes into bureaucratic mold, it becomes but a means for the advancement of its functionaries, and the pursuit of their private pleasures replaces the heroic dedication to public revolt. But all of this, thinks Fanon, while an ever-present danger, is not a necessary outcome.

The revolution can be saved provided it is not halted prematurely, and provided it remains permanent. The soft life of the city must not be allowed to corrupt the new governing elites. The city, to Fanon, is always corruption. He hates it with the traditional hatred of the peasant; it is to him the true whore of Babylon. The city represents softness and relaxation in contrast to the lean and hard energy and dedication of the countryside. Hence only geographic decentralization of power can save the revolution. Revolutionary virtue can be maintained in the village square; it will inevitably succumb to the vices of the city if power comes to be centered in the capital.

The anticolonial revolution is primarily a revolution of the peasant people, and it can maintain itself only as long as it remains rooted in that people. The party, the leaders, once arrived in power will attempt to exclude the people from participation. They will say that the people are too ignorant, that they do not understand the intricacies of political decision-making. These are self-serving lies. "Everything can be explained to the people, on the single condition that you really want them to understand . . . when the people are invited to partake in the management of the country, they do not slow the movement down but on the contrary speed it up." Hence the birth of a national bourgeoisie or of a privileged caste of bureaucrats must be vigorously opposed. The masses must be educated so that they can form the politically decisive arms of the revolution. If this is done, the nation will become a living reality to each of its citizens.

The book closes with a violent diatribe against European civilization. "Europe undertook the leadership of the world with ardor, cynicism, and violence. . . . Europe has declined all humility and all modesty; but she has also set her face against all solicitude and all tenderness . . . she has only shown herself parsimonious and niggardly where men are concerned; it is only men that she has killed and devoured . . . today we know with what sufferings humanity has paid for every one of their [the Europeans'] triumphs of the mind." European civilization, Fanon argues, by its very success in taming the forces of nature, has only succeeded in dehumanizing man—colonial man in the first place, but ultimately, European man also. Hence Fanon's message, and this distinguishes him from almost all previous colonial rebels, rejects the whole heritage of Europe. He declines to accept guidance even from the West's revolutionaries. Corrupted to the core, the West can teach nothing but death of the soul. "So, comrades," says Fanon on his last page, "let us not pay tribute to Europe by creating states, institutions, and societies which draw their inspiration from her." Most previous colonial revolutionaries paid tribute to the West in the very act of revolting against it. Fanon's myth involves a much more profound rejection than do the ideologies of a Gandhi or of a Nehru, a Lenin, or a Stalin. He warns the nations of the Third World that they should not create a Third or Fourth Rome, a pale imitation of a civilization decaying at its very roots.

Spengler coined the term "historical pseudomorphosis" to "designate those cases in which an older alien culture lies so massively over the land that a young culture, born in this land, cannot get its breath and fails not only to achieve pure and specific expression-forms, but even to develop fully its own self-consciousness. All that wells up from the depth of the young soul is cast in the old molds, young feelings stiffen in senile works, and instead of rearing itself up in its own creative power, it can only hate the distant power with a hate that grows to be monstrous." It is to prevent such a state of affairs that Fanon has fashioned his myth.

If, contrary to Sorel's prescription, one compares actual accomplishments with the mythical images that Fanon set forth only a few years ago, one is brought up against the fact that the book is already dated. The Algeria of Boumédienne bears but little resemblance to the peasant democracy of which Fanon dreamed. The tough military men who now run independent Algeria presumably look at men like Fanon as ideologists whose usefulness to the regime has long been exhausted. African rulers have grown fat on resources pumped out of the countryside, and they have flocked to the central cities where they build skyscrapers and airports, slavishly imitating Western models. The peasants have fallen back into the immemorial routines of traditional life-styles; sometimes they are prodded into the world of modernity by tax collectors, recruiting sergeants, or party organizers. The peasants' lot differs in the various new nations, to be sure, but in none of them have they become history-making subjects, as Fanon expected and hoped. Everywhere they are the subjects of historical processes over which they have, at best, only minimal control. The specific weight of the peasantry in the political life of the underdeveloped nations is low indeed, and the tutelary power of the new states comes to lie as heavily on today's peasantry as it rested upon them in the colonial past.

Fanon's picture hardly fits the contemporary reality. Yet it would be foolish to dismiss his work as a mere regressive fantasy —though it may be that, too. The myth that he has helped to create will stay alive, I believe, precisely because the reality of the new nations departs so very crucially from the image he has drawn. The peasantry does make up the great majority in these nations and will remain so for a very long time to come. Peasant discontent will persist as a consequence of the dislocation of traditional styles of life which the modernizing regimes attempt to institute. Fanon was quite right, of course, when he noted that the young working class and the bulk of the Westernized intelligentsia would not, as a whole, play a revolutionary role in the history of the new nations. They have tasted power or gained at least a modicum of higher standards of living, and they are most probably not willing to risk these. But it is conceivable that dissatisfied peasants may come to learn of this book in due course and make it a kind of breviary for their aspirations. Yet while the future, contrary to what Fanon believed, belongs to the city and not the countryside, the death throes of traditional peasant society will last for a very long time and may well be punctured by uprisings and revolts, a variey of peasant *Jacqueries*. And even though I believe these peasant revolts ultimately doomed to failure, they may for a time, perhaps in alliance with disaffected city intellectuals, create large revolutionary movements. Africa may see a repeat performance of Europe's peasant revolts before it enters the new world of modernity. For quite some time to come, the new rulers of the African nations will be faced by the specter of peasant uprisings and disaffection—and Fanon's myth will haunt them, much as the *Communist Manifesto* and its myth haunted the millowners of Victorian Europe.

In the West this book will be read for a long time and will become a bible for romantic rebels and sophisticated university students in quest of primeval revolutionary innocence. Jean-Paul Sartre's incredibly naive introduction gives a foretaste of what may be in store. A man who can speak in earnest about North African Arabs, of all people, "recovering their lost innocence" can believe anything—anything, that is, which feeds his anti-Western masochism.

It seems hardly necessary to say here that I consider Fanon's myth an evil and destructive vision. I find his view of violence as a healer profoundly mistaken. Violence may sometimes be necessary, but those who wield it systematically cannot help becoming brutalized by it. And this holds true for colonizer and native alike. Similarly, I think that the course Fanon charts for the new nations is not only morally dubious but politically inept and self-defeating. What I have tried here is to convey Fanon's symptomatic importance rather than engage in refutations of his views.

One must never forget while reading Fanon's book that it was written in anguish and heartbreak, even though one might recognize in it elements of a "paranoid style" with which we have become familiar in many a sinister context. The vision which informs the book may be profoundly repellent, but we must not forget that the violence and hatred it breathes on every page is a reactive violence, a testimony to the havoc the white man has loosed upon Africa. Finally, one might hope that the myth Fanon has wrought may move some Western men to that compassion and sense of fraternity with the downtrodden of Africa which Fanon—who expected only white hatred and, at best, condescension—plainly believed impossible.

2. NECHAEV IN THE ANDES

"The emancipation of the working class is the work of the working class itself," wrote Marx and Engels in the *Communist Manifesto*.

One of the tragic paradoxes of the Marxist movement has been that impatient revolutionaries—appalled by the sluggishness of history and the apparent unwillingness of the working class to be interested in its alleged interest—have ever since been in search of substitute agents of historical transformation.

Lenin, convinced that unaided working-class spontaneity could create trade-union but not political consciousness, bent all his energies to organizing a devoted sect of professionals who would become the real agents of the revolutionary transformation, even though initially they might be mainly intellectuals of middle-class origin. The emancipation of the working class, Lenin believed, could never be accomplished except through the Bolshevik party. And in due course, the party substituted itself for the working class.

In Lenin's day the Russian working class was numerically small, almost drowned in a sea of peasants. But it carried considerable specific weight due to its high degree of social concentration. In China, by contrast, when the Chinese Communist party was created, there was hardly an industrial working class at all. In consequence, after the bloody repression of revolutionary attempts in a few port cities, Mao Tse-tung turned to the peasantry, which was led by cadres of *déclassé* intellectuals, as the major revolutionary force. That very peasantry toward which Marx had expressed his withering contempt, and that he had judged to be incapable of concerted action due to its isolation from the major centers of political and economic power, became the basis for the second major revolution to call itself—such are the ironies of history—"Marxist."

In our day a significant theorist of revolution in the underdeveloped countries, Frantz Fanon, created a powerful myth according to which, the proletariat having been corrupted and softened by the exploiting colonialists, only a pure and uncontaminated peasantry allied to the *Lumpenproletariat* of the city—that *Lumpenproletariat* Marx had thought incapable of any constructive political initiative—would constitute the motor force of revolutionary transformation.

But the end is not yet. *The Monthly Review*, the organ of Paul Sweezy, a man who thinks of himself as the upholder of Marxist orthodoxy in the United States, published a special issue (July–August 1967) presenting a full translation of Régis Debray's book *Revolution in the Revolution*, in which it is argued that neither the working class nor the peasantry, neither professional political revolutionaries nor city *Lumpen*, but armed guerrillas made up of students and revolutionary intellectuals will "initiate the highest forms of class struggle." Debray and Sweezy thus have come full circle in their distorted form of "Marxism"; the emancipation of the working class is now to be the work of *déclassé* intellectuals.

Yet Debray's work is by no means without historical precedent. He is a lineal descendant of that long line of Russian revolutionary terrorists and *enragés* from Nechaev to Tkachev, who, appalled by the weakness of the liberal bourgeoisie, the subservience of the enlightened nobility, and the primordial passivity of the peasantry, concluded that only the heroic deeds of small elites of dedicated revolutionaries could propel Russian society into freedom. Despairing of the slow course of history, despairing

also of all existent social forces, they concluded that only terroristic acts of a self-chosen few would be able to mold the resist-
ant paste of social reality.

Since history was unwilling to go in the direction of their desires, they would have to rape it. They would take it upon
themselves to break the thick cake of customary resistance, they
would pit their naked will against the inert force of history. And
they would prevail.

> Neither in the present nor in the future [wrote Tkachev],
> can the people, left to their own resources, bring into exis-
> tence the social revolution. Only we revolutionists can ac-
> complish this. . . . Social ideals are alien to the people;
> they belong to the social philosophy of the revolutionary
> minority.

Debray is a follower of these Russian revolutionaries, though
he seems to suffer under the strange illusion that he is a Marxist.
A young French philosopher of impeccable upper-class origin,
he has turned his intellectual gifts to developing the theoretical
underpinnings for Castro's political adventurism in Latin America.

His book is not without its pathos. One sometimes feels sympathy for this young revolutionary who is engaged in what he himself surely considers a promethean effort at liberation in the face
of hard and seemingly untractable realities. Nevertheless, what
strikes one most forcefully in the book is his deep and abiding
contempt for the common run of humanity.

All previous Marxist theory took as its point of departure an
assessment of the preparedness, or readiness for basic change, of
the class or classes which were to be the targets of revolutionary
agitation and propaganda. Though they may have differed as to
the extent to which voluntaristic action by the vanguard elite
could hasten the process of radicalization in the population, no
Marxist theorist ever considered it possible or desirable to engage in revolutionary activity without the assurance of large-
scale disaffection and at least an inchoate desire for fundamental
change among oppressed classes.

Debray breaks with that tradition. He is basically unconcerned with the wishes and desires of the people. His revolutionary guerrilla units are to be "organizationally separate from the civilian population." They will function in its midst, but they will "not assume the direct defense of the peasant population." In other words, they will not feel responsible if this population is subject to reprisal by virtue of nearby guerrilla actions. Debray, in fact, is at pains to point out that the revolutionary warfare he advocates has nothing to do with the age-old tradition of peasant self-defense. "Self-defense," he argues, "is partial; revolutionary guerrilla warfare aims at total war by combining under its hegemony all forms of struggle at all points within its territory."

The guerrillas are not responsible to the peasants among whom they fight; nor are they responsible to urban-based political party leaders. Debray, like Fanon, distrusts the city; it softens and corrupts. "These lukewarm incubators [of the cities] make one infantile and bourgeois." Or: "When a guerrilla group communicates with city leadership or its representatives abroad, it is dealing with 'its' bourgeoisie." The city, that whore of Babylon, is lost; parties, being city-based organisms, are inherently suspect.

Not only can the armed units of youthful adventurers operating in the remoteness of the hinterland not trust the city; they cannot even trust older men, no matter what their politics or previous experience. "There is a close tie between biology and ideology. . . . That an elderly man should be proven militant—and possess revolutionary training—is not, alas, sufficient for coping with guerrilla existence, especially in the early stages. Physical aptitude is the prerequisite for all other aptitudes."

In Debray's picture, the guerrilla fighter who presumes to unleash the forces of revolution looks a bit like a caricature of a Nietzschean superman. He needs to be young lest he suffer from "the vices of excessive deliberation," and "a perfect Marxist education is not at the outset an imperative condition." If he can shoot straight, he need not be burdened with theoretical baggage. Too much ratiocination may only cramp his style.

"The guerrilla army assumes the prerogatives of political leadership" even though it is, at least in the initial stages of insurrection, cut off from all strata of the underlying population. The guerrillas "are the foreigners, lacking status, who at the begin-

ning can offer the populace nothing but bloodshed and pain."
They must live like perpetual nomads moving from camp to
camp. Mao taught that the guerrillas should remain unnoticed,
living in the midst of peasant sympathizers "like fish in water,"
but Debray thinks this impossible under Latin-American conditions. The guerrillas must cut themselves loose from all sectors of
the population, all of which are either hostile or lukewarm. The
world is corrupt, and only a tiny revolutionary elite can be
trusted. But why can they be trusted, why should they be
trusted? Because they act, because they wield guns. It is perhaps
harsh to say so, yet I cannot help but feel that Debray's view of
the matter has more affinity with the rhetoric of fascism than with
that of classical Marxism.

Nowhere is Debray's distrust of reason and his elitist anti-intellectualism more apparent than in his discussion of the relationships between the guerrilla units and the revolutionary party.
Here again he seems nearer to fascist than to Marxist thought.
For all Marxists the forging of a revolutionary party was
always a *sine qua non*, because the party and its program
embodied the theoretical and ideological thrust of the movement. Its program was the intellectual distillation of the movement's philosophy and ideology. But to Debray the party counts
for very little, because ideas and ideologies count for very little.
What Karl Mannheim once said of fascism seems eminently ap-
plicable to Debray's vision:

> At the very heart of its theory and its practice lies the
> apotheosis of direct action, the belief in the decisive *deed*,
> and in the significance attributed to the initiative of a
> leading elite. The essence of politics is to recognize and to
> grapple with the demands of the hour. . . . History is
> made neither by the masses, nor by ideas . . . but by the
> elites who from time to time assert themselves. . . . This
> idea of history as an intelligible scheme disappears in the
> face of the irrationality of the fascist apotheosis of the
> deed.

Someone once said that everywhere else armies were the instruments of states, but in Prussia the state was an instrument of

the army. Debray has a "Prussian" view of the relations between the party and the army: "The people's army will be the nucleus of the party, not vice versa." "Eventually, the future People's Army will beget the party of which it is to be, theoretically, the instrument: Essentially the party is the army." Ideology and organization, it would appear, all grow out of the barrel of a gun.

Personally, Debray may be a man of heroic cast and admirable virtues, but what he stands for is an evil and mischievous doctrine. His is a politics of despair, a politics that has lost all belief in the political capacities of ordinary human beings. His violent and apocalyptic fantasies are rooted in his distrust of men. He would force them to be free at the point of a gun. Debray thinks of the guerrillas as promethean rebels, but had they any power, they would more likely become the terroristic scourges of the people of Latin America.

Defenders of Debray's doctrine might contend that he proposes guerrilla activity in Latin America not because he is drawn to such solutions in principle but only because, given the reality of Latin-American dictatorships, other methods are not available. How can you consult the masses, they might argue, if they are gagged by a military regime? Debray's defenders may so argue, but it is important to note that he himself does not employ this rationale. He makes no distinction whatever between political activities in relatively democratic countries, such as Venezuela and Chile, and in military dictatorships, such as Bolivia. He offers the same terroristic solution for all of them—and hence shows quite clearly that he has only contempt for democratic methods and alternatives.

There is no doubt in my mind that the liberation of Latin America from internal and external oppression will be a prolonged ordeal. It would be foolish to expect that this will not be accompanied in many situations by violence and bloodshed. Guns will probably have to be used. But recourse to guns always corrupts, absolute reliance on guns corrupts absolutely, and those who make a mystique out of guns are already corrupted in advance.

Ché Guevara was killed after his guerrilla band was discovered by the Bolivian military. And Régis Debray faced a military

court in Bolivia, which accused him of having been a participant
in guerrilla activities and sentenced him to thirty years' imprisonment—the maximum penalty according to Bolivian law. What
has been reported about the proceedings of the court does not
give one the impression that it acted with anything resembling
judicial impartiality. International pressures should be brought
upon the Bolivian junta to induce it to expel Debray from the
country rather than impose so severe and vindictive a sentence.

In the meantime it ought to be said without equivocation:
Those of us who sympathize with the Latin-American masses,
and are moved by the misery and oppression in which they now
live, must hope that they will not fall prey to the sick adventurist fantasies of Debray and his ilk. Whatever the Andes need, it
is not Nechaevs from Paris.

[1968]

A DAY IN THE LIFE OF A SOCIALIST CITIZEN

by Michael Walzer

Imagine a day in the life of a socialist citizen. He hunts in the morning, fishes in the afternoon, rears cattle in the evening, and plays the critic after dinner. Yet he is neither hunter, fisherman, herdsman nor critic; tomorrow he may select another set of activities just as he pleases. This is the delightful portrait that Marx sketches in *The German Ideology* as part of a polemic against the division of labor. Socialists since have worried that it is not economically feasible; perhaps it isn't. But there is another difficulty that I want to consider: that is, the curiously apolitical character of the citizen Marx describes. Certain crucial features of socialist life have been omitted altogether.

In light of the recent discussions about participatory democracy, Marx's sketch needs to be elaborated. Before hunting in the morning, this unalienated man of the future is likely to attend a meeting of the Council on Animal Life, where he will be required to vote on important matters relating to the stocking of the forests. The meeting will probably not end much before noon, for among the many-sided citizens there will always be a lively interest even in highly technical problems. Immediately after lunch, a special session of the Fishermen's Council will be called to protest the maximum catch recently voted by the Regional Planning Commission. And the Marxist man will participate eagerly in these debates, even postponing a scheduled discussion of some contradictory theses on cattle-rearing. Indeed, he will probably love argument far better than hunting, fishing, *or* rearing cattle. The debates will go on so long that the citizens will have to rush through dinner in order to assume their roles as critics. Then off they will go to meetings of study groups, clubs, editorial boards, and political parties where criticism will be carried on long into the night.

Socialism, Oscar Wilde once wrote, would take too many evenings. This is, it seems to me, one of the most significant criticisms of socialist theory that has ever been made. The fanciful sketch above is only intended to suggest its possible truth. Socialism's great appeal is the prospect it holds out for the development of human capacities. An enormous growth of creative talent, a new and unprecedented variety of expression, a wild proliferation of sects, associations, schools, parties: This will be the flowering of the future society. But underlying this new individualism and exciting group life must be a broad, self-governing community of equal men. A powerful figure looms behind Marx's hunter, fisherman, herdsman, and critic: the busy citizen attending his endless meetings. "Society regulates the general production," Marx writes, "and thus makes it possible for me to do one thing today and another tomorrow. . . ." If society is not to become an alien and dangerous force, however, the citizens cannot accept its regulation and gratefully do what they please. They must participate in social regulation; they must be social men, organizing and planning their own fulfillment in spontaneous activity. The purpose of Wilde's objection is to suggest that just this self-regulation is incompatible with spontaneity, that the requirements of citizenship are incompatible with the freedom of hunter, fisherman, and so on.

Politics itself, of course, can be a spontaneous activity, freely chosen by those men and women who enjoy it and to whose talents a meeting is so much exercise. But this is very unlikely to be true of all men and women all the time—even if one were to admit what seems plausible enough: that political life is more intrinsic to human nature than is hunting and cattle-rearing or even (to drop Marx's rural imagery) art or music. "Too many evenings" is a shorthand phrase that describes something more

than the sometimes tedious, sometimes exciting business of reso-
lutions and debates. It suggests also that socialism and participatory democracy will depend upon, and hence require, an extraordinary willingness to attend meetings, and a public spirit and
sense of responsibility that will make attendance dependable
and activity consistent and sustained. None of this can rest for
any long period of time or among any substantial group of men
upon spontaneous interest. Nor does it seem possible that spontaneity will flourish above and beyond the routines of social regulation.

Self-government is a very demanding and time-consuming
business, and when it is extended from political to economic and
cultural life, and when the organs of government are decentralized so as to maximize participation, it will inevitably become
more demanding still. Ultimately, it may well require almost
continuous activity, and life will become a succession of meetings. When will there be time for the cultivation of personal
creativity or the free association of like-minded friends? In the
world of the meeting, when will there be time for the tête-à-
tête.

I suppose there will always be time for the tête-à-tête. Men
and women will secretly plan love affairs even while public business is being transacted. But Wilde's objection isn't silly. The
idea of citizenship on the Left has always been overwhelming,
suggesting a positive frenzy of activity, and often involving the
repression of all feelings except political ones. Its character can
best be examined in the work of Jean Jacques Rousseau, from
whom socialists and, more recently, New Leftists directly or indi-
rectly inherited it. In order to guarantee public-spiritedness and
political participation, and as a part of his critique of bourgeois
egotism, Rousseau systematically denigrated the value of private
life:

> The better the constitution of a state is, the more do pub-
> lic affairs encroach on private in the minds of the citizens.
> Private affairs are even of much less importance, because
> the aggregate of the common happiness furnishes a
> greater proportion of that of each individual, so that there
> is less for him to seek in particular cares.

Rousseau might well have written these lines out of a deep awareness that private life will not, in fact, bear the great weight that bourgeois society places upon it. We need, beyond our families and jobs, a public world where purposes are shared and cooperative activity is possible. More likely, however, he wrote them because he believed that cooperative activity could not be sustained unless private life were radically repressed, if not altogether eradicated. His citizen does not participate in social regulation as one part of a round of activities. Social regulation is his entire life. Rousseau develops his own critique of the division of labor by absorbing all human activities into the idea of citizenship: "Citizens," he wrote, "are neither lawyers, nor soldiers, nor priests by profession; they perform all these functions as a matter of duty." *As a matter of duty:* Here is the key to the character of that patriotic, responsible, energetic man who has figured also in socialist thought, but always in the guise of a new man, freely exercising his human powers.

It is probably more realistic to see the citizen as the product of collective repression and self-discipline. He is, above all, *dutiful,* and this is only possible if he has triumphed over egotism and impulse in his own personality. He embodies what political theorists have called "republican virtue"—that means, he puts the common good, the success of the movement, the safety of the community, above his own delight or well-being, *always.* To symbolize his virtue, perhaps, he adopts an ascetic style and gives up every sort of self-decoration: He adopts a sansculotte style or wears unpressed khakis. More important, he foregoes a conventional career for the profession of politics; he commits himself entirely. It is an act of the most extreme devotion. Now, how is such a man produced? What kind of conversion is necessary? Or what kind of rigorous training?

Rousseau set out to create virtuous citizens, and the means he chose are very old in the history of republicanism: an authoritarian family, a rigid sexual code, censorship of the arts, sumptuary laws, mutual surveillance, the systematic indoctrination of children. All these have been associated historically (at least until recent times) not with tyrannical but with republican regimes: Greece and Rome, the Swiss Protestant city-states, the first

French republic. Tyrannies and oligarchies, Rousseau argued, might tolerate or even encourage license, for the effect of sexual indulgence, artistic freedom, extravagant self-decoration, and privacy itself was to corrupt men and turn them away from public life, leaving government to the few. Self-government requires self-control: It is one of the oldest arguments in the history of political thought.

But if that argument is true, it may mean that self-government also leaves government to the few. For, if we reject the discipline of Rousseau's republicanism (as we have, and for good reasons), then only those men and women will be activists who volunteer for action. How many will that be? How many of the people you and I know? How many ought they to be? Certainly no radical movement or socialist society is possible without those ever-ready participants, who "fly," as Rousseau said, "to the public assemblies."

Radicalism and socialism make political activity for the first time an option for all those who relish it and a duty—sometimes —even for those who don't. But what a suffocating sense of responsibility, what a plethora of virtue would be necessary to sustain the participation of everybody all the time! How exhausting it would be! Surely there is something to be said for the irresponsible nonparticipant and something also for the part-time activist, the half-virtuous man (and the most scorned among the militants), who appears and disappears, thinking of Marx and then of his dinner? The very least that can be said is that these people, unlike the poor, will always be with us.

We can assume that a great many citizens, in the best of societies, will do all they can to avoid what Mel Tumin has nicely called "the merciless masochism of community-minded and self-regulating men and women." While the necessary meetings go on and on, they will take long walks, play with their children, paint pictures, make love, and watch television. They will attend sometimes, when their interests are directly at stake or when they feel like it. But they won't make the full-scale commitment necessary for socialism or participatory democracy. How are these people to be represented at the meetings? What are their rights? These are not only problems of the future, when popular

participation has finally been established as the core of political
and economic life. They come up in every radical movement;
they are the stuff of contemporary controversy.

Many people feel that they ought to join this or that political
movement; they do join; they contribute time and energy—but
unequally. Some make a full-time commitment; they work every
minute; the movement becomes their whole life and they often
come to disbelieve in the moral validity of life outside. Others
are established outside, solidly or precariously; they snatch hours
and sometimes days; they harry their families and skimp on their
jobs, but yet cannot make it to every meeting. Still others attend
no meetings at all; they work hard but occasionally; they show
up, perhaps, at critical moments, then they are gone. These last
two groups make up the majority of the people available to the
movement (any movement), just as they will make up the majority of the citizens of any socialist society. Radical politics radically increases the amount and intensity of political participation, but it doesn't (and probably oughtn't to) break through the
limits imposed on republican virtue by the inevitable pluralism
of commitments, the terrible shortage of time, and the day-to-day
hedonism of ordinary men and women.

Under these circumstances, words like citizenship and participation actually describe the enfranchisement of only a part, and
not necessarily a large part, of the movement or the community.
Participatory democracy means the sharing of power among the
activists. Socialism means the rule of the men with the most evenings to spare. Both imply also an injunction to the others: Join
us, come to the meetings, participate!

Sometimes young radicals sound very much like old Christians, demanding the severance of every tie for the sake of politics. "How many Christian women are there," John Calvin once
wrote, "who are held captive by their children!" How many
"community people" miss meetings because of their families! But
there is nothing to be done. Ardent democrats have sometimes
urged that citizens be legally required to vote: That is possible,
though the device is not attractive. Requiring people to attend
meetings, to join in discussions, to govern themselves: That is
not possible, at least not in a free society. And if they do not
govern themselves, they will, willy-nilly, be governed by their

activist fellows. The apathetic, the occasional enthusiasts, the part-time workers: All of them will be ruled by full-timers, militants, and professionals.

But if only some citizens participate in political life, it is essential that they always remember and be regularly reminded that they are . . . only some. This isn't easy to arrange. The militant in the movement, for example, doesn't represent anybody; it is his great virtue that he is self-chosen, a volunteer. But since he sacrifices so much for his fellowmen, he readily persuades himself that he is acting in their name. He takes their failure to put in an appearance only as a token of their oppression. He is certain he is their agent, or rather, the agent of their liberation.

He isn't in any simple sense wrong. The small numbers of participating citizens in the United States today, the widespread fearfulness, the sense of impotence and irrelevance: All these are signs of social sickness. Self-government is an important human function, an exercise of significant talents and energies, and the sense of power and responsibility it brings is enormously healthy. A certain amount of commitment and discipline, of not-quite-merciless masochism, is socially desirable, and efforts to evoke it are socially justifiable.

But many of the people who stay away from meetings do so for reasons that the militants don't understand or won't acknowledge. They stay away not because they are beaten, afraid, uneducated, lacking confidence and skills (though these are often important reasons), but because they have made other commitments; they have found ways to cope short of politics; they have created viable subcultures even in an oppressive world. They may lend passive support to the movement and help out occasionally, but they won't work, nor are their needs and aspirations in any sense embodied by the militants who will.

The militants represent themselves. If the movement is to be democratic, the others must *be represented*. The same thing will be true in any future socialist society: Participatory democracy has to be paralleled by representative democracy. I'm not sure precisely how to adjust the two; I am sure that they have to be adjusted. Somehow power must be distributed, as it isn't today, to small groups of active and interested citizens, but these citizens must themselves be made responsible to a larger electorate.

Nothing is more important than that responsibility; without it we will only get one or another sort of activist or *apparatchik* tyranny. And that we have already.

Nonparticipants have rights; it is one of the dangers of participatory democracy that it would fail to provide any effective protection for these rights. But nonparticipants also have functions; it is another danger that these would not be sufficiently valued. For many people in America today, politics is something to watch, an exciting spectacle, and there exists between the activists and the others something of the relation of actor and audience. Now for any democrat this is an unsatisfactory relation. We rightly resent the way actors play upon and manipulate the feelings of their audiences. We dislike the aura of magic and mystification contrived at on stage. We would prefer politics to be like the new drama with its alienation effects and audience participation. Fair enough.

But even the new drama requires its audience, and we ought not to forget that audiences can be critical as well as admiring, enlightened as well as mystified. More important, political actors, like actors in the theater, need the control and tension imposed by audiences, the knowledge that tomorrow the reviews will appear, tomorrow people will come or not come to watch their performance. Too often, of course, the reviews are favorable and the audiences come. That is because of the various sorts of collusion which presently develop between small and co-opted cliques of actors and critics. But in an entirely free society, there would be many more political actors and critics than ever before, and they would, presumably, be self-chosen. Not only the participants, but also the nonparticipants would come into their own. Alongside the democratic politics of shared work and perpetual activism, there would arise the open and leisurely culture of criticism, second-guessing, and burlesque.

It would be a mistake to underestimate the importance of all these, even if they aren't marked, as they generally won't be, by responsibility and virtue. They are far more important in the political arena than in the theater. For activists and professionals in the movement or the polity don't simply contrive effects; their work has more palpable results. Their policies touch us all in material ways, whether we go or don't go to the meetings. And those who don't go may well turn out to be more effective critics than those who do: No one who was one of its first guessers can usefully second-guess a decision. That is why the best critics in a liberal society are men-out-of-office. In a radically democratic society they would be men who stay away from meetings, perhaps for months at a time, and only then discover that something outrageous has been perpetrated that must be mocked or protested. The proper response to such protests is not to tell the laggard citizens that they should have been active these past many months, not to nag them to do work that they don't enjoy and in any case won't do well, but to listen to what they have to say. After all, what would democratic politics be like without its kibbitzers?

[1968]

ONE-DIMENSIONAL PESSIMISM:

A Critique of Herbert Marcuse's Theories

by Allen Graubard

Herbert Marcuse's *One-Dimensional Man* appeared four years ago. Since then it has been widely and, on the whole, favorably reviewed, read, and discussed. Accepted by many as the long-awaited work that "tells it like it is," Marcuse's essay has assumed near-canonical status among some of the most serious and thoughtful of the New Left. An incisive and original discussion of community organizing in *Studies on the Left* led off by announcing that *One-Dimensional Man* was to be assumed as the theoretical underpinning for the detailed and specific analysis that followed—though the philosopher's theory could be taken to be sometimes downright incompatible with the authors' practice. In *New Left Notes*, the SDS internal journal, Marcuse's special philosophical vocabulary appears as unproblematically as if it were part of ordinary language. Marcuse's reputation in Europe is tremendous, as attested by a news item in *The New York Times* in the summer of 1967 described the tumultuous reception he received from crowds of Berlin students. A weighty *Festschrift* for Marcuse has also appeared, and a front-page review in the Sunday *New York Times Book Review* section proclaimed him as "the foremost philosopher of the New Left." Even in the "bourgeois" press, Marcuse has made it.

Clearly the work has wide appeal. But in my view it is a great disappointment. Given the real and pressing needs of theory-hungry American radicalism and the danger of overvaluing any attempt, especially one which seems to be deeply rooted in profound if obscure philosophical traditions, it is worthwhile even at this time to try to account for both the appeal and the disappointment. *One-Dimensional Man* is an attempt to give a "total" analysis of our society, encompassing all major aspects of thought and action. It claims to unmask hopes for any significant possibilities of change from within the system. The note of pessimism struck is so profound that to be critical is to appear superficial, unaware of the despair which must accompany true insight. An example can serve to show how the tone of the book can evoke such feelings. At one point, Marcuse inserts a quote from Ionesco, without comment, though clearly with approval.

> The world of the concentration camps . . . was not an exceptionally monstrous society. What we saw there was the image, and in a sense the quintessence, of the infernal society into which we are plunged every day.

The quote is not explicitly related to the discussion of technological rationality in the midst of which it appears. What should one say? My feeling is *no*, but I feel hesitant and defensive about it. I do think the camps were exceptionally monstrous, and I don't think they are, even "in a sense," the "quintessence" of the society I am plunged into daily (or Professor Marcuse either). Which isn't to defend the goodness of this society unless one's position is so "profound" that "not as bad as Auschwitz" is considered a positive defense.

The kind of position here taken by Marcuse makes profundity a little too easy and smothers analysis. From such a stance all qualifications can seem unessential, petty, and superficial. The total statement is tougher, more absolute, more powerful, and more satisfying; but finally, if offered as description and explanation, it fails. For precisely the differences and qualifications it overlooks are essential for understanding our situation, especially if understanding is related to decision and action. The vision of pessimism may express part of our mood, as in the Beckett novels which Marcuse commends, but offered as multidimensional analysis it can be numbing. It can lead to a sense that no action is really relevant or significant in a situation so totally awful and devoid of possibilities.

The book is an essay in philosophical sociology, an attempt to grasp the essential defining characteristics of a form of society by means of an analysis of its ideology. Marcuse's mode is to specify *the* ideology of the society as a whole in terms of particular realizations of general categories. We are given descriptions of particular uses of propaganda as exemplifications of the general category of "*the* language of the society," a particular view of modern atomic physics as *the* philosophy of science, a particular style of philosophy now dominant in England and important in America as *the* philosophy of "advanced industrial society," a particular approach to method in social science ("functionalism" and "behaviorism") as *the* social science of the society, and so on.

This style is carried through even in the more rhetorical passages, as in Marcuse's statement that *the* face of our time is seen in the novels of Samuel Beckett. The unqualified nature of this style incorporates fundamental ambiguities, empirical and methodological. First, a characterization of the general category—Art, Philosophy, Science, Language—is stated. As usual, such general descriptions of what Art or Philosophy has always been are at best dubious. Then the realization of the general category for advanced industrial society is described in terms of the root metaphor of "one-dimensionality." *The* art, *the* politics, *the* language, *the* social science, *the* philosophy are one-dimensional; they lack the possibility of transcendence or negation, possibilities always present in previous societies. These realizations are expounded in terms of particular examples, often extreme examples, the worst aspects of whatever activity or category is being considered. The argument is not an inductive empirical one, though empirical pronouncements are often made in the course of the argument. (We are told what *the* people think, how *Time* magazine affects *the* leader. No empirical basis for such claims is given, no qualifications are offered; exceptions are not analyzed.)

The effect of the empirical claim is really dependent upon the conceptual claim that the "totalizing" syntax is justified; that the examples or particular realizations of the general category are the defining, essential ones. No real argument justifying the "essential" constructions is, in fact, given (just as there is no argument to support the claim that the Nazi death camps are the quintessential image of the society we live in). What drives the discussion along is the repetition of the root image, the emotional appeal of extreme and powerful examples, and crucial confusions between empirical and conceptual questions involved in notions like "prevailing universe of discourse and action," and "possibility of transcendence."

However difficult the language often is to those who are not at ease in Marcuse's Hegelian idiom, the general thesis and overall structure of the argument are quite clear. The thesis is as follows:

The avance of modern post-Galilean science and the technology based upon this science have made possible an industrial society that is able to achieve a tremendous and constantly increasing productivity. Politically, the effect of this development has been to destroy the basis of revolutionary protest, to damp down social conflict to the point where historical agencies of social change disappear. In Marcuse's words:

> Contemporary society seems to be capable of containing social change—qualitative change which would establish essentially different institutions, a new direction of the productive process, new modes of human existence.
>
> . . . the capitalist development has altered the structure and function of these two classes [bourgeoisie and proletariat] in such a way that they no longer appear to be agents of historical transformation. An overriding interest in the preservation of the institutional status quo unites the former antagonists in the most advanced areas of contemporary society.

What follows is the disappearance of meaningful protest as a society develops which instills the false needs it then satisfies. Society conditions a population to support its own irrational domination while thinking itself to be free and rational.

> . . . the technological controls appear to be the very embodiment of Reason for the benefit of all social groups

and interests—to such an extent that all contradiction
seems irrational and *all* counteraction impossible. . . .
The intellectual and emotional refusal "to go along" appears neurotic and impotent. This is the socio-psychologi-
cal aspect of the political event that marks the
contemporary period: the passing of the historical forces
which, at the preceding stage of industrial society, seemed
to represent the possibility of new forms of existence.

(Italics added.)

The result is a false consciousness, a deceptive "Happy Consciousness," a "preconditioning," an indoctrination which se-
curely integrates the society around its productive apparatus and
makes impotent or meaningless any protest.

Thus emerges a pattern of *one-dimensional thought and
behavior* in which ideas, aspirations, and objectives that
by their content transcend the established universe of discourse and action are either repelled or reduced to terms
of this universe. They are redefined by the rationality of
the given system and its quantitative extension.

At the conclusion of the book, Marcuse writes:

The enchained possibilities of advanced industrial society
are: development of the productive forces on an enlarged
scale, extension of the conquest of nature, growing satisfaction of needs and faculties. But these possibilities are
gradually being realized through means and institutions
which cancel their liberating potential, and this process
affects not only the means but also the ends. The instruments of productivity and progress, organized into a totalitarian system, determine not only the actual but also the
possible utilizations.

Marcuse's discussions of particular topics are designed to illustrate and substantiate this general theme. The metaphor of
"one-dimensionality" expresses the disappearance of fundamental
oppositions in our society, those oppositions which can be indi-

cated by such traditional pairs as "fact-value," "is-ought," "reality-appearance," "potential-actual." The dimension which is dissolving is that of man's perception of the injustice, irrationality, and oppression which characterize the actual existence of all historical societies. This perception was always accompanied by a vision of a better, truer, freer existence, as has been conceived in art, philosophy, and religion; though such vision was presented necessarily in a disguised and sublimated form.

This metaphor expresses Marcuse's sense of the frightening uniqueness of advanced industrial society. The very society which has, in Marxian terminology, produced the material means for the leap from the realm of necessity into the realm of freedom, has accomplished this in such a manner as to perpetuate "domination." Even more important, this domination, characteristic of "technological rationality," destroys the possibility of transcending the domination. This unique closing-off of possibility, this destruction of an entire dimension of human existence cannot but be the most frightening and depressing development in man's history. In an obvious sense—implies Marcuse—this is the best and the worst of times, but the "bestness" is superficial and the "worstness" profound.

The first "study" in the book is of "one-dimensional society." The thesis is that technological society has made it possible to incorporate the proletariat into the system, in fact as well as in consciousness, by means of the welfare state. Using as background this conception of the welfare state as a stable form of oppression, Marcuse describes the concomitant cultural integration under the heading "The Conquest of the Unhappy Consciousness: Repressive Desublimation." The claim here is that "high culture," by being absorbed by the system which uses it as a commodity, loses its essential function of being sublimated protest. The alienation, the embodying of the tension between the actual and the possible, beauty as the *promesse de bonheur*—these essential characteristics of all art are disappearing. The massification of culture as a by-product of democratization and technological advance has undermined the very substance of art, its critical potential, and its alienated truth.

In the sphere of sexuality also, apparent progress is seen as really a worsening of the situation. Admittedly, erotic energy is freed in contemporary society. But Marcuse conceives of the "sexual revolution," the "desublimation," as worse than the former repression since

> the greater liberty involves a contradiction rather than extension and development of instinctual needs . . . it works *for* rather than *against* the status quo of general repression—one might speak of "institutionalized desublimation."

Pleasure is allowed, but only in acceptable forms which dissolve those claims that are unreconcilable with the established society. In this manner, further submission is generated. The result is "The Happy Consciousness," "the belief that the real is rational and that the system delivers the goods."

Marcuse extends this cultural analysis to the "closing of the universe of discourse." He wishes to show how "behaviorism" and "functionalism" characterize the language and thought of our society and destroy the capacity for critical two-dimensional language and thought.

> Discourse is deprived of the mediations which are the stages of the process of cognition and cognitive evaluation. The concepts which comprehend the facts are losing their authentic linguistic representation. Without these mediations language tends to express and promote the immediate identification of reason and fact, truth and established truth, essence and existence, the thing and its function.

Marcuse uses the term "operationalism," as expounded by the physicist P. W. Bridgman, to characterize the identification of a concept with a set of operations. This "total empiricism" restricts the meaning of concepts to the representation of particular operations and behavior. Marcuse considers this type of "operationalism" and its counterpart "behaviorism" to be the "predominant trend in philosophy, sociology, and other fields."

This is a very substantial claim, but Marcuse does little to substantiate it. Bridgman's views, along with the logical positivist position of which they were the most extreme expression, have been subjected to quite devastating critiques, both from within and without the "neo-positivist" tradition. Similarly, such method-ologies in social science continue to receive effective criticism; and for many scientists and philosophers, such extreme behavior-ism as Marcuse constructs is a thoroughly refuted position. (See, for example, Noam Chomsky's brilliant and scathing review of Skinner's *Verbal Behavior,* and Charles Taylor's *The Explanation of Behavior,* a subtle attack on behaviorism in psychology writ-ten by an analytical philosopher who was a leading figure in the English New Left of the late 1950s.) The same dialectical situa-tion of accepted position and critique applies to anthropology, sociology, and political science as well.

In a broader and vaguer sense of "behaviorism" and "positiv-ism" than Marcuse's, there is such a predominance in American social science. The kind of "scientism" with its proclaimed "value neutrality," which characterizes much work in social science, often cloaks ideological support for the system in the guise of "scientific objectivity," as Marcuse shows in unmasking some ex-amples of such work. But this sort of predominance is not star-tling to a radical, especially one who is conscious of Marx's con-tributions to the theory of ideology. This society is not exceptional in having key institutions like universities dominated by trends and approaches that are ideologically tied to and sup-portive of the status quo. What would be exceptional and uniquely "one-dimensional" is the disappearance of an opposi-tion. But Marcuse does not demonstrate this, and the book misses what would be helpful and revealing in this context, namely a sense of the dialectic of the disputes and radical cri-tiques being made within the disciplines.

Marcuse's view would clearly be that my comments are totally superficial; that these positions are not merely dominant but ac-tually definitive of the activity for *this* society because they are truly the expression of the form of Reason which is embodied in advanced industrial society. The opposition is ignored and im-plicitly ruled out of being part of *the* society, and the ideological and institutional dominance is transformed into a monolithic conceptual bind. This form of argument comes out quite clearly in the use of examples. The author explicitly puts forward his ex-

amples as illuminatingly representative, although little argument
is offered other than the feel of how, being extreme examples,
they appeal to and reflect our fears. What results is a kind of
armchair sociology of knowledge, a truncation of reality, and a curious ambiguity in the extension of crucial terms.

For example, in the discussion of "functional," "operational,"
and "behavioral" language referred to, Marcuse wants to characterize the "prevailing modes of speech" as making the expression
of opposition impossible. The explication of concepts in terms of
functions is said to result in a one-dimensional language of
"magic-ritual formulas."

Marcuse attempts to illustrate the thought-impeding style of
this language in terms of advertisements for luxury fallout shelters, RAND Corporation "war game" instructions, specimens of
political huckstering, news-column heads, and a passage from
Time. The claim is that "clean bomb" and "harmless fallout" are
"only extreme creations of a normal style." The passage from
Time, also noted as an "extreme example," is analyzed in this
manner:

> A hyphenated attributive construction creates a fixed syn-
> drome: "Georgia's high-handed low-browed governor . . .
> had the stage all set for one of his wild political rallies
> last week." . . . The governor, his function, his physical
> features, and his political practices are fused together into
> one *indivisible* and *immutable* stucture which, in its natu-
> ral innocence and immediacy, overwhelms *the reader's*
> mind. . . . Terms designating quite different spheres or
> qualities are forced together into a solid, *overpowering*
> whole. . . . The effect is again a *magical* and *hypnotic*
> one.

The kind of "good" language characterizing the possibilities of
previous societies is exemplified for Marcuse by *The Communist
Manifesto.* (I think this might be called "loading the comparison.") Are we to take it that *the* language of nineteenth-century
bourgeois-feudal Germany, the "prevailing universe of discourse," is best represented by the writings of Karl Marx and
Friedrich Engels? If not, why this particular sort of comparison?

A critical aspect of this *a priori* sociology can be brought out by noting an ambiguity in the reference of crucial terms, a tacit amendment to the "total" claims of Marcuse's syntax. Take the analysis of *Time* language: *The* reader's mind is "overwhelmed," the structure is "indivisible and immutable," the whole is "solid and overpowering," the effect is "magical and hypnotic." At another point, Marcuse says: "The people recognize themselves in their commodities; they find their soul in their automobile, hi-fi set, split-level home, kitchen equipment." The tacit amendment to such characterizations is that neither the author nor the radical reader is included in "the reader" or "the people" (even if one sometimes looks, with anger and disgust, at an issue of *Time,* or if one owns a car and a stereo). My question is—how does Marcuse know so much and so exactly about *the* reader's responses? From a brief analysis of *Time*-ese, from the evidence of syntax? The sociological questions—who reads *Time,* what variety of responses are there, is there skepticism, do the same "language" and response characterize, say, *The New Yorker, Scientific American, Partisan Review, Fortune,* and *Ramparts*—are immediately raised in my mind. The author, however, does not seem to feel that there is anything more to be learned or that what might be discovered could make a difference in one's understanding.

But Marcuse also says: "The new touch of the magic-ritual language rather is that people don't believe it, or don't care, and yet act accordingly." Is it really all so clear? Is there any range between being hypnotized and "not believing"? No complexity or shading of response? Isn't there anything to be discovered about the nature of compliance and support, the apathy, the areas of dissent? What is the implication of the fact that *we* are not included—we have seen through it, we fight against it, write critical books, publish magazines, organize "free universities"? Why is it that the others don't (can't, won't)? Marcuse's "totalizing" analysis of extreme examples is not a sufficient answer.

The most detailed critique of the possibilities of the "language" of the society is presented in the central section of the essay, the discussion of "one-dimensional thought." This is the most "ideological" of the analyses, for Marcuse assumes that "it is the sphere farthest removed from the concreteness of society which may show most clearly the extent of the conquest of thought by society."

Unfortunately, this section is the weakest part of the book. The subjects are no less than science and philosophy in general and specifically in our society. The discussion of the essential nature of philosophy and its origins among the Greeks is extremely compressed, and, for me, almost impossible to follow with any confidence. The intent is to characterize good philosophy as "two-dimensional," dialectical, contradictory, able to come "to grips with reality," in Marcuse's phrase. Only "dialectical thought," he seems to be saying, retains the tension between "is" and "ought" (and of the other oppositions mentioned at the beginning of this article). This kind of thought emphasizes the necessity of changing the apparent reality in order to bring into being a truer, more rational, and hence more real reality. (In Marcuse's words, "Dialectical thought understands the critical tension between 'is' and 'ought' first as an ontological condition, pertaining to the structure of Being itself.") This "two-dimensionality" involves the notion of "another logic," "another universe of discourse."

There is good rhetoric here, but not much more. At no point does Marcuse clarify the notion of a "logic" or of "laws of thought." This would be necessary if one wanted to show how "formal logic" is a narrow and essentially conservative mode of thinking, a "logic of domination," "nontranscendent in its very structure."

The discussion depends upon unexamined ambiguities in the use of "logic," "contradiction," "real," and other related terms. Although we are supposedly given a contrast between "good" logic and "bad" logic, at no point is the formal study of "logic," as in Aristotle or Frege, distinguished from the idea of "logic" as referring to coherence and consistency of thought and communication. "Logic," in this general sense of deductive logic or rules of inference, seems to exist in all languages and in all societies. In this sense, "logic" is a "linguistic universal." The "dialectic" as a style, a recommendation to conceive the world in terms of conflicting forces, within a context which should always be seen as characterized by possibilities for transformation, is not, therefore, a question of "logic," properly conceived. It is one of intelligence and insight. A logical contradiction will be invalid even in a good society, when all social "contradictions" will have been dissolved.

The discussion of "good" thought is the context for an analysis of the nature of science and its philosophy. The line taken is the familiar one that science took man out of nature, separated value and fact, destroyed a nature conceivable in terms of "final causes," dissolved matter into abstract equations.

Marcuse's analysis of mathematical physics and the philosophy associated with it is singularly unenlightening. It is dogmatically stated, based on a pastiche of quotes from various philosophers and philosophically minded scientists. We get little sense of the kind of discussions these quotes may be part of; or why a certain philosopher's statement, say W. V. Quine's personal and controversial formulation that "objects continue to persist only as 'convenient intermediaries,' as 'obsolescent cultural posits,'" is to be taken as properly and essentially characterizing the general terms "physics" and "modern philosophy of science." ("Obsolescent" is Marcuse's own misinterpretive interpolation.) Without a proper "dialectical" sense of the debates, such use of quotes gives only an arbitrary picture of Marcuse's own construction, especially misleading if it can be assumed that most readers don't know much about quantum mechanics or special relativity theory.[1]

The key claim is that science "develops under the *technological a priori* which projects nature as potential instrumentality, stuff of control and organization." For Marcuse this means that

---

[1] It is interesting to note that this approach to science and its philosophy is almost identical with that given by Hannah Arendt in *The Human Condition*, a book which in many ways resembles *One-Dimensional Man*. (Neither writer will thank me for this comparison.) The same essays by Heisenberg, giving philosophical interpretations that are highly controversial and are in any case obscurely and inadequately argued, are accepted without question as definitive of modern science and its philosophy. There are also striking similarities in the respective analyses of "functionalism" and "behaviorism" and the dreaded but expected "brave new world"-style behavioristic future for postindustrial mass society. But ironically, Miss Arendt writes from a profoundly conservative antirevolutionary perspective while Marcuse is revolutionary and utopian.

scientific rationality determines a society of technological domination in which everything, including man, is treated "function-
ally" and "instrumentally." He wants

> to demonstrate the *internal* instrumentalist character of
> this scientific rationality by virtue of which it is *a priori*
> technology, and the *a priori* of a *specific* technology —
> namely, technology as a form of social control and domi-
> nation. . . . Science, *by virtue of its own method* and con-
> cepts, has projected and promoted a universe in which the
> domination of nature has remained linked to the domina-
> tion of man.

Since Marcuse's discussion of science and its philosophy is so in-
adequate and mistaken, the claimed connection between science
in general and domination is left completely undemonstrated.

But isn't the question itself wrongly posed? Science has not
led to domination, even to a particular form of domination. It
has been a crucial factor, of course, in the material and ideological transformation of the West, and now, increasingly, of the entire world. But the activity of science arose in a society which
was characterized by all sorts of tyrannies and domination, and
many of the liberating forces of our age are essentially related to
ideas of science and the various ways in which these have been
interpreted. These include the development of socialism, Marxism, psychoanalytic theory. I don't mean to say hurrah for science; like logic, it is part of the general framework in which we
think and act. The question should not be how science has maintained domination, which would have been better maintained by
"non-science," but why didn't the development of scientific
thought, by and of itself, lead to the free society? To ask the
question this way is to see immediately that blaming or exonerat-
ing science is unhelpful at best. Why should science have accomplished this? What about everything else—the social institutions,
character structures, beliefs, vested interests—which characterized the society within which science developed? What we need
and Marcuse doesn't supply is a sense of the interplay between
scientific ideas, technological developments, and the beliefs and
values of man, as this interplay works itself out in history.

For Marcuse, the "one-dimensional thought" toward which science has led is seen most clearly in the "positive thinking" of "one-dimensional philosophy." This philosophical ideology, the "school" of linguistic analysis, is claimed to be a travesty, a pseudophilosophy, at best inconsequential, at worst tragically dangerous.

Marcuse's discussion of linguistic philosophy raises the general question of ideological analysis, as much by what it doesn't say as by what it does. If we take examples of ideological analysis like Mannheim's study "Conservative Thought" or Sutton's *The American Business Creed,* we find an analysis of "ideological productions" related to the individuals who produced them or adhere to them. These individuals are described as members of particular groups, characterized in terms of roles, institutions, and social structure. Thought and social structure are mediated by a theory of some sort—crude self-interest theories, Marxist theories of class interest, "strain" theories of the sort prominent in American social science.

Marcuse's critique of linguistic analysis completely ignores the questions raised by this schema of ideological analysis. Social and institutional questions are not raised. Nor are the political positions of the people involved. The national traditions of English philosophy and its relation to linguistic analysis are not discussed. The claim is that, in crucial ways, this philosophy represents a radical break with all previous philosophy, even with the "two-dimensional" empiricism it evolves from.

What Marcuse hopes to show is that this philosophy reflects the positive thinking of advanced industrial society. This project would seem to entail a subtle and accurate description and analysis of linguistic philosophy. What we find instead is another instance of the fallacious kind of argument used throughout the book.

Marcuse takes as given that linguistic philosophy is a philosophy with clear and definite doctrines. "It identifies as its chief concern the debunking of transcendent concepts; it proclaims as its frame of reference the common usage of words, the variety of prevailing behavior." According to Marcuse, such philosophy permits no negativity toward the existing practices of society.

> The self-imposed restriction to the prevalent behavioral universe makes for an intrinsically positive attitude . . .

the prebound analysis succumbs to the power of positive thinking.

How these doctrines were proclaimed we are not told. Would the God believed in by religious linguistic philosophers count as a "transcendent concept"? What exactly is meant by "debunking"? Does Marcuse mean that any attempt to criticize society is considered meaningless by the linguistic philosophers? What is meant by "the variety of prevailing behavior"? And what is his evidence for characterizing linguistic analysis as adhering to "philosophical behaviorism"? (This subject of "action" and "behavior" is one of the most important areas of dispute *within* the "style," though if Marcuse's analysis were a reader's only acquaintance with this philosophy, he would not have the slightest idea of the existence or nature of such disputes.) As usual, we find the monolithic tone—Linguistic Analysis believes this and Linguistic Analysis makes it impossible to do that.

The examples Marcuse cites to illustrate his claims are from Wittgenstein and Austin, the two major figures of postwar British philosophy. Marcuse tells us that "silly scraps of language that sound like baby talk" guide the analysis of such philosophers. For example, he says: "Wittgenstein devotes much acumen and space to the analysis of 'My broom is in the corner.'" A lengthy quote from Austin's essay "Other Minds" is added. These examples are supposed to support Marcuse's claim that this style of philosophy is destructive of philosophic thought, "and of critical thought as such."

This is a rather damning indictment, and one would have expected some sense of context, *at least* to be told what the analyses mentioned were used for. As it is, Marcuse does not give the slightest hint of the purpose of Wittgenstein's analysis of "silly scraps of language."

However, Marcuse does assure us that if such scraps appeared in Hegel, "they would be revealed as inappropriate or even false examples." But inappropriate or false examples of what? Does the sentence "My broom is in the corner" carry written on it that it will always and in all circumstances be an inappropriate or a false example? Since we are never told what Wittgenstein uses it as an example of, how are we to know even that he takes it to be a true example, in the sense that a truly profound philosopher would show it to be false? Similarly for the quote from Austin, on the basis of which a reader might think that Austin had written an essay on ways of being hesitant or on the taste of pineapples. But in fact the essay quoted deals with basic problems of epistemology. Professor Stanley Cavell, one of the most provocative interpreters of both Austin and Wittgenstein, characterizes Austin's methods and their effects in the following manner:

> He asks for the difference between being sure and being certain, but what is uncovered is an initial survey of the complex and mutual alignments between mind and world that are necessary to successful knowledge. He asks for the difference between expressing belief and expressing knowledge (or between saying "I believe" and saying "I know") and what comes up is a new sense and assessment of the human limitations, or human responsibilities, of human knowledge, and so on. (S. Cavell, "Austin at Criticism," *Philosophical Review*, April 1965.)

Of course there is disagreement even among those who are vaguely called "analytical philosophers" on the worth and implication of the work of Wittgenstein or Austin. But Marcuse is clearly not interested in this nor in recognizing how such stuff could have ever been considered as possibly fruitful philosophical activity. I think that there is a difficult and important task to be done in the analysis of thought-styles and emphases and their relation to more general social circumstances (and analytical philosophy is a good case to work on). But this implies that the works themselves must be treated with appropriate subtlety and even sympathy. To put Wittgenstein down by mentioning a sentence he uses as an example really smacks of philistinism and is unworthy of Marcuse. One could apply this sort of critique to Kant or Descartes with the same result. Making the relevant substitutions in the Marcusean argument, we come up with: "Kant devotes much acumen and space to the analysis of '5 + 7 = 12'" (a piece of second-grade arithmetic); "Descartes devotes much acumen and space to describing the melting of a piece of wax." The last step in the argument is to leave the reader to try to discover what on earth could have been in the minds of these so-called philosophers.

The crucial point in Marcuse's attack is the repeated insistence that linguistic analysis makes "negative thinking" impossible; that it surrenders to "ordinary language"; that it doesn't subvert the given facts, as true philosophy should; that it leaves language in "the repressive context of the established universe of discourse"; that it gives a "behavioral explication of meaning." The contention is that this philosophy makes it impossible to think critically about our society because of its unquestioning acceptance of "the established universe of discourse and action."

This last phrase is basic to Marcuse's critique and appears frequently throughout the book. It is based upon a fundamental ambiguity of Marcuse's analysis which emerges most clearly in his polemic against analytical philosophy. In philosophy of this sort, questions of language are in general questions of meaning, and, as Cavell emphasizes, are simultaneously questions about the "world." One concern, among others, is getting clear on how we use words and thus on the conditions and problems of meaning and understanding. This is *not* equivalent to accepting the limiting of "meaningful" to "what most people say" or what is politically or socially acceptable to the majority or to the ruling elites. What is at stake is what *we* ourselves say and mean, when we talk about pain or love or fear or truth or freedom. And it is simply not the case, as Marcuse dogmatically states, that "to begin with, an irreducible difference exists between the universe of everyday thinking and language on one side, and that of philosophic thinking and language on the other." It is not the case because I grew up and live in a "universe of everyday thinking and language," and it is by means of this language, used subtly, intelligently, and critically, that I learn valuable new concepts and new possibilities of meaning, including "philosophic" meaning.

If the difference were truly "irreducible," it would be impossible to explain the meaning of new terms, say "dialectic" or "transcendent." "The established universe of discourse and action" should be taken to mean "what can be meaningfully said and done." (This universe includes radical ideas and radical actions, as well as conforming behavior and television commercials.) The sliding between the statistical and conceptual connotations of this key phrase has been noted several times before. In the derogatory sense of "established universe," to be within it or to accept it uncritically is to lose the possibility of being negative, radical, critical, original, and so is to be "one-dimensional." But in the other sense, and it is this sense I associate with the best possibilities of analytical philosophy, there is no limit except meaningfulness (and establishing this is a problem, not an assumption to begin with).

What can be said in "ordinary language" is that this society is lousy in many ways; that it is immoral to waste vast resources in maintaining irrational and oppressive institutions while most of the world starves; that the lives of many people, both in the United States and in the countries with which it is involved, are twisted and their potentialities distorted by the prevailing values and practices of this affluent society; that there could and should be more beauty and truth and justice in the world. The refusal to accept the propaganda of the Establishment, the decision to protest and to live in socially and politically disapproved ways are as much a part of the universe of meanings as are the most conformist actions. That the number of such radicals may be small does not settle the question of what can be *meant*. It implies that, as always, those who are willing to go beyond generally accepted arrangements and values will be in a minority and can have no guarantee that their vision will win out.

This core ambiguity causes much of Marcuse's critique to miss the mark. That philosophers discuss academic topics at all instead of attacking current political and social arrangements might seem to present a problem, given Marcuse's conception of philosophy. But then every other life activity except direct political action or critique would fall under a similar criticism. Why discuss problems of causality in physics when this is the world of Hiroshima and Auschwitz; why take time listening to music and going to see movies when every minute our government is committing murderous atrocities; why produce Molière comedies or paint abstract canvases when people are starving? I don't find these questions silly, but each of us has to find and live out his own answers.

Why then does Marcuse pour so much scorn and ridicule on

this little-known part of the academy, so out of proportion as a target, given the subjects of the other parts of the book? My feeling is that Marcuse is expressing his anger and frustration at the apparent impotence of thought to break through, to bring about the necessary radical changes in consciousness he sketches in the concluding section on "The Chance for Alternatives."

This whole section should be read against the background of Marcuse's *Eros and Civilization,* an essay that developed at greater length the utopian concepts which constitute Marcuse's vision of a "good" future. In *One-Dimensional Man,* the key concepts are "pacification of existence," "freedom," "liberation." The vision is that the "project" of scientific rationality would surpass its present structure and direction, and would become "metaphysical" again; industrialization would take new forms. Values would be translated into needs that would develop on the basis of "nonrepressive sublimation." The vision must necessarily be sketched programmatically ("liberation of the imagination," "redefinition of needs"), for there is a real limitation of the established universe of discourse.

The ambiguity between the conceptual and the empirical accounts both for the power of Marcuse's vision to express despair and for the confusions of his analysis. It reappears strikingly in his somber conclusion. He reaffirms his faith in "critical reason" but finds its powerlessness a source of despair. The quality of the despair can be related to Marcuse's Marxian framework. One-dimensional society, however wasteful, ugly, oppressive, and crippling for man, seems increasingly capable, by its irrational rationality, of containing social change, and containing it by consent, as it were. This implies the disappearance of real forces, of definite social groups whose existence would compel them toward the abolition of oppression. Without these social groups, determined in their very existence by the nature of the society which brought them into being, can any change come? Can theory, however critical, become practice in some other way; by changing consciousness within the affluent society, for example?

For Marcuse it seems that the answer must be no. This is the way history *must* work. His despair and anger translate themselves into the depressing sense that thought itself is becoming impossible. Even those seemingly favorable signs, like the civil-

rights movement, must be seen as part of "the catastrophe of liberation," as signs of how totalitarian the society is becoming. For
now even the most materially oppressed groups will be brought
into the system; and whereas a blatantly oppressed and despised
Negro population was by its very existence, if not in its consciousness, a threat to the system, a Negro population with apparent political power and opportunities for seeking significant
economic advance will lose this existential aspect of "negativity."
It would seem to follow that peace movements, SDS, left-wing
magazines and books can be taken most significantly as signs of
the increasing power of the system, ways of letting off steam,
part of the society's fooling itself into thinking it is free and open
whereas the true reality is otherwise. Better, it would appear, the
old McCarthyite terror or worse, outlawing of student protests,
police censorship of political publications; at least this would
force some people to face the underlying truth.

   This contemporary version of "the worse, the better" could
hardly be more despairing and pessimistic. That hardly anyone
in his most thoughtful moods could desire such a situation seems
obvious. We want our freedoms and rights, and we think it is
worthwhile to work for simple material gains, however small, for
people whose lives are ground down by poverty. But, given the
frustrations of a commitment to a vision of radical social change,
the frequent failure to accomplish small goals—let alone the
great transformations which are the ultimate motivations of
hopefully "radical" projects like organizing a community union
project in the Newark ghetto, being a SNCC worker in Mississippi, or forming a draft resistance movement—how can one
avoid moods of deep pessimism? Such moods are not, finally, an
accurate indication of our complex sense of where we are and
what we can do. But my feeling is that much of the appeal of
the book stems from Marcuse's evocation of this mood of blan-
keting and apparently omniscient pessimism, his rooting the frustrations of failure in an impressive if obscure philosophical frame
which projects a society that makes "transcendence" in any area
impossible.

   To a great extent this Marcusean pessimism is related to a romantic involvement with the image and rhetoric of the great revolutionary moment, the kind of apocalyptic transformation

where one can see with satisfying certainty the success of one's efforts in reaching the deepest goals of the radical vision. For Marcuse, the disappearance of the possibility of realizing this vision (for all the reasons that the book notes) provides a simplifying if despairing canon of historical interpretation. If rising standards of living, the elimination of sheer material oppression, the development of a semi–welfare state, the liberation of sexuality, etc., are factors in the conditions making the vision of revolutionary transformation completely illusory, then they are finally bad. What is ignored is the actual meaning of these changes to the people who experience them as real improvements, however meager they seem in the light of the utopian vision of the end of all psychic repression and the transformation of man's instinctual structures.

The analyses in the book are attempts to justify this simplifying pessimism. But as I have tried to demonstrate, Marcuse's argument fails to support his thesis which, itself, is not interestingly new. In various forms it is the recurrent nightmare of an automated, sterile, passive "brave new world." Finally, the argument misleads by not matching our sense of the ambiguity of our situation, its confusing "two-dimensionality": as regards our political possibilities, the art we respond to, the dynamic of science, the meaning of sexuality. By denying this felt ambiguity within our own lived experience and by assuming an almost *a priori* pessimistic knowledge of the state of "the people," the meaning of increasing prosperity and welfare, the possibilities of art and sexuality, Marcuse has translated a justified sense of staggering and sometimes unique difficulties of successful "transcendence" and opposition into an unjustified vision of an almost complete conceptual impossibility. In this way, Marcuse has been able to construct a frightening metaphor of bleak pessimism.

But the real help we need is not in giving nightmares an intellectual structure. It is in beginning to answer questions about the politics of the "totalizing" and "post-totalized" society. The old agents of history may disappear or be absorbed, but what will the new social and psychic strains and discontents be like in the prosperous, postindustrial society, and how will the discontent, dissatisfiaction, and alienation be made politically relevant, at least potentially? Should the movement be one of resolute opposition, gathering in and giving activity and space to those who become conscious of their alienation, thus hopefully building an area of "negativity" in American society which could become relevant in future situations the nature of which we can't yet clearly conceive? Or should attempts be made to work at least partly within the established institutions of the society, to attempt to affect, even if only marginally, the actual and potential destructiveness of American power, and to help in the totalizing process which is going on and will provide the context for a possible new politics? These questions are hard to formulate in a clear way appropriate to the ambiguity of our situation, just as it is hard to explain the meaning of the unexpected phenomenon of the transformation not of "high culture" which Marcuse fastens on, but of mass culture in the form of, say, the Beatles or Bob Dylan or the movies.

A discouraging projection of despair built up by bad argument doesn't touch these questions; and despite the appeal of the tone to many young radicals, the analysis is indifferent between radical perspectives of community organizing and uncompromising opposition and, so to speak, "moderate" perspectives of coalition politics and working within the system. The whole spectrum of possibilities is swallowed up in the "catastrophe of liberation." We may not reach the understanding we need, but if we do, it will be with a little help from our friends; and that Marcuse, for all his intelligence, passion, and commitment, does not help, is the measure of the book's failure and my disappointment.

[1968]

REVISIONIST HISTORIANS AND THE COLD WAR

by Henry Pachter

Not only the East has its revisionists. In this country, too, and even more insistently in Western Europe, honest research has led to a thorough and often painful reappraisal of recent history. The conventional view of the so-called cold war, as it still appears in such widely used textbooks as Spanier and Lukacz,[1] is under attack. This view may be crudely presented in three propositions:

> After World War II the Soviet Union tried to expand its power through military conquest and Communist uprisings in as many countries as possible.

> But it was restrained by vigorous counteraction of the Western powers, which "contained" the Soviet advance by measures of mutual assistance short of war.

> Fortunately, United States opinion had abandoned isolationism and America now was ready to assume its responsibilities as a great world power dedicated to the principle of collective security.

[1] John Lukacz, A History of the Cold War (Garden City: Doubleday, 1961; rev. ed., A New History of the Cold War, 1966); rev. ed. somewhat more critical. John Spanier, American Foreign Policy Since World War II (New York: Praeger, 1967).

In this view we appear virtuous, restrained, and almost passive; our policy was largely defensive, and if we sent soldiers abroad, it was only to help the oppressed or to ward off aggression. Moreover, such moves were clearly meant as "deterrence." Only twice were we unfortunate enough to be drawn into military actions—in Korea and in Vietnam, both places where we had to fight under conditions not of our own choosing—and on two occasions we barely avoided military conflict: in Berlin and in Cuba. But on the whole we managed to keep the war "cool" in spite of tempting provocation, as in Hungary, Czechoslovakia, Sinai.

The professional historian will instinctively distrust such a pat presentation. He can hardly remember a twenty-year period in history where right has been consistently on one side and wrong with equal regularity on the other. He is used to the play of force and counterforce with little reference to good and evil, and he expects to see every hero debunked in due time, every patriotic myth destroyed in the light of newly found documents, and every decision that had been deemed "inevitable" or "forced upon us" after diligent research proven avoidable. Therefore, he is not surprised to read, in Mr. Louis Halle's magisterial study of *The Cold War as History* that diametric labels such as "wicked" and "virtuous," or "aggressor" and "peace-loving nation" have little meaning in a conflict that on both sides was experienced as an irreducible dilemma.[2]

Taking a cool view of the East-West conflict, Mr. Halle pleads for an understanding of the Kremlin's motives and concludes that Stalin was as much afraid of us as we were afraid of him. He does not claim that newly unearthed evidence changed his mind. Rather, his dispassionate view of both sides is a matter of interpretation, and whatever new insight is gained by his method is due to his attitude: Having participated in many cold-war decisions as a member of the State Department's Policy Planning staff, he now sits back and reflects on the impact these decisions may have had on the other side, and he comes rather close to the admission that some of the early critics of the con-

---

[2] Louis Halle, *The Cold War as History* (New York: Harper & Row, 1967). A superb work, both personal and scholarly.

tainment policy, like Henry Wallace, Water Lippmann, and P. M. S. Blackett,[3] may have had a point: The Russians refused to play the game according to our rules, and instead of being contained they strained every effort to break out of the "iron curtain" which from their side looked like "capitalist encirclement."

The view that Mr. Halle presents would contrast with the three propositions of the conventional view in the following way:

> *After the defeat of Hitler, the balance of power was not restored in Europe, and from both sides of its outer fringe, therefore, attempts were made to establish a new equilibrium.*

> *The cold war, though widened to encompass worldwide conflicts, is essentially the continuation of the international power contest which has raged from the time of the Seven Years' War through the Napoleonic wars and the two world wars of this century to the present day.*

> *The United States was drawn into this conflict because it is basically a European-Atlantic nation, and this entanglement seems to have been fatefully inevitable; but accidental outbreaks of military hostilities in Asia created a climate of "crusading" which needlessly embroiled the United States in areas where it had little interest, less power, and no traditional ties.*

Even before Mr. Halle, similar views had been expressed by conservative critics like George Kennan and Hans Morgenthau who warned that the cold war must not be escalated into a military confrontation, must not be extended to areas outside Eu-

---

[3] Walter Lippmann, *The Cold War* (New York: Harper, 1948). Consists of 12 articles originally printed in the *New York Herald Tribune* in reply to George F. Kennan's "Mr. X" article. P. M. S. Blackett, *Fear, War and the Bomb: Military and Political Consequences of Atomic Energy* (London, 1948; New York: McGraw-Hill, 1949). The famous British weapons expert was the first to criticize the concepts of nuclear deterrence. Henry Wallace, former Vice President, left the Truman Administration and campaigned in 1948 on a "Peace" platform.

rope, and must not be conducted in the name of one ideology against the other.

Mr. André Fontaine, foreign editor of the Paris *Le Monde*, also abandons the black-and-white view of history in his two-volume *History of the Cold War*.[4] Each side, he laments, sees the enemy as an outlaw against whom no holds are barred, and each feels righteous about its cause. Viewing a confrontation of two *righteous* causes makes tragedy and history close neighbors. But is the cold war so much past history that we can look at it in this way? We shall see that, on the contrary, the revision of our views on the cold war is no academic exercise—like admitting that George III was a fool rather than a tyrant—but a passionate matter of partisanship. Even the contention that the cold war is over is a partisan slogan.

Nevertheless, the new view is associated with deep-seated attitudes of the academic mind. The statesman must act from a conviction of righteousness. But a dispassionate view of our own and a compassionate view of the other side naturally appeals to intellectuals, who not only are more immune to propaganda but also disgusted by its methods and distrustful of its aims. From their vantage point, the cold war appeared as a contest between two brainwashing crews, and perhaps even as the outgrowth of hate ideologies.

However, one can go too far in trying to be fair and even-handed.

Professor Walter La Feber has rendered a valuable service in tracing the relationship between the domestic and the international phases of the cold war and in describing the struggle between the cold-war ideology and the critical forces in this country.[5] He shows how much of the cold-war anxieties and of

---

[4] André Fontaine, *History of the Cold War* (New York: Pantheon, 1968 and 1969). The scope and point of view of this brave attempt is indicated by its starting date—the October Revolution. Writing from the vantage point of French politics, M. Fontaine usefully reminds us that in 1944 Ho Chi Minh liberated part of Vietnam with the help of the CIA (or its predecessor) and that Maurice Thorez, then the French Communist leader, told the Vietnamese that he "would not like to be considered the liquidator of French positions in Indochina."

[5] Walter La Feber, *America, Russia and the Cold War 1945–1966* (New York: Wiley, 1967). Probably the best of the historical narratives.

our responses was due not to enemy action but to our interpretation of it. Regrettably, language difficulties and lack of access to
Russian documents bar him from attempting a similar study of
the cold-war climate in the Kremlin. But like other revisionists,
he tends generally to attribute too much of what happened in
the last eighty years to American initiatives. We did this, we did
that—as though diplomacy were not an interaction of many
powers. Revisionists have justly criticized the self-centered, arrogant view that this country is called to maintain the world order
single-handedly. They are no less provincial in assuming that different attitudes in this country alone could at will have changed
a course of events that was largely determined by others and by
its starting point. Mr. La Feber neither quotes the European pro-
moters and critics of the cold-war policies nor does he analyze
the *European* interests and forces that drew or pushed the
United States into the cold war. Revisionists fail to combat but
rather tend to amplify the legend that Europe was a mere object
of American policies. This is not true. Reading La Feber or any
other revisionist book, no one would guess that British Foreign
Minister Ernest Bevin did more than anybody else to muddle a
postwar settlement in Europe, or that Berlin's Mayor Ernst Reu-
ter single-handedly forced us to fight for the freedom of his city.
In 1968 our European allies asked us to punish Moscow for the
invasion of Czechoslovakia.

Nor does Mr. La Feber disclose the full measure of Stalin's
contribution to the cold war. This book begins with the statement
that in October 1945 the magazine *Bolshevik* and President Truman more or less simultaneously ("meanwhile") sounded warlike trumpets. Only in the footnote does he acknowledge that
when Truman spoke, *Bolshevik* was already three months old,
i.e., it had appeared *before* the end of World War II. Even earlier, at the time of Roosevelt's death, two public statements announced a reversal in Kremlin policies: One was Jacques Du-
clos's "Open Letter" in *Cahiers du Communisme* for April 1945;
the letter has been quoted frequently because it denounced the
wartime truce between the Allies, deposed Earl Browder as
leader of the Communist Party in the United States, and rein-
stated the slogan of fighting capitalism in all its forms. Mr.

Christopher Lasch, another revisionist, writing in the *New York Times Magazine*,[6] brushes this letter off as just a quibble about electoral tactics and takes Arthur Schlesinger, Jr., to task for considering it a key document. Mr. Lasch displays ignorance of Communist affairs; an open letter was about the most solemn announcement, next to a speech by Stalin himself, of a shift of policy in Comintern usage. Messrs. Lasch and La Feber also omit the real opening shot of the cold war—Soviet Foreign Minister Molotov's speech at the opening session of the United Nations, 26 April 1945, where he accused the Western powers of complicity with Hitler.

Leaning over backward is a laudable attitude, but this is going rather far. American intellectuals have been angered by cold-war lies; but instead of concluding, like Mr. Halle, that both sides lie, many seem to feel that if we lie, the other side must be telling the truth. Mr. Halle carefully says that in such a great conflict where two historic forces meet, it really does not matter "who started it." In fact, every experienced historian will agree that this is a question for nursery-school teachers. To the younger (and some not so young but equally naïve) revisionists, however, this question seems to matter: In order to prove the U.S. government wrong they must prove Stalin right. This calls for three kinds of operations:

Finding a suitable date for the beginning of the cold war;

finding documents which disprove Western propaganda claims and prove the claims of Soviet peacefulness;

reinterpreting or ignoring documents which up to now have formed our view of the cold war.

This endeavor goes beyond the intentions of moderate critics like Halle and La Feber. They assume that any errors of judgment or mistakes of policy were made in good faith, perhaps under the pressure of circumstances or as the consequence of honest miscalculation, misinformation, and misunderstanding;

6 *New York Times Magazine*, 14 January 1968.

that even in ideological warfare the participants believed in what they were saying and that indeed the conflict came about rather like a Greek tragedy—through a confusion of the minds wrought by jealous gods. We shall hear about those gods later on; first we must speak of the new revisionists who charge that vicious men with malicious purposes started the cold war.[7] For obvious reasons we shall give them the name they prefer, radicals.

The liberal critic of the cold war laments the alleged fumbling of our policies and deplores the fateful but involuntary military and ideological escalation; establishment historians impute all criminal initiative to Stalin—the radical says it just was not so. Nor is he content with giving merely his own interpretation to known facts. He cites a different set of facts and he sets out to prove with documents that the real course of events was quite different from what people believe. The most impressive and best documented work of this sort has been presented by Gar Alperovitz in his analysis of the Potsdam Conference of July–August 1945.[8] It will be remembered that President Truman was on his way to Potsdam when he received the "good news" from Alamogordo, that the first atomic bomb had been successfully tested. He relayed this top secret to Stalin in such a way as to minimize its importance, and he chuckled when he told Churchill that the Russian apparently had not grasped the significance

---

[7] Some have suggested that Truman could have avoided the cold war if he had not abruptly stopped Lend-Lease operations after V-E Day, or if he had granted Stalin a loan. Lend-Lease was stopped not only to Russia but to England as well since the program's authorization automatically ended when it had fulfilled its purpose—victory in Europe. As to the loan, the Kremlin could have used drawing rights in the amount of $1.5 billion had it ratified the Bretton Woods agreements. Later, Molotov appeared with a large staff of experts to participate in setting up the Marshall Plan machinery; but he was called out of the meeting by a telegram from Moscow and never returned. I cannot understand why most Americans think that peace could be bought with money.

[8] Gar Alperovitz, *Atomic Diplomacy: Hiroshima and Potsdam* (New York: Simon & Schuster, 1965). Mr. Alperovitz impresses his point of view on the reader by an excessive display of irrelevant scholarship. I have no quarrel with a careful study of the documents. But the results have been meager: The documents show only that the relations between the allies were distrustful throughout the war. This could surprise the naïve.

of the information. In fact he still chuckles when he remembers the incident in his Memoirs.[9] Mindful of the coming election year, eager to "bring the boys home" and also aware that an early victory over Japan would give "Uncle Joe" no chance to claim his part of the spoils, Truman made the fateful decision to use the bomb at once. The world has since questioned the wisdom of this decision but not the alleged reasons. These seem to me quite sufficient to explain Truman's action, given his background and position.

Alperovitz, however, amasses documents to show that the real reason for an early use of the bomb was not victory in Asia over the Japanese, but intimidation of the Russians in Europe. At Potsdam, indeed, where the powers implemented the Yalta arrangements for the future of Europe—we must now say for the partition of Europe—the Western statesmen tried to secure some measure of freedom for their friends in the Eastern countries which they had abandoned to Russian hegemony. Mr. Alperovitz shows how possession of the bomb made the Anglo-Saxons feel much more "confident" that they might be able to negotiate from strength. Lasch flatly maintains that they "asked Stalin to accept hostile governments" or even "tried to force the Soviet Union out of Europe." [10] Alperovitz tells us how: Truman wished to show Stalin his real strength; for that purpose he needed a demonstration of the awesome power of the atom. Therefore he ordered the bombing of Hiroshima—in order to gain room for maneuver in Eastern Europe!

To the odious crime of releasing the jinn that since has hovered over the future of mankind, Alperovitz adds the indictment that this was done wantonly, for an unrelated purpose, in an action that was not even directed against the enemy but against an ally. Since we agree that the use of the bomb was heinous, we are tempted to grant Mr. Alperovitz that the reason for this crime must have been at once sinister and ludicrous. Since Mr. Alperovitz names such a sinister and ludicrous reason, we are further tempted to agree that he must be right, and from there it

---

[9] Harry S. Truman, *Memoirs,* Vol. 1 (Garden City: Doubleday, 1955), p. 419.
[10] *New York Times,* 14 January 1968.

is only one step to the conclusion that, since all this is so shameful, Truman's hope to save a little democracy in Eastern Europe must also be condemned. On such notions radical revisionism builds its case against the U.S. government's actions in the early months of the cold war.

But the entire deduction is fantastic. If Truman wished to frighten Stalin, why did he chuckle instead of plopping the bomb with all its awful statistics on the conference table? Why could he not have ordered a public demonstration of its power? Why does Mr. Alperovitz fail to mention the Oppenheimer-Compton report which recommended the military use of the bomb without making reference to Europe? Why did Secretary of State Byrnes publicly concede that the "Soviet Union has a right to friendly governments along its borders" and Under-Secretary, later Secretary, Acheson even speak of "a Monroe Doctrine for Eastern Europe"? [11] Why, in fact, did they all look on meekly while brutal ultimatums expelled their friends from the governments of Bulgaria, Rumania, Poland, Hungary, and later of Czechoslovakia? All this happened while the United States still enjoyed its atomic monopoly, and Mr. Halle usefully reminds us that the United States demobilized its armies, did not prevent the development of atomic energy elsewhere, and did not try—as I think it should have—to barter its monopoly against the withdrawal of Soviet troops from Eastern Europe. In all the quotations with which Mr. Alperovitz smothers the reader, we do not find a shred of evidence for his contention that Truman tried to force Stalin's retreat from Europe, which is based on pure conjecture. Immersed in documents, he fails to look at the acts of the governments and to reconstruct the climate of the year 1945. So obsessed is he indeed with the search for secret evidence of evil that he never notices the evil which was being done in plain daylight.

Radical revisionism, we see, is not content with suggesting that wrong may be evenly distributed over both sides; it reverses the roles of hero and villain completely. Where we had pointed

---

[11] *New York Times,* 1 and 15 November 1945. Mr. Alperovitz indeed has an answer: Byrnes was trying to lull Stalin into complacency. That kind of logic can prove anything.

an accusing finger at Stalin, charging him with bland disregard of the Yalta agreements, we now find ourselves in the defendant's dock, indicted not with an isolated misdeed but with the consistent, systematic, and—one is tempted to say—congenital pursuit of Empire. Mr. Ronald Steel gives his book the angry title *"Pax Americana—The Cold War Empire,"* [12] and begins by quoting de Gaulle to the effect that the United States "feeling that she no longer had within herself sufficient scope for her energies . . . yielded in her turn to that taste for intervention in which the instinct for domination cloaked itself." The general merely was repeating the anguished outcry of his compatriot, Alexis de Tocqueville, 130 years earlier, that "there are today two great peoples which, starting out from different points of departure, advance towards the same goal—the Americans and the Russians. . . . Each of them will one day hold in its hands the destinies of half of mankind." [13]

Tempting as it may be to trace the European roots of revisionism, we must now inquire what is the nature of this American imperialism which has motivated American initiatives in the cold war. There are three main lines of thought indicating long-term American commitments:

To the first proposition of the conventional view, Professor Denna F. Fleming answers that the world need not be concerned with Soviet expansionism—but with the systematic and consistent encirclement policies of the West, beginning with the interventions of 1917–20, and later methodically enlarged to form coalitions threatening the Soviet Union with atomic destruction and organizing the cold war as a holy crusade.[14] No Soviet actions but the mere existence of the Soviet Union called up Western ire.

To the second proposition Professor William Appleman Williams replies that American interventionism abroad needed no provocation by the Soviets.[15] He maintains that it dates back to

---

[12] Ronald Steel, *Pax Americana* (New York: Viking, 1967).

[13] See concluding page of Vol. 1 of *Democracy in America*.

[14] Denna F. Fleming, *The Cold War and Its Origins 1917–1960*, 2 Vols. (Garden City: Doubleday, 1961).

[15] William Appleman Williams, *The Tragedy of American Diplomacy* (Cleveland: World, 1959).

well before the October Revolution, to be precise to the open-door policy of the nineties of the last century, a policy designed to "keep China sovereign for purposes of exploitation by the burgeoning U.S. industrial complex while the Russians who could not compete, tried to assure themselves political leverage by creating spheres of influence." [16]

To the third proposition David Horowitz replies that not idealism led the United States into an internationalist policy but the defense of narrow economic interests,[17] to wit those of the rich. He concludes by quoting Arnold Toynbee, that America is today "the leader of a worldwide antirevolutionary movement in defense of vested interests." [18]

In all the last-named books the scholarship is unbelievably poor. Professor Fleming's work reads in places like a scrap book of newspaper clippings; he never distinguishes between opinion and document, as he will triumphantly exhibit a silly Letter to the Editor of the *Ashville Courier* as though its author were speaking for the U.S. government, while glossing over the most important statements by Lenin, Stalin, and their successors. Mr. Horowitz requotes Fleming's quotes with admiration and adds nothing but vulgar Marxist explanations or plain misinformation. For instance, he wishes to show that Stalin did not plan to hold on to the imposed Communist regime in East Germany; for that purpose he quotes Molotov's unification plan of 10 March 1952. But he fails to mention that Molotov refused to allow free elections under U.N. supervision. Moreover, he fails to mention that the entire "peace plan" was nothing but a desperate, last-minute bait to prevent West Germany from joining NATO. I happen to think that the Western powers should have taken Molotov's

---

[16] La Feber, op. cit; see also the contributions by Lloyd Gardner and Robert Freeman Smith to the New Left anthology *Towards a New Past*, Barton J. Bernstein, ed. (New York: Pantheon, 1968). All three authors acknowledge W. A. Williams as their master. With the exception of Professor Genovese's contribution, the scholarship in Mr. Bernstein's volume leaves much to be desired.

[17] David Horowitz, *The Free World Colossus* (New York: Hill & Wang, 1965).

[18] Arnold Toynbee, *America and the World Revolution* (New York: Oxford University Press, 1961).

offer and trusted the dynamics of further development—the German uprising a year later then might have been a different affair!
Had Horowitz analyzed the episode instead of quoting propaganda notes, he would have seen that it provides an argument
for, not against cold-war tactics: Molotov had never made even
as limited an offer as his 10 March plan until the Germans actually threatened to join NATO! If Acheson needed proof for his
theory of "positions of strength," it is here; but though German
revisionists have asked why Molotov failed to follow suit, American revisionists remain silent—for good reason; they try to avoid
the issue of power.

Mr. Horowitz's treatment of the episode is a rather typical example of the half-truths on which much revisionist writing is
based. As for his teacher Fleming, his file of episodes, which
throws a bad light on Western governments, may be a good
thing to have handy when a government apologist offers nothing
but a similar file indicting the Soviet government. But as a serious historical work the Fleming book is beneath discussion. A series of episodes does not show consistency of a policy; by merely
suppressing the long periods of coexistence, by ignoring the differences between the attitudes of various Western governments
in their relations with the Soviet Union, and by taking the Sovi-
et-Western relationships out of the context of the constantly
shifting play of coalitions and constellations, Mr. Fleming misses
every point.

Moreover, if Fleming is right, William Appleman Williams
must be wrong: If the United States interventions antedate the
October Revolution, as Mr. Williams maintains, they cannot
have been provoked by it, as Fleming will have it. As George
Kennan has shown,[19] Wilson's decision to intervene had no
cold-war motivation.

Professor Williams, the most influential writer in this field, ostensibly follows the classical lead of Scott Nearing,[20] in his attempt to reduce U.S. foreign policy to economic causes. He is no

---

[19] George F. Kennan, *The Decision to Intervene* (Princeton: Princeton University Press, 1958; paper, New York: Atheneum, 1967).
[20] Scott Nearing and Joseph Freeman, *Dollar Diplomacy: A Study in
American Imperialism* (New York: Viking, 1925).

Marxist however, but a Christian populist who became a convert to mercantilism. He is fanatically devoted to the idea that closed economic areas are healthy for development and for peace. Whatever disturbs this imaginary idyll is bad, above all the American efforts to prevent any pieces of geography from being fenced off as empire. He calls the open-door policy "anticolonialist imperialism" and condemns the Marshall Plan as another attempt to force a door open—an attempt which apparently left Stalin no choice but to save Europe from U.S. control.

As to the economic motive, the trouble is that our China trade never lived up to the expectations of the "hundred million lamps," [21] but remained 1–2 percent of our total imports and exports. Nor were American capitalists eager to invest in China as the modern theory of the "surplus" would require. At the beginning of the century the State Department vainly tried to encourage American bankers and railway magnates to help in offsetting the Japanese and European influence; but to no avail. Far from practicing "dollar imperialism" the United States was not even capable of practicing dollar diplomacy—the use of dollars for political ends. The indifference of U.S. capital made it necessary for Dr. Sun Yat-sen to turn to Lenin for help.

Nor has Professor Williams been very fortunate in the quality of his followers. Robert F. Smith descends to the following trick [22]: To show that U.S. policy was antisocialist even when it

---

[21] Title of a prewar book exhorting America to deny the great Chinese market to the Japanese. Critics of U.S. Asian policies have always argued that we have no substantial "interests" there. If this is true, Professor Williams would have to postulate that potential development of hypothetical interests has the same effect on policy-making decisions as actual interests. I am not contending, of course, that the "open-door" policy was disinterested or that it was morally superior: In fact, the United States demanded no real open door but only equal rights with the Japanese and other colonialists. However, it so happened that U.S. interests coincided with Chinese interests. Many critics of U.S. policies think their job has been done when they can prove an "interest." They forget that all business relations between people, institutions, and states are based on "interest," which may be beneficial either to both or to only one side. Opprobrium should properly be cast not on interests as such but on exploitative interests that subordinate other interests.

[22] Bernstein, op. cit., p. 247.

seemed to be antifascist, he quotes *Foreign Affairs* for July 1937 to the effect that "capitalism is lost where it is not built on liberalism." On closer inspection, the quoted passage turns out to be by a German exile, editor of a respected business magazine, trying to warn American business to beware of Hitler. In the cold war, too, the economic tools of propaganda and of diplomacy are often mistaken for ends or motivations. Thus Professor La Feber quotes A. A. Berle testifying in 1947 that "within four years the world will be faced with surplus production." He then proceeds to interpret this threat as "one paramount motivation" for the Truman Doctrine and the Marshall Plan.[23] It is, of course, much more correct to say that the Marshall Plan was the economic arm of the Truman Doctrine. Berle then was Under-Secretary for Economic Affairs, and he was particularly concerned with promoting the "Point Four" program which was designed to win the friendship of underdeveloped countries in the world struggle between the United States and the USSR for supremacy. The aim of this policy, including its economic measures, was not economic penetration but the preservation of independent states in all areas of the world. So much for "the economic motive," the search for which only shows that American liberals rarely understand power as a motive. Now let us see how power has been understood by U.S. policy-makers.

As originally conceived, the policy of containment meant the creation of strong, self-reliant states along the periphery of the Soviet empire, but especially in Europe. It meant measures short of war, and there was then no premonition of NATO or other military confrontations. Therefore, Bernard Baruch quipped that we were engaged in a "cold war"; he was varying the coinage "dry war," which had been used before World War I.

This policy was consistent with Wilson's policy of creating independent national states in place of the old empires, and with FDR's anticolonial thrust during and after World War II. Long before he had ever heard of Bolshevism, Colonel House warned Woodrow Wilson that "an Entente victory would mean domina-

---

[23] La Feber, op. cit., p. 43.

tion of Russia on the Continent,"[24] and thirty years later George Kennan expressed the same fear in the now-famous "long telegram." As a remedy he recommended the "containment" policy spelled out in the controversial "Mr. X" article.[25]

This indeed has been the red-white-and-blue thread that runs throughout American foreign policy. Shorn of the anti-Communist rhetoric to which Kennan objected, this was the message of the Truman Doctrine of which Kennan approved. It said "hands off" to Stalin, and so did Eisenhower in his first inaugural, as had FDR's "Quarantine Speech": Irrespective of the expansionist's philosophy, the United States has been opposed to closed doors indeed, everywhere and at all times. There is something incomprehensibly sectarian in the revisionist charge that all American and indeed all Western policies have always been directed against Russia. The open-door policy clearly was directed first of all against Japan, second against Western colonialists, and only third against Russia, imperial as well as Soviet. For we are dealing here with the kind of tension between powers that is the usual stuff of history. Its permanence is reflected, for instance, in A. J. P. Taylor's title *The Struggle for Mastery in Europe 1848–1918*. Ideology has done very little to embitter or alleviate these conflicts. World War I started between nations of like ideology, and World War II saw nations with opposing ideologies allied nevertheless. The United States conducted the cold war by helping Tito, a Communist—but Mr. La Feber can quote senatorial diaries endlessly to the effect that Acheson was staunchly anti-Communist, yet forget to mention that he supported Tito's Communist economy. (Since this was written, Acheson's memoirs have appeared, reminding us that at the time the Right attacked Acheson as "fool of Communism.")

In a strange way, revisionists reflect the mirror image of their opponents: Both think that "ideology" was the cause of the cold war or that some conspirational power was hiding behind the ideology—be that power the Communist world leadership, or

---

[24] Quoted by La Feber, from A. S. Link, *Wilson: The Struggle for Neutrality* (Princeton: Princeton University Press, 1960), p. 48.
[25] *Foreign Affairs*, July 1947. Both documents are now contained in his *Memoirs* (Boston: Little, Brown, 1967).

America's military-industrial complex. They find it difficult to admit that conflicts arise out of the fact that "we live in a system of states" (Lenin), and that in such a system of conflicting and converging interests all combinations are possible.

The cold war is such a conflict for the "mastery of Europe" in which political, diplomatic, psychological, and economic pressures are the principal weapons but military deployment is used in a symbolic and logistic fashion short of warlike action. It makes no sense to apply the term "cold" war to the hot wars in Korea and Indochina or to areas where no such conflict rages. The Asian and African wars must be explained in terms of their specific origins; they were fought in a different area, with different means, and against a different enemy. But there is not the slightest connection between "Communism" or "anti-Communism," and the quarreling factions in, say, the Congo or Nigeria.

Cold-war ideologists, of course, like to subsume all the post-1945 wars under the heading of anti-Communism or of the "Sino-Soviet bloc." These efforts must be strongly resisted—if only for the practical reason that one may disagree with U.S. conduct in Asia while agreeing with it in Europe, or agree in 1950 but not today. It is regrettable that the revisionists here do not go far enough. Instead of accepting Mr. Rusk's cold-war generalizations—which they denounce in another context—they should analyze each of these wars in terms of its particular condition, its weapons and conduct, its particular ideology, and, above all—its particular enemy. It will then be found that the cold war proper, as we knew it in the forties and fifties, may soon be over. Like many great wars, it was not settled, had no victors or vanquished, but is simmering down. Both sides in that war recognized rather early in the game that its solution could only be a confirmation of the status quo: For all his propaganda antics about the "liberation" of "captive nations" and the "rollback" of the Iron Curtain, the late John F. Dulles did the most to "freeze" the cold war where it stood. In Asia, on the contrary, even the most ardent Kremlin partisan of coexistence never wavered in his support of "wars of liberation."

Back to the cold war. This conflict arose out of the postwar situation: Russia had just emerged from her most excruciating trial. Even without resorting to Stalin's paranoia one must understand his desire for a protective glacis. The United States, on the other hand, could not allow any power to combine the potential of a reconstructed Europe with the resources of Asia. She is always opposed to the building of empires, as we saw.

But it was not just the actual fear and the recent experience which determined Stalin's expansionism. Rather, Mr. Halle impresses on our sympathetic heart, the Russians are suffering from a deep-seated, historical encirclement complex, an anxiety which the Western powers have clumsily fostered instead of allaying. The Cold War, Mr. Halle gravely informs us, cannot be understood unless we go back into history—not to Churchill's Fulton speech that some use as the date of its beginning, nor to Yalta that to me seems the most reasonable date, not even to 7 November 1917, as Messrs. Fontaine and Fleming suggest, and not to the Pan-Slav agitation that led to World War I. No, we must go back to the Day of Creation when Nature failed to endow Russia with frontiers that can easily be defended. The rulers of her wide-open plains, we learn, could protect themselves only by seizing adjacent territory, a strategy called "defensive expansionism." What with the understandable reaction of her neighbors Russia unhappily acquired, over the centuries, that feeling of insecurity and the resulting ferocity which can be appeased only by giving her mastery over other nations. (Never mind how *their* anxiety is to be soothed.) The pattern which the Czars established reproduced itself in the relations of the Bolsheviks with their neighbors and even (this was written at the peak of the Czechoslovak crisis) with other "socialist" countries. Long before the end of World War II, it was therefore clear to Professor Halle, who then was in the State Department, that ultimately a confrontation between the victors could not be avoided: "The dynamics of the postwar situation produced an expansion of Moscow's tyranny that was not altogether voluntary but provoked a reaction in the West that in turn awoke Moscow's persecution mania. Had it not been for this persecution mania, the Western reaction might have provided the basis for a settlement." The finger of God driving men into mad confusion and conflagration!

With all due respect to Professor Halle's eminence and scholarship, this is history stood on its head. Russia's open plains indeed were invasion roads for Napoleon and Hitler. But the Tatars had come through the inhospitable Urals; the Varangians and the Swedes had come across the sea, and so did the allies in the Crimean War. On the other hand, Russia's open frontiers permitted the Cossacks to invade Poland-Lithuania and to conquer Asia. It was Russia's neighbors who had reason to complain about Nature's disfavor, and Russia's belligerency was a product of her military, absolutist state rather than of her geography. Neither Lenin nor—emphatically—Trotsky needed any "persecution mania" to conceive of the Soviet state as a revolutionary bastion in a worldwide uprising of the underprivileged proletarians and colonial peoples. Zhdanov revived these conceptions when the power vacuum in postwar Europe opened an opportunity, and Stalin felt "secure" only with Communist governments installed in each European capital. Khrushchev felt encircled by the free city of West Berlin, and today Brezhnev does not feel secure behind the Carpathian mountains. "In a conquered country," Stalin varied Machiavelli, "each of the hegemonic powers must install its system." As Engels said, no border is ever strategically safe.

An important function of the cold war was to keep the bloc allies in line. This aspect has been very little commented upon by the revisionists although it is the one which is least likely to disappear so soon, and it is also the one that keeps the cold-war ideology alive. I do not think the Russians had to march into Czechoslovakia because they were afraid of internal reform—after all, the Czech economy is still one hundred percent socialist and Czech agriculture is the most collectivized of all the satellites. What the Russians were unable to tolerate was the softening of Czech relations with West Germany, and for that reason they had to insist on ideological conformity throughout the satellite empire, too.

The revisionists' ability to empathize with Stalin's tender nerves is at times limitless. Christopher Lasch laments that it was inconsiderate of Mikolajczyk to inquire how four thousand Polish officers came to be buried in a mass grave in Katyn. Could Stalin really be expected to tolerate such a man in a Polish cabinet, even a cabinet totally dominated by Communists? Small nations, on the other hand, have no right to tender nerves. Exalting Stalin's magnanimity, Mr. Brian Thomas reminds us that Groza was not even a Communist.[26] Correct! Nor was Laval a Nazi. Groza was only the man on top of the list of the ministers which Vishinsky handed the king of Romania with an ultimatum to appoint them within two hours.

The examples of revisionist writers exculpating Soviet policies by psychosociological explanations, or even by doing a touch-up job on the events, are as numerous as the apologetic somersaults of our Establishment champions. After all, reasoning from insecurity is available to all parties and every nation may need "defensive expansion."

This is the domino theory in reverse, and we must ask ourselves how far it may lead. Would it not justify a Hitler, too? Strangely enough, some revisionist writers have drawn this uncouth consequence. It is not Dean Rusk who proposes the false analogy between Hitler and Stalin or Ho Chi Minh; it is Mr. Robert Freeman Smith, writing in a New Left collection, who suggests that the conformist interpretation of World War II supports the cold-war arguments.[27] Mr. Smith is amused by "simplistic" people who still believe in "the Adolf Hitler syndrome"; he cannot conceive that Hitler and Hirohito had any design to rule the world, and Pearl Harbor to him "revealed the full implication of [Brooks Adams's] imperial logic," which also made the cold war inevitable. For it was not Japan but the United States which "in 1941 rigidly asserted that any order in Asia would have to be in terms of its objectives." Again, history stood on its head.

Professor A. J. P. Taylor, in his turn, author of a book which absolved Hitler of all guilt in unleashing World War II,[28] writes in—of all places!—the *New York Review of Books:*

"Germans were no more wicked in aspiring to dominate Europe . . . than others were in resolving to stop them. They were in a sense less wicked. For their domination was achieved with little physical destruction and comparatively few casualties, whereas the effort to resist them produced general devastation."

---

[26] Brian Thomas, in the *Journal of Contemporary History* (London), January 1968.

[27] Bernstein, op. cit., p. 237.

[28] A. J. P. Taylor, *The Origins of the Second World War* (New York: Atheneum, 1962).

The wanton destruction of Guernica in the Spanish Civil War, of Lidice, of Coventry, of Amsterdam, and Kharkov—all brought about by the wicked resistance of the victims. The six million Jews were so wicked as not to see that Hitler was merely trying to do them a favor. Not the murderer but the victim is guilty! This atrocious statement is followed by more sick jokes and by an interesting aside which reveals the purpose of Taylor's revisionist effort. Citing Poland's quixotic refusal to become either Hitler's or Stalin's satellite, he says: "Western historians exaggerate Soviet faults as much as they condone Polish ones. This is only to be expected in the era of the cold war, which historians are still loyally fighting when most sensible people have forgotten about it." [29]

Professor Taylor meant to buy peace for England by encouraging Hitler to acquire an Eastern empire. He still thinks that in September 1939 the peace might have been preserved if Poland had yielded some territory and in exchange had been compensated, perhaps, with a piece of the Ukraine. The English have always been very generous with land that did not belong to them —but why does the *New York Review* lend its columns to this kind of eighteenth-century statecraft? Do the revisionists of World War I, World War II, and of the cold war have more in common than the name?

It may be possible to point to an aversion which they share— the fear of ideologies and in particular of the idea of collective security. The Astor set had to resist the pressures which came from the Popular Front in the name of both antifascism and collective security. These two themes were intimately linked with each other since the fascist governments were by nature and ideology aggressors, and to resist them was tantamount to the creation of international police forces against the disturbers of the peace.

One needs no imagination to see the trap here: The cold war,

---

[29] *New York Review of Books*, 6 June 1968. Taylor claims that he was no member of the famous Astor clique but "denounced it often." I cannot find any evidence of this, the last occasion to denounce Chamberlain was his *English History 1914–1945* (London: Oxford University Press, 1965). There he defends Chamberlain's policy of appeasement and specifically denies (p. 436) that Hitler's policy was aggressive.

too, has been fought on this side under the ideology of collective security against a power that had openly proclaimed itself as the challenger of the status quo. The New Left, which accepts the arguments of radical revisionism, sees the similarities between the cold-war ideology and the ideologies which were used to bring America into both world wars:

In all three cases the United States was defending the status quo against challengers who attacked the traditional power of the Western, colonialist states.

In each case ideology was used more or less deliberately to proclaim a "crusade" against a militant force of change.

In each case the notion of collective security was propagated to justify American involvement in alliances which allegedly were contrary to its interests and which perhaps overtaxed its power.

We can now understand the importance of this ideological identification. To the liberal it matters whether Ho Chi Minh can be compared to Stalin or maybe even to Hitler; to the radical it does not matter at all. He may even find it easier to proclaim his solidarity with a frankly revolutionary Ho Chi Minh than with a pacific one. What matters to him is not whether this country has obligations to come to the aid of others, but that it returns to the isolationist stance which was imparted to it in George Washington's Farewell Address.

Liberals usually know that this is not possible. Conservatives and radicals cherish the pious legend that once this country lived in a state of innocence but at some point evil spirits—power-hungry politicians and greedy capitalists—contrived to entangle it in foreign alliances and wars. Though a superficial glance at nineteenth-century history should dispel such fantasies, most criticism of U.S. policies is based on some version of a Fall. A particularly flattering version of the legend is the Woodrow Wilson myth: that a misguided "idealism," an arrogant, puritanical sense of mission drove this country to assume the mantle of world policeman, which sat awkwardly on its shoulders; it had not been created to "take up the white man's burden" and was not fit for empire. The country was able, therefore, to play a role in world politics only if armed with a righteous ideology. The late John Foster Dulles, with his solemn countenance, was ide-

ally suited to make this image plausible. But let us note that for
all his talk about brinkmanship Dulles failed to come to the aid
of East Berlin in 1953, or Hungary in 1956; he kept Chiang Kai-
shek on the leash and made no move to get the Russian armies
out of Europe. He concluded armistices in Korea and Vietnam
and seemed reasonably happy with a world divided between
"theirs" and "ours": His rhetoric was no guide to his politics,
which were defensive and unimaginative. While he sought to
contain the Communists, he also recognized that they were containing us.

Moreover, this policy was bipartisan. Rusk took it over from
his predecessor, and Stevenson endorsed it shortly before his
death (in a letter to Paul Goodman).

Dean Acheson makes it clear in his memoirs that to him and
Marshall, the essence of this policy was not ideology or anti-
ideology, but collective security (even the Communist scare was
mobilized only to make containment acceptable to a reluctant
Congress and a war-weary public). As formulated by Niebuhr:
For peace we must risk war. In the less poetic language of the
Secretary of State Rusk: "Let no would-be aggressor suppose
that the absence of a formal defense treaty . . . grants immunity
to aggression." [30]

The "cool," sophisticated postwar generation feels superior to
the generation of its parents which stumbled into two or three
wars because they either believed in ideas or placed their faith
in collective security. The New Left rejects these illusions: Containment policy, the Truman Doctrine, the Marshall Plan, and
NATO have led to other alliances and to wars in Asia; they have
dispelled the world political dream of the liberals that peace can
be won by power. Conservative and radical critics of the cold
war may differ on the precise phase of it which they began to reject: Some started the day Henry Wallace was fired, others after
the proclamation of the Truman Doctrine, the more moderate
would still go along with the European confrontation until after
the death of Stalin, [31] or even side with the U.S. government in

---

[30] Senate Preparedness Committee, quoted in *The Washington Post,* 26
August 1966.
[31] Ronald Steel, op. cit.

the first phase of the Korean War [32]—but all share an almost pathological contempt for "idealism":

> He [Rusk] is a meliorist, a liberalist and moralist . . . the heir to the Wilsonian tradition. . . . Ultimately it was Wilson's effect to convert the First World War, initially a European [!] dynastic and commercial carnage, into a war for the unattainable goal of universal peace and justice. . . . It has escaped notice that the "war to end all wars," that black joke of the Wilson era, has emerged once more in our day as the war to end all insurgency.[33]

It may not be easy to recognize in this caricature the person of the unflamboyant Dean Rusk but it is not difficult to recognize the bastard that conservative *realpolitik* has begotten on Populist pacifism. The noblest principle of American foreign policy, or perhaps the noblest principle in the foreign policy of all ages, has been ridiculed in order to disparage the policies of a particular Secretary of State. Instead of attacking him for misapplying the principle, the principle itself is attacked; instead of denouncing the use of great ideas for petty ends, ideas as such are held up to ridicule.

The revisionists are poor historians if they don't understand the importance of principles and ideas, either in guiding or in moving the men who act.[34] No part of history, not even foreign

---

[32] Edmund Stillman and William Pfaff, *The New Politics* (New York: Harper, 1961), and *The Politics of Hysteria* (New York: Harper, 1964).
[33] Edmund Stillman, "Dean Rusk: In the American Grain," *Commentary*, May 1968, p. 36.
[34] Revisionists of the conservative school reject "ideologies" but at least are aware that "principles" or political concepts are necessary to understand and to shape foreign policy. Such a principle is the old-fashioned "balance of powers." A more modern one would be "collective security"; very ancient ones are "empire" and "hegemony." The New Left, in its general waste land of theory, does not understand the difference between ideologies, which supply rationalizations or justifications for action, and theories or concepts and principles, which are tools. A genuine difficulty is that some principles may be used as ideologies. A perfectly good tool of foreign policy, such as "arbitration," may be used as an excuse for having no policy. But even such debased principles are easy to distinguish from ideologies, such as Com-

policy, is a game on a checkerboard where every move can be figured out coldly with all its consequences. The responsible statesman is distinguished from the chess player in that he does not
see all his enemy's forces on the board and has no way of knowing his true intentions. The revisionist, who can study the ar-
chives at his leisure, has the advantage over the statesman who
was in the middle of the rumble. He knows what each of the acting governments should have done, and he can read all the perti-
nent documents but can ignore the pressures of time, opinion,
and other business that act on the statesman. Nor do his documents reveal the anxieties of contemporaries.[35]

Professor Taylor can calmly assure us that we only needed to
give Hitler one more country to have eternal peace—he does not
choose to remember the anxious moments when Hitler's, Mussolini's, and Hirohito's ultimatums followed each other with the
inexorable regularity of a military march. Mr. La Feber may
blame Acheson for throwing the Communist scare into the Congress debate when obdurate isolationists like Taft would not
grant Greece the aid she needed; fortunately Mr. Halle, writing
from personal memories, conveys the sense of urgency that set
the pace for those who had to respond to a sudden change of the
situation. He also makes it clear that the somewhat confused
message which soon was to be called "the Truman Doctrine"
was hardly conceived as the blistering *pronunciamento* which it
seems in retrospect.

To the orderly mind of the political scientist, historical events
always seem to be planned, or at least conceived, to suit some
idea or conception. In real history nothing ever happens that
way. No one had conceived of the "cold war"; the statesmen re-
acted to situations into which they tumbled. No one seemed to

---

munism and anti-Communism, which cannot serve as guides for a policy and
never have served so, but merely described an imputed motivation.

[35] There is no more dangerous trap for the inexperienced historian, nor any
more dangerous weapon in the hands of the experienced propagandist, than
the pseudo-fact: a well-documented record of irrelevant events. Fortunately,
Professor H. Stuart Hughes has undertaken the necessary and ungrateful task
of setting the record straight in the August 1969 issue of *Commentary*
magazine. He re-creates the atmosphere in which the decisions of 1946–48
were taken.

have planned a crusade, many wondered later on how they came to be in one. We have to accept as the lesson of history that forces that were more or less blind and guided by their own dynamism clashed in conflict and therefore had to hate each other. It was the diplomats' business to keep this conflict under control, not to fan it. We must judge them by their success in disentangling the entanglement, because they could not avoid it in the first place.

This does not mean, of course, that we must absolve the governments of the charge that they blundered, or that at least some of the blunders were avoidable. But the revisionists have failed to prove that the postwar coexistence could be anything but antagonistic; it might even be possible to argue that the cold confrontation was among the milder forms which that antagonism was capable of taking. In certain respects it might even be said that the phrase "cold war" exaggerates the gravity of the situation. There was no war plan and no concerted effort to achieve well-defined aims; no proof has been given that either Stalin or Truman was having designs for the destruction of the other's power. What we see, rather, is a series of disconnected actions which happened at opportune moments, of opportunities seized and of weaknesses exploited. We also see a certain awareness on both sides to spare the other's susceptibilities and to carry provocations just to the threshold but not beyond. This must be said even of Dulles, whose often misquoted simile emphasized the need to step to the brink *and back.*

Speaking of Dulles, finally, one remembers the worst feature of the cold war, its ideological aggressiveness, its crusading spirit, its grandiloquent militancy. Well, Homer's heroes are hollering at each other when they are not giving battle, and ideology in the cold war served the most degrading purpose to which an ideology can finally be put—as a cover for inaction. We won all the battles of righteousness but, thank God, the cold war did not really break out into a hot war. Most of it was shouting.[36]

---

[36] U.N. debates provide good examples of "cold war" language signifying nothing. After the invasion of Czechoslovakia by the armies of five Warsaw Pact powers, Mr. George Ball, our delegate in the Security Council, deplored, berated, and condemned the Soviet Union, but carefully avoided key words such as "aggression" which might have obligated the United

Ideologies rarely are the cause of action; they provide rationalizations for actions, they justify the division into parties. Once created, however, ideas may transcend the immediate propaganda purpose and become myths or rigid doctrines which tend to alienate the faithful from reality, freeze hostilities whose real causes have long been forgotten, and prolong loyalties that no longer make sense. By searching for the sources of the cold war, revisionists might contribute to the thawing-out process, to loosening up the ideological rigidities, and on the whole to deideologizing the antagonisms.

Unfortunately, most revisionists are doing the exact opposite: Instead of understanding how the ideologies were first manipulated and then began in turn to manipulate the manipulators, the revisionists have become victims of the ideological impact. Instead of separating the cold-war ideologies from the power conflict, they have carried them into more areas of conflict, such as the wars in Africa and in the Middle East. They have fallen down on their self-assigned task; instead of questioning the ideological foundations of the crusade, they have simply changed the labels of villain and victim.

[1968]

States to take or support countermeasures. The invasion of Hungary in 1956 was subjected to the same "cold war" treatment. Yet, some political scientists still seize upon such rhetoric to prove that there is a "cold war." One may criticize this rhetoric on many grounds, except on the assumption that the Russians take it seriously. This they leave to our simpletons on the Right and Left.

"MIDDLE-CLASS" WORKERS AND THE NEW POLITICS

by Brendan Sexton

Much of my life has been split between two worlds: blue-collar unions and the intellectual-academic arena—a sort of long-haired working stiff, or at least an uncommon marginal man.

Born in a tough Irish working-class neighborhood and reared on Catholicism, Irish rebellion, and later socialism, I fell into the life of an organizer during the great depression and the early days of the CIO. As a reader of everything in reach, I have followed with great regret the growing schism between organized labor and middle-class liberals during the past decade. Like others, I was stunned to see the old liberal coalition finally fragment during the presidential election under the separate discontents of workers (out of sight and mind to most observers, but not, alas, to George Wallace) and the middle-class liberal antagonists of LBJ. What the consequences of the fragmentation will be only Nixon and Agnew may know.

Yet I continue to believe, in my old-fashioned, radical-populist way, that a broad alliance between these two groups at their center remains the best hope for reconstructing our society along democratic-humanist lines.

Many issues need clarifying if we are to halt a national move to the Right. I wish to explore only one here: the assumption that blue-collar workers are "middle-class" and sitting pretty. I'd also like to suggest some of the political consequences of both the assumption and the reality of workers' lives.

In December of 1967 the "average production worker" with three dependents took home $90.89 for a full week's work. Measured against the previous year, his dollar income rose about $2.34 a week. In fact, however, his actual purchasing power *declined by about six cents per week*. He was worse off in 1967 than in 1966, and probably even more so in 1968.

Now $90.89 take-home is not "middle-class," especially if you are an "average" family head with three dependents. If such a man puts aside $25 a week for house or rent payments (a modest enough sum), he's left with a little less than $66 a week to pay for food, clothing, medicines, school supplies, etc., for two adults and two children. That comes to roughly $2.37 per day, per person, for a family of four—about the amount a big-city newspaper reporter (or any of us in the real middle class) is likely to spend for lunch.

These figures are distorted a bit by the inclusion of Southern, and largely unorganized, workers. But in 1967, *manufacturing* workers (most of whom are organized) with three dependents averaged only $101.26 in take-home pay. As against the previous year, they also experienced a slight dip in real income and purchasing power.

In New York, the locale of many observers who write so expertly about "middle-class" workers, manufacturing workers averaged a gross income of $114.44. Only in Michigan, among all continental states, where the weekly gross was $145.78, could an average manufacturing worker come close to the national family median (about $8,000) with a full year of work.

At the other end of the scale, retail workers averaged just slightly less that $7 per week during 1967. The retail worker, if he worked a full year, earned a gross income high enough to lift him barely above the "poverty line" of $3,000, but low enough to leave him with less than half the national family median income. This is the extreme example. Still, there are more than eight million workers in retail trade. Even when they wear white collars, they can't, at this rate, be factored into the middle class.

Skilled workers are the aristocrats of labor, yet the median earnings of male craftsmen who were employed full-time in 1966

were only $6,981.[1] Of course, a good many of the elite and
highly organized urban craftsmen—electricians, typographers,
lithographers, etc.—rise to and above $10,000 a year. For a blue-
collar worker, this is really "making it." For the new college professor, fresh out of graduate school, it's just so-so.

Where affluence begins and ends no one knows, but it must be
above the levels cited. In late 1966, the U.S. Department of
Labor said that an income of $9,191 would enable a city family of
four to maintain "a moderate standard of living." Only about
one-third of *all* American families reach that now-dated standard. Certainly, the typical production worker is much better off
than a Mississippi farm tractor driver or a city mother living on
welfare, but he hardly lives opulently. He treads water, financially and psychically.

The myth of the "middle-class" worker is kin to the Negro of
folklore who "lives in the slums but drives a big new Cadillac."
He's there, all right, but his numbers are grossly exaggerated.

Workers with small families and two or more paychecks coming in each week may be able to make it. Among all American
families with incomes of $10,000, the multi-incomes are twice as
numerous as the single income. Still, millions of families combine
two or even three paychecks and yet earn less than $5,000 a year.

The young worker is hardest hit and hence most discontented.
He often holds down the lower-paid and more onerous jobs. He is
somewhat less likely to work overtime at premium rates and
more likely to be caught in temporary layoffs, though in some
union contracts he is now protected against loss from the latter.

No less than others of his generation, the young worker expects more. Why not? He belongs to a generation with rapidy rising expectations. As long as he's single, his first paychecks may
give him more money than he's ever seen before. He dresses
well, owns a new car, and generally lives it up.

But once married, his problems multiply. He furnishes a home,
perhaps buys it. He does it "on time." He pays more for furniture
and appliances than anyone ever did before. The house that cost
his father $12,000, with a mortgage at five percent, now may sell

---

[1] Gaps of a year or more sometimes occur in government statistics. In all
cases, I have used the most recent annual reports available.

for twice that and be financed at seven percent. The young married worker age twenty-five or thirty will probably carry twice the burden of debt as the worker age forty or forty-five. When children come, the wife of the young worker will probably drop out of the labor market, leaving him as sole support for perhaps fifteen or twenty years. In these years, his financial needs increase with the size of his family, but his paycheck does not respond to need.

These economic realities confront workers with a long list of harrowing problems. How, for example, do they provide equal opportunity for their children? How do they shelter them against the draft for four years when the cost of sending a son to the state university now averages nearly $2,000 a year? *Perhaps less than a quarter of all high school graduates who are children of factory workers enter college.* (The myth that something like half of all young Americans go to college is very nearly unshatterable. Actually, 46.3 percent of the 18- and 19-year-olds, but only 19 percent in the age group of 20–24 are "in school." U.S. Office of Education reports are so unclear here that I suspect the agency of misleading us regarding the accessibility of college opportunities.)

Children of workers are overrepresented in the mass of those excluded from college. Working-class kids make their trips abroad as members of the armed forces, while some middle-class youths, student deferments in hand, spend a junior year at European universities. While the college boy steps on an escalator that moves rapidly upward, the worker's son may step on his father's assembly line and into a job without much promise.

Relatively few colleges, social agencies, schools, or other public institutions mount programs to meet special needs of workers. In many places, even the services provided by "Red Feather" agencies seem more closely geared to middle- than working-class needs.

Inevitably, many workers come to feel they are being dunned and taxed for the benefit of others. Considering the notorious imbalance of our tax structure, they have a point. *In general, the rate of taxation declines as income rises.* This is most obviously true of the state sales taxes. It is almost as true of the federal income tax, under which, in the most extreme cases, some individuals and corporations pay little or no tax at all, though their incomes may exceed $5 million annually. Estimates of total tax loads indicate that thirty-three percent of the income of those earning $3,000 to $5,000 goes to taxes, and only twenty-eight percent of those earning $15,000 or more.

So we have the case of the "invisible" and aggrieved worker. Many of his breed are even found among Mike Harrington's invisible poor. In fact, about one-third of all heads of impoverished families hold down full-time jobs. They are generally not organized, but they are workers. While millions of workers live in poverty, millions more barely escape it. Most are in income brackets between $3,000 and $10,000 (which include some fifty-six percent of all American families), with probably more workers near the bottom than the top.

Reporters often talk about the sweeper who "makes more than a teacher." True, a sweeper in an auto plant in Michigan or New Jersey probably earns more than a teacher in a backwoods school in Mississippi, but his pay is hardly a pot of gold. The sweeper seems to fit a set of hidden assumptions according to which the society is divided, at a magical line, between rich and poor. The premise of this stereotype is that our class structure is a dualism—rich and poor. In this simplified pseudo-Marxian schema, organized workers are seen as part of the richer half, along with bankers, businessmen, professionals. They are, it is assumed, well fed, well cared for, up to their hip in "things," and all-around partners in an open and affluent society.

According to this hidden assumption, all or nearly all the poor are black. They are mostly mothers of large families living on welfare in big city ghettos. The rest (except for a few Appalachian whites) are young blacks who can't find jobs because they are school dropouts or because they are excluded from unions by corpulent and corrupt union bosses. So goes this version of things, especially popular in some college circles. But in fact about eighty percent of the poor are white, and a startling proportion of them work full-time.

In real life the typical worker has lived on a treadmill, except where union contracts have protected him from rises in the cost of living. Everyone else—including the poor and the militant blacks (at least as their image was cast by the media)—*seemed* to be moving forward, while only *they* stood still, waiting in a twilight zone somewhere between hunger and plenty. Some comforts came to them through expanded consumer credit, but the credit exacted high costs in tension, insecurity, and interest rates. They gave increasing taxes to the government, their sons to the army. They seemed to get little in return: only conflict, and sometimes mortal combat with the emerging black poor over jobs, neighborhoods, and schools.

Here is fertile soil for the growth of resentment. For a time, it grew like a weed under the cultivation of George Wallace. A turning point in the presidential campaign may have come when Hubert Humphrey began to see something Wallace always understood: that while many "experts" said the "old issues" were dead, millions of American workers angrily disagreed and wanted a better life. Many workers were ready, in short, for a campaign resembling Harry Truman's historical effort of 1948, a hell-raising campaign about the "old" economic issues (social justice, more and better jobs, more opportunity, good schools, health care, and so forth).

The trap almost sprung by Wallace was set by those "opinion-makers" who dismissed all Wallace supporters as red-necked bigots and opponents of Negro aspirations. Fortunately, they were mistaken. While many workers have no doubt been shook up quite a bit by the black revolt, they have been even more shaken by their own failure to get on in life. Being far wiser than we think, they knew this was not the fault of blacks.

Sadly, some of the Wallaccite resentment was, of course, turned against the poor and the black. Yet it is possible that Wallace's exposed bigotry finally did him in among Northern workers. Industrial workers generally have closer relations with Negroes than any other class, and the big factories in steel, auto, rubber, glass, etc., are probably the most integrated workplaces in the society. Most workers who were drawn to Wallace because he spoke their economic language must have had problems of conscience about blacks with whom they worked and had friendly relations. As Wallace's campaign became more violent in tone, many of them probably grew uneasy and fell away from his camp.

When "opinion-makers" bothered to talk with workers, they

found to their surprise that not all were racists. After talking with Wallace supporters in Flint, Michigan (said to be a hotbed of Wallace sentiment), Mike Hubbard, a student editor of the University of Michigan *Daily*, wrote:

> Certainly these Americans do not identify with red-necked racism. . . . No one ever taught them Negro History, but they grew up with blacks. . . . They don't dislike blacks, they just feel black men shouldn't be given a bigger break than anyone else. The white UAW members as a whole do not believe Wallace is a racist. All they know is what he told them, and he never said he hated blacks. Even the most militant Negro workers I talked to didn't feel there was large-scale prejudice in the Union. They dislike Wallace, but not the men who are voting for him.

Others found many Wallace supporters who would have preferred Robert Kennedy, and some even Eugene McCarthy. *Time* found many such in its 150 interviews across the country, and Haynes Johnson of *The Washington Star* reported this comment from a leader of the Wallace movement in Duluth, Minnesota: "The reason I got into this actually was when Robert Kennedy was shot. . . . That assassination—plus that of Martin Luther King—pointed up for me just how sick it was in this country, and I decided to do something for my country."

The "new issues"—the war on poverty and bureaucracy, the struggles for racial justice and world peace—can be lost unless they are paralleled by campaigns on issues that are important to those millions who are often ignored except by demagogues.

The mythology that obscures the realities of working-class life derives in large part from the success story of unions and what various observers have made of that story. Unions have made great gains in wages, working conditions, fringe benefits, politics; but they started from very far back, and they are still very far from the millennium. Since our society has been late and miserly in providing social insurance, unions have had to push hard in collective bargaining for benefits that don't show up in paychecks. Their focus on such goals has had some negative side effects. Fringe benefits mean more to older than to younger workers—and it is the young who are drawn to men like George Wallace.

Unless unions were to act irresponsibly toward the aging (one of the most impoverished and helpless groups among us), pensions had to be won. Pensions cost money, and that money was subtracted from the wage package won at the bargaining table. Also, older workers need and make more use of hospitalization, medical, and sickness insurance. These too came out of the total package, leaving less for wages. It was humane to help the older worker, and it helped him retire and make way for younger workers. But it was costly. *In the UAW alone, more than 200,000 members have retired and received pension benefits of over $1.5 billion.* Unions sometimes may have overresponded to the older workers, as in seniority and vacation benefits, but one can hardly look at the life of the aging worker and say he has too much.

Unions need to make a new beginning, paying more attention to the needs of the young. An aging and sometimes feeble union leadership needs to refresh itself with activists and new leadership recruited among younger generations. Unless the young become partners in the union movement, they may end up wrecking it. The dramatic rise in the rate of rank-and-file rejection of union contract settlements is a clear signal of distress among workers. Usually, veteran unionists report, the increased rejections result from organized opposition among young workers.

Unions need to do a lot of things, far more than I can mention in this piece. I come from a union that has split from the AFL over some of these issues, including foreign policy, interest in the poor and minorities, and general militancy. I have opposed the Vietnam war, and I think labor should have. I have been involved in the war on poverty, along with many other unionists—though it is remote from many others. Still, one observer says, "If the labor movement in this country moves to the Right, it's not least the fault of those, like Sexton, who will not say a word of criticism of its policies." I leave nothing to the imagination of readers, for we are all deeply aware of the shortcomings of unions. I do not dwell on these flaws for another reason: Whatever their blemishes, unions have given workers the only support and attention they have had—and they needed a lot.

Unions are, however, limited in what they can do for members. They are limited by their own willingness and that of their members to go into battle, to strike. They are limited by the public's willingness to accept strikes. The middle-class liberal himself is often offended, sometimes outraged, by strikers. He may say, "They're selfish and out for themselves." When the desperately poor hospital worker strikes, the liberal will see only the patient as victim; but he will offer no clues as to how else the hospital worker can win a measure of justice. When subway and sanitation workers in New York strike for a modest $3.50 or so an hour (to perform some of the most disagreeable jobs known to man), many middle-class liberals complain bitterly, without also noting that New York's affluent can afford to pay men decent wages to do hard, often dangerous, always unpleasant work.

Many liberals dismiss as unimportant, if not irrelevant, every claim workers make for their attention and support. In few cases do they distinguish workers from union leaders, for some of whom their contempt may be warranted. It is not surprising, considering their mentors, that so much of the young New Left seems to despise the working class.

Not since the early and dramatic days of the CIO have liberals and intellectuals (with some honorable exceptions) shown much sympathetic interest in workers or unions. Now workers come sharply to their view only when they threaten to make life inconvenient or dangerous. A subway strike, shutdown at *The New York Times*, a large vote for Wallace may do the trick—momentarily.

I believe that liberals and moderate leftists—in whose circle opinion-makers are heavily represented—are out of touch with the reality of American working-class life. Many of them live at rarified levels where almost everyone's income is at least $15,000 a year. *Less than ten percent of the nation's families earn that much;* still, they form a mass of between 18 and 20 million people. Those who live within it can easily come to think that all

Americans, except the poor, are living just about as they and their colleagues and neighbors do. Having little contact outside their own circles, and having heard so much about the great gains of unions, they may naturally assume that workers have made it too.

Many of these opinion-makers are men of my generation or near it. Forgetting the ravages of inflation, they may think of $6,000 a year as a fairly substantial income. They may remember maintaining a modest existence on even less. I recall that I was thirty-five years old when I first earned $5,000 a year as president of the nation's second largest local union. Now when I hear that auto workers gross more than $8,000, I too sometimes forget the dollar's decline and assume they've got it made. Relative to most other workers, they have; but they are still far from well-off. These opinion-makers greatly influence what appears in periodicals and dailies, and what is said on TV and radio. They often draft political platforms and write candidates' speeches. When they don't, their readers do. They think of themselves as open-minded and sensitive, and sometimes they are. But too often their politics are introspective—concentrated only on issues that touch them, plus a now-fashionable interest in the poor. . . .

Young workers outnumber all college students, and there are perhaps fifteen or twenty of them for every one disaffected youth upon whom various advocates of a New Politics are counting. The big three in auto alone employ about 250,000 workers who are thirty or under. Total UAW membership of that age group may reach 600,000, with perhaps half of these under twenty-five. Among organized workers, possibly five million are young people under thirty.

Young workers seem to be tougher and to have more staying power than students. Their stake in social change may turn out to be greater and more compelling. Most will never experience the softening effects of well-paid, high-status jobs in the professional, academic, artistic, or business worlds—jobs to which most student rebels are on their way. Knowing they're unlikely to escape individually, workers can grow desperate when denied political hope.

One pollster puts many workers in the "no change" coalition. He misunderstands. Workers simply oppose changes that benefit or seem to benefit others while increasing their own burdens.

The auto industry average wage of $3.80 per hour, though the highest in manufacturing, still does not mean affluence, The UAW (like many other unions) has won comprehensive medical protection, including coverage for psychiatric care of a million members. Its contracts now provide tuition remission plans for members who wish to take classes that may help them escape from dead-end factory jobs. In December of 1968, the hourly wage system came close to ending for perhaps a million UAW members; thus, in one industry, workers have almost scaled an important barrier between them and the middle class; they will be salaried rather than hourly workers. UAW contracts have moved toward the guaranteed annual income and retirement with decent security. Gains have been made, yes; but even auto workers still have far to go.

One friend tells me, "intellectuals still cling to a hopeful and perhaps incorrect view, idealizing the union members as an instrument of class struggle." What members and their unions try to do, at best, is not class struggle in any classic sense. Their conscious antagonists are the employer and the conservative legislator, not the "capitalist system." Yet their efforts have profoundly influenced American life. And unionists have tasted enough of victory so that they generally do not believe in the "final conflict" for which the "prisoners of starvation" must arise.

Those publicists who seek such an apocalypse will not find unionists mounting the barricades with the swiftness and pleasure of student rebels or black militants. Unionists have learned a hard lesson after almost a century of fierce bloodletting on the picket line: *That combat is the last, not the first, resort.* Unionists have possibly been too moderate in this respect, for open conflict sometimes is the only way to rally people and get what you want. But they have learned many other good ways to get on with it. They will not be found burning down their own neighborhoods to prove a point, or otherwise sacrificing their own ranks in unproductive, self-destructive conflict. In this respect, interestingly, some black militants seem to be taking a rather active interest in labor studies. Most militants, coming from poor families, are interested in the "old issues" (opportunity, jobs, etc.) and in ways of organizing people for effective action. A similar interest in unions has not come to the campus, thanks to the myth of the middle-class worker and other academic folklore.

Workers and their unions have many problems and they need lots of help. On the other side, the middle-class Left may find itself isolated if it accepts the standard mythology about workers. If they are to create a New Society, liberals and radicals need to become aware of socially excluded workers and find avenues of communication with them, as well as with Negroes, Latin Americans, and the oppressed poor generally.

[1969]

BLACK STUDIES:

Trouble Ahead

by Eugene D. Genovese

No problem so agitates the campuses today as that posed by the growing pressure for black studies programs and departments. The agitation presents special dangers since it can be, and sometimes is, opportunistically manipulated by the nihilist factions of the radical white student movement. For the most part, black students have shown considerable restraint in dealing with dubious white allies and have given strong indication of being much more interested in reforming the universities than in burning them down. The black student movement, like some parts of the white radical student movement and very much unlike others, represents an authentic effort by young people to take a leading role in the liberation of an oppressed people and, as such, exhibits impressive seriousness and developing sophistication. The political forms that the agitation takes and the deep frustrations from which it stems nonetheless open the way to reckless elements among black, as well as white, student militants.

The universities must now choose between three courses: a principled but flexible response to legitimate black demands; a dogmatic, repressive adherence to traditional, liberal, and essentially racist policies; and a cowardly surrender to all black demands, no matter how destructive to the university as an institution of higher learning or to American and Afro-American society in general. This last option, which has been taken in a notable number of places, ironically reflects as much racism in its assumptions and implications as the second, and it takes little skill in prophecy to realize that its conclusion will be a bloodbath in which blacks are once again the chief victims. Yet the debate over black studies proceeds without attention to the major features of the alternatives; it proceeds, in fact, in a manner that suggests the very paternalistic white racism against which so many blacks are today protesting.

The demand for black studies and for special black studies departments needs no elaborate explanation or defense. It rests on an awareness of the unique and dual nature of the black experience in the United States. Unlike European immigrants, blacks came here involuntarily, were enslaved and excluded from access to the mainstream of American life, and as a result have had a special history with a profoundly national-cultural dimension. Unlike, say, Italo-Americans, Afro-Americans have within their history the elements of a distinct nationality at the same time that they have participated in and contributed immensely to a common American nationality. Despite the efforts of many black and some white scholars, this paradoxical experience has yet to be explored with the respect and intellectual rigor it deserves.

This essential justification for black studies, incidentally, raises serious questions about the demands by white radicals for "ethnic studies" and for special attention to people from the "third world," especially since the term "third world" is, from a Marxist and revolutionary point of view, a reactionary swindle. These demands, when sincere, have their origin in a proper concern for the fate of Mexican-Americans, Puerto Ricans, Asians, and other ethnic groups in a white-racist culture, but the study of the attendant problems does not, at least on the face of it, require anything like an approach similar to that of black studies. For the most part, the discrimination against these groups is largely a class question, requiring sober analysis of class structure in America; for the rest, much of the racism directed against these minorities can be traced directly to the by-products of the enslavement of blacks by whites and the ideology derived therefrom. In any case, the issues are clearly different, for the black question is simultaneously one of class and nationality (not merely minority ethnic status), and it is therefore a disservice to the cause of black liberation to construct a politically opportunist equation that can only blur the unique and central quality of the black experience in the United States.

The duality of the black experience haunts the present debate and leads us immediately into a consideration of the ideological and political features of the black studies programs. It is, at best, irrelevant to argue, as DeVere E. Pentony does in the April 1969 issue of the *Atlantic*, that all professors of history and social science bring a particular ideology and politics to their classroom and that a black ideological bias is no worse than any other. There is no such thing as a black ideology or a black point of view. Rather there are various black-nationalist biases, from left-wing versions such as that of the Panthers to right-wing versions such as that of Ron Karenga and other "cultural nationalists." There are also authentic sections of the black community that retain conservative, liberal, or radical integrationist and antinationalist positions. Both integrationist and separatist tendencies can be militant or moderate, radical or conservative (in the sense generally applied to white politics in relation to social questions). The separatists are riding high today, and the integrationists are beating a retreat; but this has happened before and may be reversed tomorrow. All these elements have a right to participate in the exploration of black historical and cultural themes. In one sense, the whole point of black studies programs in a liberal arts college or university ought to be to provide for the widest and most vigorous exchange among all these groups in an atmosphere of free discussion and mutual toleration. The demand for an exclusively black faculty and especially the reactionary demand for student control of autonomous departments must be understood as demands for the introduction of specific ideological and political criteria into the selection of faculty and the composition of programs. Far from being proposals to relate these programs to the black community, they are in fact factionally based proposals to relate them to one or another political tendency within the black community and to exclude others. The bloody, but by no means isolated, feud between black student factions on the UCLA campus ought to make that clear.

One of the new hallmarks of white racism is the notion of one black voice, one black experience, one black political community, one black ideology—of a black community without an authentic inner political life, wracked by dissension and ideological struggle. In plain truth, what appears on the campuses as "what the blacks want" is almost invariably what the dominant faction in a particular black caucus wants. Like all people who fight for liberation, blacks are learning the value of organizational discipline and subordination to a firm and united line of action. Sometimes, the formulation of particular demands and actions has much less to do with their intrinsic merits or with the institution under fire than with the momentary balance in the struggle for power within the caucus itself. This discipline presents nothing unprincipled or sinister, but it does present difficult and painful problems, which must be evaluated independently by those charged with institutional and political responsibility in the white community.

The pseudo-revolutionary middle-class totalitarians who constitute one temporarily powerful wing of the left-wing student movement understand this dimension, even if few others seem to. Accordingly, they support demands for student control as an entering wedge for a general political purge of faculties, a purge they naïvely hope to dominate. These suburban putschists are most unlikely to succeed in their stated objectives of purging "reactionaries," for they are isolated, incoherent, and without adequate power. But they may very well help to reestablish the principle of the campus purge and thereby provide a moral and legal basis for a new wave of McCarthyism. The disgraceful treatment of Professors Staughton Lynd and Jesse Lemisch, among many who have been recently purged from universities by both liberal and right-wing pressure, has already set a tone of renewed repression, which some fanatical and unreasoning left-wing militants are unwittingly reinforcing. If black studies departments are permitted to become political bases and cadre-training schools for one or another political movement, the door will be open for the conversion of other departments to similar roles; that door is already being forced in some places.

Those blacks who speak in harsh nationalist accents in favor of all-black faculties, departmental autonomy, and student power open themselves to grave suspicions of bad faith. The most obvious objection, raised sharply by several outstanding black educators in the South, concerns the systematic raiding of black colleges by financially stronger white ones. The shortage of competent black specialists in black history, social science, and black culture is a matter of general knowledge and concern. Hence, the successful application of the all-black principle in most universities would spell the end of hopes to build one or more distinguished black universities to serve as a center for the training of a national Afro-American intelligentsia. One need not be partial to black nationalism in any of its varieties to respect the right of black people to self-determination, for this right flows directly from the duality of their unique experience in the United States. Even those who dislike or distrust black nationalism as such should be able to view the development of such centers of higher education as positive and healthy. If there is no place in the general American university for ideological homogeneity and conformity, there is a place in American society for universities based on adherence to a specific ideology, as the Catholic universities, for example, have demonstrated.

Responsible black scholars have been working hard for an end to raiding and to the scattering of the small number of black professors across the country. Among other obstacles, they face the effort of ostensibly nationalist black students who seek to justify their decision to attend predominantly white institutions, often of high prestige, by fighting for a larger black teaching staff. The outcome of these demands is the obscurantist nonsense that black studies can and should be taught by people without intellectual credentials since these credentials are "white" anyway. It is true that many black men are capable of teaching important college-level courses even though they do not have formal credentials. For example, the Afro-American tradition in music, embracing slave songs, spirituals, blues, jazz, and other forms, could probably be taught best by a considerable number of articulate and cultured, if sometimes self-taught, black musicians and freelance critics who are largely unknown to the white community. But few good universities have ever refused to waive formalities in any field when genuine intellectual credentials of a non-academic order could be provided. What has to be resisted firmly is the insanity that claims, as in one recent instance, that experience as a SNCC field organizer should be considered more important than a Ph.D. in the hiring of a professor of Afro-American history. This assertion represents a general contempt for all learning and a particular contempt for black studies as a field of study requiring disciplined, serious intellectual effort—an attitude that reflects the influence of white racism, even when brought forth by a black man.

The demand for all-black faculties rests on the insistence that only blacks can understand the black experience. This cant is nothing new: It forms the latest version of the battle cry of every reactionary nationalism and has clear antecedents, for example, in the nineteenth-century German Romantic movement. To be perfectly blunt, it now constitutes an ideologically fascist position and must be understood as such. The general reply to it —if one is necessary—is simply that the history of every people can only be written from within and without. But there is a specific reply too. However much the black presence has produced a unique and distinctly national Afro-American experience, it has also formed part of a broader, integrated national culture. It would be absurd to try to understand the history of, say, the South without carefully studying black history. Any Southern historian worth his salt must also be a historian of black America —and vice versa—and if so, it would be criminal to deny him an opportunity to teach his proper subject. Certainly, these remarks do not add up to an objection to a preference for black departmental directors and a numerical predominance of blacks on the faculty, if possible, for every people must write its own history and play the main role in the formation of its own intelligentsia and national culture. These measures would be justified simply on grounds of the need to establish relations of confidence with black students, for they involve no sacrifice of principle and do not compromise the integrity of the university. But preference and emphasis are one thing; monopoly and ideological exclusion are quite another.

We might mention here the problem of the alleged "psychological need" of black people to do this or that or to be this or that in order to reclaim their manhood, reestablish their ostensibly lost dignity, and God knows what else. There is a place for these questions and in certain kinds of intellectual discussions and in certain political forums, but there is no place for these questions in the formation of university policy. In such a context they represent a benevolent paternalism that is neither more nor less than racist. Whites in general and university professors and administrators in particular are not required to show "sympathy," "compassion," "understanding," and other manifestations of liberal guilt feelings; they are required to take black demands seriously—to take them straight, on their merits. That is, they are required to treat political demands politically and to meet their responsibility to fight white racism while also meeting their responsibility to defend the integrity and dignity of the university community as a whole.

Only if the universities have a clear attitude toward themselves will they be able to fulfill their duty to the black community. Our universities, if they are to survive—and their survival is problematical—must redefine themselves as institutions of higher learning and firmly reject the role of cadre-training schools for government, business, or community organizations of any kind. Blame for the present crisis ought to be placed on those who, especially after World War II, opened the universities to the military, to big-business recruitment, to the "fight against Communism," to the CIA, and to numerous other rightist pressures. If Dow Chemical or ROTC belongs on a college campus, so does the Communist Party, the Black Panthers, the John Birch Society, the Campfire Girls, or the Mafia for that matter. Students have a clear political right to organize on campuses as Democrats, Republicans, Communists, Panthers, or whatever, provided their activities are appropriate to campus life, but the universities have no business making special institutional arrangements with this or that faction off campus and then putting down other factions as illicit. And government and business represent political intrusions quite as much as do political parties. The same is true for the anachronistic and absurd practice of having American universities controlled by boards of trustees instead of by their faculties in consultation with the students. In short, the black studies question, like the black revolt as a whole, has raised all the fundamental problems of class power in American life, and the solutions will have to run deep into the structure of the institutions themselves.

What the universities owe to black America is what they owe to white America: an atmosphere of freedom and dissent for the pursuit of higher learning. Black people have largely been excluded in the past, for the atmosphere has been racist, the history and culture of black people have been ignored or caricatured, and access to the universities themselves has been severely circumscribed. Black studies programs, shaped in a manner consistent with such traditional university values as ideological freedom and diversity, can help to correct this injustice. So can scholarships and financial assistance to black students and special facilities for those blacks who wish to live and work with some degree of ethnic homogeneity. But no university is required to surrender its basic standards of competence in the selection of faculty or the admission of students. If not enough black students are equipped to enter college today, it is because of atrocious conditions in lower education. The universities can take a few steps to correct this injustice, but the real fight must take place elsewhere in society and must be aimed at providing black communities with the financial resources, independence, and autonomy necessary to educate their people properly from the earliest appropriate ages. There are limits to what a particular institution like a university can do, and it dare not try to solve problems that can be solved only by the political institutions of society as a whole. And above all, no university need surrender its historical role and essential content in order to right the wrongs of the whole political and social system; it need only reform itself to contribute to a solution of the broader problems in a manner consistent with its character as a place of higher learning with limited functions, possibilities, and responsibilities.

Black studies programs have two legitimate tasks. First, they can, by their very nature, provide a setting within which black people can forge an intelligentsia equipped to provide leadership on various levels of political and cultural action. Black studies programs themselves can do only part of this job. For that reason many able and sophisticated sections of the Black Student Alliance organizations wisely call on their brothers and sisters to participate in these programs, but also to specialize in medicine, engineering, sociology, economic analysis, or in fact any scientific or humanistic field. They know that only the emergence of a fully developed intelligentsia, with training in every field of knowledge, can ultimately meet the deepest needs of the black community. In this respect, notwithstanding strong elements of nihilism in their own organizations, their seriousness, maturity, discipline, and realism stand in striking contrast to the childish anti-intellectualism of those bourgeois whites who currently claim to speak for the radical student movement and who impose upon it their own version of generational revolt.

Second, black studies can help immeasurably to combat the racism of white students. The exclusion of whites from the faculty and student body of the black studies programs would therefore defeat half the purpose of the programs themselves. Undoubtedly, there are problems. To the extent that black students view these courses as places of refuge where they can rap with their brothers, they are certain to resent the white presence, not to mention a possible white numerical predominance among the student body. Black students who want an exclusively black setting are entitled to it—in a black university. They are not entitled to tear any institution apart to suit their present mood. The universities owe black people a chance to get a liberal or technical education, but that debt can only be paid in a way consistent with the proper role of the university in society. Beyond that, no university may safely go. If it tries, the result can only be the end of any worthwhile higher education. The inability of so many radical whites to grasp this obvious point is especially galling. It ought to be obvious that the elite schools will protect themselves from this kind of degradation, even if they continue to accept the degradation that accompanies complicity with the war machine and with big business. It is the others—the ones serving the working-class and lower-middle-class youth—that will perish or be transformed into extensions of low-grade high schools. Universities must resist the onslaught now being made against them by superficially radical bourgeois students who have exploited the struggles over black studies programs to advance their own tactical objectives. Fortunately, these elements do not speak for the radical student movement as a whole but represent only a tendency within it; the internal diversity of organizations like SDS, for example, far exceeds the level revealed in the press.

No matter how painful some of the battles are or will become, the advent of black studies programs represents a momentous step toward the establishment of relations of equality between white and black intellectuals. But if these programs are to realize their potential in support of black liberation and in the fostering of genuinely free and critical scholarship, our universities must resolve honestly the questions of limits and legitimacy. Those who blindly ignore or cynically manipulate these questions, and the reforms they imply, corrupt the meaning of black studies and risk the destruction of institutions necessary to the preservation of freedom in American life.

[1969]

THE CASE FOR PROFESSIONALISM

by Robert Brustein

In such a state of society [a state of democratic anarchy], the master fears and flatters his scholars, and the scholars despise their masters and tutors; young and old are alike; and the young man is on a level with the old, and is ready to compete with him in word and deed; and old men condescend to the young and are full of pleasantry and gaiety; they are loth to be thought morose and authoritative, and therefore they adopt the manners of the young. . . .

PLATO, *The Republic*, BOOK VIII

Among the many valuable things on the verge of disintegration in contemporary America is the concept of professionalism—by which I mean to suggest a condition determined by training, experience, skill, and achievement (by remuneration, too, but this is secondary). In our intensely Romantic age, where so many activities are being politicized and objective judgments are continually colliding with subjective demands, the amateur is exalted as a kind of democratic culture hero, subject to no standards or restrictions. This development has been of concern to me because of its impact upon my immediate areas of interest —the theater and theater training—but its consequences can be seen everywhere, most conspicuously in the field of liberal education. If the amateur is coequal—and some would say, superior

—to the professional, then the student is coequal or superior to the professor, and "the young man," as Plato puts it in his discourse on the conditions that lead to tyranny, "is on a level with the old, and is ready to compete with him in word and deed."

As recently as five years ago, this proposition would have seemed remote; today, it has virtually become established dogma, and its implementation is absorbing much of the energy of the young. Although student unrest was originally stimulated, and rightly so, by such external issues as the war in Vietnam and the social grievances of the blacks and the poor, it is now more often aroused over internal issues of power and influence in the university itself. Making an analogy between democratic political systems and the university structure, students begin by demanding a representative voice in the "decisions that affect our lives," including questions of faculty tenure, curriculum changes, grading, and academic discipline. As universities begin to grant some of these demands, thus tacitly accepting the analogy, the demands escalate to the point where students are now insisting on a voice in electing the university president, a role in choosing the faculty, and even a place on the board of trustees.

I do not wish to comment here on the validity of individual student demands—certainly, a student role in university affairs is both practical and desirable, as long as that role remains advisory. Nor will I take the time to repeat the familiar litany of admiration for the current student generation—it has, to my mind, already been sufficiently praised, even overpraised, since for all its intrinsic passion, intelligence, and commitment, the proportion of serious, gifted, hardworking students remains about what it always was (if not actually dwindling, for reasons I hope soon to develop). I do want, however, to examine the analogy, which is now helping to politicize the university, and scholarship itself, because it seems to me full of falsehood.

Clearly, it is absurd to identify electoral with educational institutions. To compare the state with the academy is to assume that the primary function of the university is to govern and to rule. While the relationship between the administration and the faculty does have certain political overtones, the faculty and administration can no more be considered the elected representatives

of the student body than the students—who were admitted after
voluntary application on a selective and competitive basis—can
be considered freeborn citizens of a democratic state: The relationship between teacher and student is strictly tutorial. Thus,
the faculty member functions not to represent the student's interests in relation to the administration, but rather to communicate
knowledge from one who knows to one who doesn't. That the
reasoning behind this analogy has not been more frequently
questioned indicates the extent to which some teachers are refus-
ing to exercise their roles as professionals. During a time when
all authority is being radically questioned, faculty members are
becoming more reluctant to accept the responsibility of their wisdom and experience and are, therefore, often willing to abandon
their authoritative position in order to placate the young.

The issue of authority is a crucial one here, and once again we
can see how the concept of professionalism is being vitiated by
false analogies. Because *some* authority is cruel, callow, or indifferent (notably the government in its treatment of certain urgent
issues of the day), the Platonic *idea* of authority comes under attack. Because some faculty members are remote and pedantic,
the credentials of distinguished scholars, artists, and intellectuals
are ignored or rejected, and anyone taking charge of a classroom
or a seminar is open to charges of "authoritarianism." This explains the hostility of many students toward the lecture course—
where an "authority" communicates the fruits of his research,
elaborating on unclear points when prodded by student questioning (still a valuable pedagogical technique, especially for beginning students, along with seminars and tutorials). Preferred
to this, and therefore replacing it in some departments, is the discussion group or "bull session," where the student's opinion
about the material receives more attention than the material itself, if indeed the material is still being treated. The idea—so
central to scholarship—that there is an inherited body of knowledge to be transmitted from one generation to another loses
favor because it puts the student in an unacceptably subordinate
position, with the result that the learning process gives way to a
general free-for-all in which one man's opinion is as good as another's.

The problem is exacerbated in the humanities and social sciences with their more subjective criteria of judgment; one hardly senses the same difficulties in the clinical sciences. It is unlikely (though anything is possible these days) that medical students will insist on making a diagnosis through majority vote, or that students entering surgery will refuse anesthesia because they want to participate in decisions that affect their lives and, therefore, demand to choose the surgeon's instruments or tell him where to cut. Obviously, some forms of authority are still respected, and some professionals remain untouched by the incursions of the amateur. In liberal education, however, where the development of the individual assumes such weight and importance, the subordination of mind to material is often looked on as some kind of repression. One begins to understand the current loss of interest in the past, which offers a literature and history verified to some extent by time, and the passionate concern with the immediate present, whose works still remain to be objectively evaluated. When one's educational concerns are contemporary, the material can be subordinated to one's own interests, whether political or aesthetic, as the contemporary literary journalist is often more occupied with his own ideas than with the book he reviews.

Allied to this problem, and compounding it, is the problem of the black students, who are sometimes inclined to reject the customary university curriculum as "irrelevant" to their interests, largely because of its orientation toward "white" culture and history. In its place, they demand courses dealing with the history and achievements of the black man, both in Africa and America. Wherever history or anthropology departments have failed to provide appropriate courses, this is a serious omission and should be rectified: Such an omission is an insult not only to black culture but to scholarship itself. But when black students begin clamoring for courses in black law, black business, black medicine, or black theater, then the university is in danger of becoming the instrument of community hopes and aspirations rather than the repository of an already achieved culture. It is only one more step before the university is asked to serve propaganda purposes, usually of an activist nature: A recent course, demanded by black law students at Yale, was to be called something like "white capitalist exploitation of the black ghetto poor."

On the one hand, the demand for "relevance" is an effort to make the university undertake the reparations that society should be paying. On the other, it is a form of solipsism, among both black students and white. And such solipsism is a serious threat to that "disinterestedness" that Matthew Arnold claimed to be the legitimate function of the scholar and the critic. The proper study of mankind becomes contemporary for future man; and the student focuses not on the outside world, past or present, so much as on a parochial corner of his own immediate needs. But this is childish, in addition to being Romantic, reflecting as it does the student's unwillingness to examine or conceive a world beyond the self. And here, the university seems to be paying a debt not of its own making—a debt incurred in the permissive home and the progressive school, where knowledge was usually of considerably less importance than self-expression.

In the schools, particularly, techniques of education always seemed to take precedence over the material to be communicated; lessons in democracy were frequently substituted for training in subjects; and everyone learned to be concerned citizens, often at the sacrifice of a solid education. I remember applying for a position many years ago in such a school. I was prepared to teach English literature, but was told no such subject was being offered. Instead, the students had a course called *Core*, which was meant to provide the essence of literature, history, civics, and the like. The students sat together at a round table to dramatize their essential equality with their instructor; the instructor—or rather, the coordinator, as he was called—remained completely unobtrusive; and instead of determining answers by investigation or the teacher's authority, they were decided upon by majority vote. I took my leave in haste, convinced that I was witnessing democracy totally misunderstood. That misunderstanding has invaded our institutions of higher learning.

For the scholastic habits of childhood and adolescence are now being extended into adulthood. The graduates of the *Core* course, and courses like it, are concentrating on the development of their "life styles," chafing against restrictions of all kinds (words like "coercion" and "co-option" are the current jargon), and demanding that all courses be geared to their personal requirements and individual interests. But this is not at all the function of the university. As Paul Goodman has observed, in *The Community of Scholars,* when you teach the child, you teach the person; when you teach the adolescent, you teach the subject through the person; *but when you teach the adult, you teach the subject.* Behind Goodman's observation lies the assumption that the university student is, or should already be, a developed personality, that he comes to the academy not to investigate his "life style" but to absorb what knowledge he can, and that he is, therefore, preparing himself, through study, research, and contemplation, to enter the community of professional scholars. In resisting this notion, some students reveal their desire to maintain the conditions of childhood, to preserve the liberty they enjoyed in their homes and secondary schools, to extend the privileges of a child- an ' youth-oriented culture into their mature years. They wish to remain amateurs.

One can see why Goodman has concluded that many of the university young do not deserve the name of students: They are creating conditions in which it is becoming virtually impossible to do intellectual work. In turning their political wrath from the social world, which is in serious need of reform (partly because of a breakdown in professionalism), to the academic world, which still has considerable value as a learning institution, they have determined, on the one hand, that society will remain as venal, as corrupt, as retrogressive as ever, and, on the other hand, that the university will no longer be able to proceed with the work of free inquiry for which it was founded. As an added irony, students, despite their professed distaste for the bureaucratic administration of the university, are now helping to construct—through the insane proliferation of student-faculty committees—a far vaster network of bureaucracy than ever before existed. This, added to their continual meetings, confrontations, and demonstrations—not to mention occupations and sit-ins—is leaving precious little time or energy either for their intellectual development, or for that of the faculty. As a result, attendance at classes has dropped drastically; exams are frequently skipped; and papers and reports are either late, underrescrached, or permanently postponed. That the university needs improvement goes without saying. And students have been very helpful in breaking down its excesses of impersonality and attempting to sever its ties with the military-industrial complex. But students need improvement too, which they are hardly receiving through all this self-righteous bustle over power. That students should pay so much attention to this activity creates an even more serious problem: The specter of an ignorant, uninformed group of graduates or dropouts who (when they finally leave the academic sanctuary) are incompetent to deal with society's real evils or to function properly in professions they have chosen to enter.

It is often observed that the word *amateur* comes from the Latin verb "to love"—presumably because the amateur is motivated by passion rather than money. Today's amateur, however, seems to love not his subject but himself. And his assault on authority—on the application of professional standards in judgment of his intellectual development—is a strategy to keep this self-love unalloyed. The permanent dream of this nation, a dream still to be realized, has been a dream of equal opportunity —the right of each man to discover wherein he might excel. But this is quite different from that sentimental egalitarianism which assumes that each man excels in everything. There is no blinking the fact that some people are brighter than others, some more beautiful, some more gifted. Any other conclusion is a degradation of the democratic dogma and promises a bleak future if universally insisted on—a future of monochromatic amateurism in which everybody has opinions, few have facts, nobody has an idea.

[1969]

THE BLACK PANTHERS

by Theodore Draper

The Black Panther Party was formed in Oakland, California, in October 1966 by two young black nationalists, Huey P. Newton, then twenty-five, and Bobby Seale, five years older. The guiding spirit and dominant personality was—and is—Newton. His family, which he once described as "lower class, working class," moved from Louisiana, where he was born, the youngest of seven children, to California. He graduated from two-year Merritt College, in Oakland, where he met Seale. At the school they took their first step toward nationalist political activity by joining a local Afro-American Association, which soon proved insufficiently militant for them. Newton wanted to become a lawyer, Seale an actor. About a year at San Francisco Law School convinced Newton that he was not cut out to be a lawyer. Seale spent almost four years in the army, the last six months in the stockade because, he later claimed, "I opposed racism in the top brass, [in] a lieutenant colonel," and he was given a "bad conduct discharge" one month before the end of his four-year term. He then drifted from odd job to odd job without getting very far in his chosen career. One evening, during an argument at a party, Newton slashed a black auto worker with a steak knife, and spent eight months in jail for the assault. After his release, he and Seale got together again, and according to one version, Seale stimulated his renewed political activity by giving him *The*

Wretched of the Earth by Frantz Fanon to read.[1] When some of their younger friends at Merritt formed a Soul Students Advisory Council to demand a "black curriculum," they took an interest in it. An incident in Berkeley apparently led them to go much further. It seems that a white policeman tried to arrest Seale for reciting poems from a chair at an outdoor café and thereby blocking the sidewalk. A fight ensued; no one was arrested. But Newton and Seale thereupon decided to give up the Soul Students Advisory Council and to form a broader organization called the Black Panther Party for Self-Defense. The panther reference came from the symbol of the Lowndes County Freedom Organization which had been launched in Alabama six months earlier. The name was later shortened to Black Panther Party to emphasize a larger goal than "self-defense." While working in the Poverty Office in Oakland in October 1966, they wrote a 10-point Platform and Program for the new party.

The Panthers seemed at first little more than another self-appointed local band of black nationalists in an urban ghetto Their chief claims to publicity were their armed patrols which drove through the streets of Oakland and their mannerism of saying "right on" as often as possible.[2] Their first important con-

---

[1] Fanon is another author who might be read more carefully by some black nationalists in America. Of the first congress of the African Cultural Society held in Paris in 1956, he wrote: "But little by little the American Negroes realized that the essential problems confronting them were not the same as those that confronted the African Negroes. The Negroes of Chicago only resemble the Nigerians or the Tanganyikans in so far as they were all defined in relation to the whites. But once the first comparisons had been made and subjective feelings were assuaged, the American Negroes realized that the objective problems were fundamentally heterogeneous. . . . Negritude therefore finds its first limitation in the phenomena which take account of the formation of the historical character of men. Negro and African-Negro culture broke up into different entities because the men who wished to incarnate these cultures realized that every culture is first and foremost national, and that the problems which kept Richard Wright or Langston Hughes on the alert were fundamentally different from those which might confront Leopold Senghor or Jomo Kenyatta." *The Wretched of the Earth* (New York: Grove Press, 1964), p. 216.
[2] "Well, its time for us right now to decide what we're gonna do, where we gone do it, how we gone do it, and when we gone do it. If you ain't decided whether if you gone do it, then go on home, right on. Because when

vert early in 1967 was Eldridge Cleaver, author of *Soul on Ice,* who, like Malcolm X, had been converted to Elijah Muhammad's Black Muslims in prison and had sided with Malcolm X after the latter's break with them. Newton impressed Cleaver, who was then working for *Ramparts,* by leading a group of armed Panthers into the office of the magazine and daring a policeman to shoot him. The police flinched that time, but in a shoot-out in Oakland in October 1967, Newton was wounded, one policeman was killed, another was wounded, and Newton was given a two-to-fifteen year sentence for manslaughter.

From this unlikely beginning, the Black Panthers have become a formidable national movement. In three years, they claimed to have set up about thirty chapters, the largest in the Oakland-San Francisco area and Chicago, which may have had a membership of about five thousand at its peak, but this was probably cut to about half or less by the end of 1969 as a result of police persecution. Besides Cleaver, the movement was able to win over, though only for a time, such well-known figures as H. Rap Brown and Stokely Carmichael of SNCC. It entered into a coalition with the white-based Peace and Freedom Party, which ran Cleaver for President in the 1968 election. Its program of black nationalism was endorsed by the Students for a Democratic Society in March 1969, and it precipitated the SDS split in June that same year. It is allied with a new League of Revolutionary Black Workers, which has sprung up in the automobile industry and particularly threatens the United Auto Workers' Union. It has provided much of the inspiration, leadership, and program of the black student unions in universities, colleges, and high schools.

The Black Panther ideology, which is all that concerns us here, is only partially revealed by the official platform and rules. Point 1 of the 10-point Platform and Program adopted in October 1966 reads: "We want freedom. We want power to determine the destiny of our Black Community." Other points call for full employ-

---

we say free Huey, that's only the first step to freeing all people. . . . Huey's gonna be set free or nobody gone be free, right. Right on. If Huey can't be free what goddamn bit of difference does it make if you're free, right on. FREE HUEY NOW." (Kathleen Cleaver at the May Day 1969 rally in San Francisco, *The Black Panther,* 11 May 1969, p. 11.)

ment, decent housing, education, and the liberation of all black prisoners from all prisons and jails. Point 10, the most nationalistic, states: "We want land, bread, housing, education, clothing, justice, and peace. And as our major political objective, a United Nations-supervised plebiscite to be held throughout the black colony in which only black colonial subjects will be allowed to participate, for the purpose of determining the will of the black people as to their national destiny." The rest of the document hints at the meaning of this demand by quoting the justification for secession in the Declaration of Independence of 1776. But this was hardly a fully thought out program of black nationhood. It left the decision to a vaguely formulated plebiscite, and even if the "black colony" decided to "dissolve the political bands" connecting it to the existing United States, it did not make any effort to suggest what the next step might be.

The full Black Panther ideology emerges only in the pages of its official organ, *The Black Panther,* published weekly in Berkeley, California, and especially in the articles, speeches, and interviews of its main leaders. Some early columns by Newton in *The Black Panther* in 1967, before he was imprisoned, have been collected in a little pamphlet. These essays show that Newton's basic ideas were formed before his shoot-out with the Oakland police and derived mainly from Fanon, Malcolm X, Mao Tsetung, and Fidel Castro.

For Newton, the "Black colony of Afro-America" has a unique and universal mission. "The Black people in America are the only people who can free the world, loosen the yoke of colonialism, and destroy the war machine." No other country can defeat this "monster" as long as it continues to function. "But Black people can make a malfunction of this machine from within." In order to do so, however, "they must have the basic tool of liberation: the gun"—a lesson attributed to Mao Tse-tung and Malcolm X. Guerrilla warfare is the tactical method that goes with the basic tool. As a self-styled "Vanguard Party," the Black Panthers do not think they have to do the whole job by themselves. They need only set an example and the masses will follow. Newton's own example leaves little to the imagination: "When the masses hear that a gestapo policeman has been executed while sipping coffee at a counter, and the revolutionary executioners fled without being traced, the masses will see the validity of this type of approach to resistance." The pamphlet, however, tells little about the ultimate objective beyond proposing that "Black people must now move, from the grassroots up through the perfumed circles of the Black bourgeoisie, to seize by any means necessary a proportionate share of the power vested and collected in the structure of America."

Since 1967, Black Panther ideology has become a more fully developed, if not essentially different, system. In essence, it is a hybrid made up of revolutionary black nationalism and what is by now an old friend, "Marxism-Leninism." As a result, it is not quite like any other black nationalism or any other Marxism-Leninism. For example, no other "Marxist-Leninists" have ever identified themselves with the *Lumpenproletariat*, the most rootless and degraded elements in capitalist society, whom Marx and Engels regarded as a "dangerous class" whose conditions of life destined it to play a reactionary role.[3] The peculiar "amalgam," as Trotsky would have called it, of bits and pieces from Frantz Fanon, Malcolm X, Mao Tse-tung, Ernesto Che Guevara, Régis Debray, and others, is typical of the kind of do-it-yourself Marxism-Leninism that has come into vogue.[4] It is especially charac-

---

[3] A statement by Chief of Staff David Hilliard was headed "Lumpen-Proletarian Discipline Versus Bourgeois Reactionism," the former representing the Panther ideal. (*The Black Panther*, 9 August 1969, p. 11.) Later, Hilliard wrote of "our duty as revolutionaries, as members of the lumpen proletariat (field niggers)." (Ibid., 6 September 1969, p. 2.) According to Gene Marine, Huey Newton's brother Melvin recalled that Huey from the outset "saw the Panthers even then as a potential mass movement, something that the *Lumpenproletariat* could relate to. Huey had a lot of confidence in the *Lumpenproletariat*; he believed it could be rallied to its own cause." (Gene Marine, *The Black Panthers*, New York: New American Library, 1969, p. 37.) In *The Communist Manifesto* of 1848, Marx and Engels referred to the *Lumpenproletariat* as follows: "The 'dangerous class,' the social scum, that passively rotting mass thrown off by the lowest layers of old society, may, here and there, be swept into the movement by a proletarian revolution; its conditions of life, however, prepare it far more for the part of a bribed tool of reactionary intrigue." (Section 1: "Bourgeois and Proletarians.") I know of no other self-styled Marxist or Marxist-Leninist group which has ever before tried to glorify the *Lumpenproletariat*.
[4] The Panthers are nothing if not catholic in their revolutionary taste. To the list above should be added Lumumba, Garvey, Ho Chi Minh, as well as

teristic of movements that have invited themselves into the
Marxist-Leninist tradition from the outside, bringing with them
their own national or particularist folkways and shopping among
all the current versions of the doctrine for those features or formulas which happen to suit or please them the most. In this respect Black Pantherism resembles Castroism but has gone much
farther in asserting its individuality.

Organizationally, the party also shows its hybrid makeup. It is
headed by a Central Committee, a term traditionally used in the
Communist movement. But unlike such parties, which are
headed by Secretaries or General Secretaries, the Panthers' No. 1
leader is the Minister of Defense—Huey P. Newton. The idea
that the top leadership should reside in the military commander,
who simultaneously fulfills the chief political role, derives di-

---

Marx, Lenin, Stalin, and Trotsky, judging from the following testimonials:

George Murray: "Our thinking is inspired by Che Guevara, Malcolm X,
Lumumba, Ho Chi Minh and Mao Tse-tung." (*The Black Panther*, 12 Octo-
ber 1968, p. 14.) Huey P. Newton: "Brother Mao put that quite well, and
we will follow the thoughts of Chairman Mao." (Ibid., 3 March 1969, p. 2.)
Field Marshal D. C. [Don Cox]: "And we dig on all the people that held up
the light before: Marx, Lenin, Stalin, Mao, Fidel, Che, Lumumba and
Malcolm. And we dig on all the people who are holding up the light now,
Ho Chi Minh, those brothers and sisters in Al Fatah, those bad Palestinian
Guerrillas, those comrades in arms in Asia and Latin America. . . ." (Ibid.,
20 April 1969, p. 16.) Bobby Seale: "You got your Red Books, hold your
Red Books up and tell the brothers where we getting some new ideology
from. We're saying like Huey P. Newton said, 'that we're going to follow
the thoughts of Chairman Mao.'" (Ibid., 11 May 1969, p. 11.) Ray "Masai"
Hewitt: "We dig Chairman Mao, Ho Chi Minh, we have a profound love
for Fidel Castro." (Ibid., 31 May 1969, p. 16.) For Trotsky, see footnote 9.

Toward the end of 1969, *The Black Panther*'s favorite foreign Communist seemed to be Kim Il Sung, President of North Korea, judging from
the space alloted to his statements and speeches.

As for supporting Al Fatah, the Panthers are so anti-Israel that their
organ attempted to justify the assassination of Senator Robert Kennedy
instead of President Richard Nixon or California's Governor Ronald Reagan
on the ground that "Kennedy was a fence-sitter on the Middle East situation," whereas "the Nixons and Reagans are consistent, open fascists." *The
Black Panther* explained: "But when a liberal asks for respect from third-
world people by 'helping' and then deceived them by representing enemy
interests, the liberal can expect retaliation." ("Sirhan—A Revolutionary,"
ibid., 23 March 1969, p. 14.)

rectly from Régis Debray. After Newton comes Bobby Seale, the Chairman, reminiscent of Mao Tse-tung's favorite title. The next in line is the Minister of Information, Eldridge Cleaver (in absentia). No. 4 is the Chief of Staff, David Hilliard, an ex-longshoreman. The Central Committee also contains Field Marshals (Underground); Minister of Education, Ray "Masai" Hewitt; Minister of Foreign Affairs (unnamed); Minister of Justice (unnamed); Prime Minister (unnamed); Communications Secretary, Kathleen Cleaver, wife of Eldridge Cleaver; and Minister of Culture, Emory Douglas, who is also the party's Revolutionary Artist.[5] With Newton in prison and Cleaver in exile, the two main leaders have been Seale and Hilliard. Local Panther groups duplicate the national setup with a Deputy Chief of Staff and Deputy Ministers.

What is most individual about the Black Panthers is, of course, what concerns them most—the "national liberation" of the "black colony" in the "white mother country."

The last term was apparently originated by Eldridge Cleaver —probably out of Frantz Fanon, who also used the term "mother country" for the French colonial regime. It indicates the difference between the Panthers and the Back-to-Africa nationalists. The mother country of the Panthers' black colony is white America, not Africa. Since the mother country is not Africa, there is no reason to go back to it. Without denying the existence of vestigial ties with Africa, the Panthers strongly reject and oppose the Back-to-Africa line, even in an attenuated form which they contemptuously call "cultural nationalism."

Newton has sternly disapproved of the return to African culture.

---

[5] On 11 February 1968 Eldridge Cleaver announced publicly that the Black Panthers and SNCC had "worked out a merger." SNCC sources claimed that he had gone too far and that the two groups had merely formed an "alliance." In any case, three SNCC leaders were appointed to leading posts in the Panthers' Central Committee—Stokely Carmichael as Prime Minister, H. Rap Brown as Minister of Justice, and James Forman as Minister of Foreign Affairs. Brown and Forman resigned from their posts in August 1968, Carmichael in July 1969. For a version of the Panthers-SNCC tie-up and possible misunderstanding, see Julius Lester, *Revolutionary Notes* (New York: Richard W. Baron, 1969, pp. 144–49).

Cultural nationalism deals with a return to the old culture of Africa and that we are somehow freed by identifying and returning to this culture, to the African cultural
stage of the 1100s or before then. . . . Somehow they
[cultural nationalists] believe that they will be free
through identifying in this manner. As far as we are concerned, we believe that it's important for us to recognize
our origins and to identify with the revolutionary Black
people of Africa and people of color throughout the world.
But as far as returning per se to the ancient customs, we
don't see any necessity in this.

Other Panther leaders have been less polite. Former Minister
of Education George Mason Murray has called this kind of pro-
African cultural nationalism "a fixation in a people's development like a half-formed baby," "reactionary and insane and
counterrevolutionary," "a bourgeois-capitalist scheme, to confuse
the masses of people, so that they will not assault the city halls,
the bank tellers, and managers, or seize control of community
schools." A programmatic article in *The Black Panther* ridiculed
the "fools running around who declare that they are 'just trying
to be black' by wearing dashikis and bubas and who tell black
people that they should relate to African customs and African
heritage that we left 300 years ago, that this will make them free,
that reading black history will make them better."

Ironically, therefore, the Panthers have decided that the emphasis on Black Studies programs has gone too far. In May 1969
the present Minister of Education, Ray "Masai" Hewitt, denounced Black Studies as a "new trick bag." He told of having
talked with "many brothers from Africa" who "are not hung up
on Swahili or Arabic." Of the new vogue for the "natural head,"
he reported: "Very few of the African brothers that we met had
what could be called a 'Natural head.' They just had hair. You
couldn't call it one of those custom-tailored natural heads. They
never spoke Swahili and every time we told them that there
were brothers here studying Swahili for the revolution, they
burst out laughing." He added: "The movement toward Black
Studies in colleges and other Black cultural programs have become a fixation. At one point in the revolutionary development
of our people it was a revolutionary step. Instead of taking it as

a beginning step many cultural nationalist opportunist boot-licking cowards and freaks have latched onto it."

The nationalist side of the Panthers' ideology makes them emphasize black unity; the "Marxist-Leninist" side makes them emphasize a social revolution by both blacks and whites. Unlike other nationalist groups, the Panthers do not believe that the "black colony" can liberate itself alone. "We have two evils to fight, capitalism and racism," Newton says. "We must destroy both racism and capitalism." The Panthers realize that they cannot destroy capitalism and install socialism in the black community without destroying capitalism and installing socialism in the white community. As a programmatic statement put it: "There must be a revolution in the white mother country, led by white radicals and poor whites, and national liberation in the black and third-world colony here in America. We can't triumph in the colony alone because that is just like cutting one finger off a hand. It still functions, you dig it. No, when we deal with this monster we must deal with it totally."

This suggests that the Panthers expect the black nationalist revolution to be part of, or accompanied by, a larger white social revolution. In this respect, therefore, they do not belong in the line of pure black nationalist movements, such as Garvey's. In fact, by the summer of 1969, Newton seemed to be appealing to all "people," not merely to black people. In a significant restatement of his party's position in a Negro magazine of mass circulation, he immediately struck a populist, rather than a nationalist, note: "The Black Panther Party is the people's party. We are fundamentally interested in one thing, that is, freeing all people from all forms of slavery in order that every man will be his own master." He blamed capitalism for all that was wrong, and made socialism the precondition for freedom of any kind, including self-determination. "All members of the working class must seize the means of production," he wrote. "This, naturally, includes black people." He might have added that this, naturally, includes even more white people. Though the Black Panthers remained a purely black organization, its leaders found a way around that restriction, too. In July 1969, they sponsored a National Conference for a United Front Against Fascism in Oakland, California, out of which came local National Committees to Combat Fascism. One black-nationalist organ noted caustically that over ninety percent of those attending the Oakland conference were white. These National Committees were designed to take in whites, especially those who, as Chairman Seale put it, had been asking why they could not join the Panther Party. "We see the National Committees as the political organizing bureaus of the Black Panther Party," Seale declared. In another period, these committees might have been called front organizations, but something was different—this was a black movement with a white front instead of a white movement with a black front. At the conference itself, Seale also disclosed that the Panthers favored creating a "new party, the new workers' party, or what have you," on the model of the "liberation fronts" in Africa and Latin America, "an American Liberation Front composed of all the people of this nation." The National Committees were presumably conceived as "organizing bureaus" of the new party as well as of the Black Panther Party.

Thus the Panthers had changed in three short years from a largely black nationalist organization to a black revolutionary organization, and the latter in turn had led it to become a black organization with white appendages. Nevertheless, at the Oakland conference and elsewhere, Panther leaders have always made clear that they consider themselves to be the vanguard of the social as well as of the nationalist revolution. Those white organizations which recognize their leadership must expect the treatment meted out to the Students for a Democratic Society at the Oakland conference. When the SDS delegates objected to the Panther proposal for "community control of the police," they were given a dose of the special brand of Pantherite polemics. Seale soon called them "those little bourgeois, snooty nose motherfucking S.D.S.'s." [6] Only that faction in the SDS which was willing to accept this type of "criticism" and come back for more

---

[6] Panther political style is *sui generis*. In his rebuke of the SDS, Seale continued: ". . . And that we're gonna kick their motherfucking ass, if they don't freeze on their shit, and we want to make that clear to them. . . . And we'll beat those little sissies, those little school boy's ass if they don't try to straighten up their politics. So we want to make that known to S.D.S. and the first motherfucker that gets out of order had better stand in line for some kind of disciplinary actions from the Black Panther Party." (*The Black Panther*, 9 August 1969, p. 12.) Another Panther leader once defined the revolution as follows: "The only way we can do this is to pick up the

was permitted to remain in the Panthers' good graces. The Panthers' relations with various white organizations and groups have varied from time to time. At the Oakland conference, the Panthers found the official American Communist Party most useful, and a well-known party intellectual, Dr. Herbert Aptheker, who has specialized in American Negro history, was permitted to make an interminable theoretical address to the meeting. Seale later explained that the American Communists had taken the Panther's criticism to heart and had done more work for the conference than any other white organization.[7]

Despite these good marks for the American Communists, the Panthers' favorite white revolutionary group continued to be the Young Patriots, a band of transplanted young Southerners located in Chicago. Another Chicago-based group, the Young Lords Organization, originally a street gang in a Puerto Rican community, has also been recognized by the Panthers as authentically revolutionary. A Chinese-American "Red Guard" in San Francisco has copied the Panthers' style and program, and there is an American Indian satellite group known as NARP.

This Pantherite shift in line—or, at least, in emphasis—was primarily behind the resignation of Stokely Carmichael. In June 1967, Carmichael had been the beneficiary of Executive Mandate

---

gun. We are gonna walk all across this motherfucking government and say Stick 'em up, motherfuckers—this is a hold up: we come to get everything that belongs to us." (Virgil Morrell, Ibid., 12 October 1968, p. 5.) And in an order purging nineteen members from the Jersey City branch: "The Party will no longer tolerate these counterrevolutionary m——f——s, who by their deeds are harming the interest of the Party and the People. These degenerates have aroused the anger of the people, the people will kill them, and we gonna kill every m——f—— who went along with their s——t." (Ibid., 4 May 1969, p. 7.) The language of "Marxism-Leninism" was never like this.

[7] Seale's exact words were: "And that's just a fascist pig tactic to try to say that the Black Panther Party is led by the Communist Party, and we're not against Communism—we dig Communism. And we have criticisms of the American Communist Party, and lately they're relating to the criticism because we told them they had to put more things into practice, and it seems that they did better than some of the other organizations, because they actually came out and did some degree of work to put the conference over, when we sat down and talked to them." (*The Black Panther*, 9 August 1969, p. 13.)

(as Minister of Defense Newton's early *pronunciamentos* were called) No. 2. In recognition of his distinguished services "in the struggle for the total liberation of Black people from oppression in racist white America," it had invested him with the rank of Field Marshal. In February 1968, Carmichael was elevated to the largely ornamental post of Prime Minister. But Carmichael had come into the Panthers from SNCC, which he had purged of all whites during his chairmanship. He never seems to have been reconciled to the Panthers' idea of coalition with white organizations, let alone a black-white social revolution, and the break on this issue came in July 1969. From his self-imposed "exile" in Guinea, Carmichael charged that the Panthers were "dogmatic, dishonest, vicious and in collusion with whites"—of which derelictions the last was probably the least forgivable. Carmichael charged: "The alliances formed by the party are alliances which I cannot politically agree with, because the history of Africans living in the U.S. has shown that any premature alliance with white radicals has led to complete subversion of blacks by the whites through their direct or indirect control of the black organizations." Cleaver answered for the Panthers that "you cats in SNCC" suffered from a "paranoid fear" of whites because they had had to wrest control of their organization from whites, unlike the Panthers, who had never been in that situation. In fact, the difference between them was not so much that of white control of black organizations as of a black-against-white nationalist revolution versus a black-and-white social-plus-nationalist revolution. The Panthers' "coalitions" with whites have thus far been arranged on the Panthers' terms, though Carmichael obviously doubted that they could continue to have their way in a white-black mass movement "of all the people of this nation." Once Carmichael broke away from the Panthers, he was denounced as nothing more than "a running dog and a lackey."

The loss of Carmichael to the Panthers was less important for the man than for the policy which he represented. The Carmichael-Cleaver dispute reminded one black nationalist editor of the Garvey-Du Bois feud almost fifty years earlier. In both cases, pure-and-simple black nationalism that totally rejected whites was opposed by a more complex and social-minded black nationalism which linked the fates of black and white. In this sense, a historic rift in black nationalism was taking a new but no less irreconcilable form.

Nevertheless, the membership of the Panthers is wholly black, and for that reason they may stand or fall on the persuasiveness of their black nationalist program. Yet it is precisely in this area that they are ideologically most vague and uncertain.

The original proposal in the Platform and Program of October 1966—to hold a United Nations-supervised plebiscite—was clearly an evasion of the issue. It is, of course, highly improbable that the U.N. would or could hold such a plebiscite; at best the proposal passed the problem on to the black voters; and it did not tell them how the Panthers wanted them to vote. There is reason to believe that this evasiveness was deliberate and that the Panther strategists considered any more concrete position premature. At a Peace and Freedom Party forum on 11 February 1968, Cleaver remarked: "It's very important to realize that in moving to gain power, you do not conceal or repudiate the land question, you hold it in abeyance. What you're saying is that we must first get ourselves organized, and then we can get some of this land." Since then, the Panther leaders seem to have had a hard time making up their minds. In an early phase, Newton would go no farther than: "Our problem is unity at this point. We have to unify ourselves. We can handle the colony better than anyone else. We are a colonized people. Many Black communities are like decentralized colonies throughout this country." But what this implied for black American nationhood, he did not say.

A later effort by Chairman Seale at the Anti-Fascist Conference in Oakland in July 1969 was also somewhat tantalizing, if seemingly more definite:

> We are not saying that self-determination of the black people in the black communities is not correct. It is necessary. But we are not saying that black people are a nation just because they are black. We are saying that black people are a nation because they have the same economic oppression that they are subjected to; because they have, number two, a basic psychological makeup in how they react to that environment they exist in; third, because

they describe what's happening; because black people in
the black community, understanding genocide (with number 4 coming up) that the language, psychological
makeup, economic conditions and the (4) geographical
location that black people exist in, generally defined as
ghettos. The geographical location defines, with all four
of those points, black people as a nation, defines Mexican
American people as a nation where they are. Whether
they're split or divided because we are colonialized, because the Third World people are colonialized. That's
what defines a nation. We are not basing it on racism. We
understand nationalism in terms of what a nation is, and
we understand internationalism.[8]

Whatever may be thought of Seale's reasons, this statement
seemed to commit him to the proposition that there was a black
nation in the United States, as well as a Mexican-American nation, even if they were made up of congeries of far-flung
ghettos.[8] Soon afterward, Chief-of-Staff Hilliard added a new
note for which he may go down in history as the originator of a
genuinely novel concept in the annals of international socialism.
He was talking about the SDS opposition to the Pantherite demand for community control or decentralization of the police,
when it occurred to him to say:

To decentralize the community imperialists, and imple-
ment probably on just the community level—Socialism.
And that's probably too Marxist-Leninist for those motherfuckers to understand, but we think that Stalin was very
clear in this concept—that socialism could be implemented in one country, we say it can be implemented in
one community.

And so, if Stalin could have "socialism in one country," the
Panthers, if their Chief of Staff can be trusted, see no reason
why they cannot have "socialism in one community." [9]

---

[8] I have thought it best to give Seale's statement in his own words. *The
Black Panther*'s practice of publishing verbatim texts of verbal statements
makes for colorful if sometimes confusing reading.
[9] This is not the first time that Hilliard invoked the name of Stalin. He had
previously "discovered" Stalin, Lenin, and Trotsky in the following way:

After all this, however, the Panthers' maximum leader, Huey P. Newton, published an article in August 1969 in which he explicitly referred to the blacks in America as a "national minority" and, inferentially, as an "ethnic minority," not a nation. He demanded the freedom "to structure our own communities so that we can determine the institutions of the community that will perpetuate our culture." But it would clearly make a difference to that structure if it were based on the concept of a nation or merely of a national minority.

In September 1969, Newton also decided to change his mind —or at least his "rhetoric"—on what being "colonized" meant. "At one time I thought that only Blacks were colonized," he announced. "But I think we have to change our rhetoric to an extent because the whole American people have been colonized, if you view exploitation as a colonized effect, now they're exploited." In effect, Newton had decided to equate "colonization" with "exploitation." Inasmuch as the whole American people were to his mind "exploited," they were at the same time "colonized." In effect, the change in "rhetoric" enlarged the formerly "black colony" to take in the whole American people, black and white. By enlarging it to take in everyone, Newton effectively emptied the concept of an internal American "colony" of all specific content. If "colonization" means nothing more than "exploitation," there is really no need of the former. Far from making the concept of "colony" more inclusive, the concept of "exploitation" does away with it altogether.

At about the same time, Newton argued that even a separate black America of five or six states could not survive if the rest of the United States remained capitalistic. "We also take into consideration the fact that if Blacks at this very minute were able to secede the union, and say have five states, or six states [sic]. It would be impossible to function in freedom side by side with

"... Our whole thing about discovering the triumvirate of Lenin, Trotsky, and Stalin. It is just a matter of trying to give a very complete picture of history. ... The reason that they fear Joseph Stalin is because of the distorted facts that they have gained through the Western press. The one thing that we respect about Stalin, is that Stalin was able to capture the will of the people." (*The Black Panther*, 20 April 1969, p. 18.) One wonders whether Stalin or Trotsky would be more displeased by the company he was made to keep.

a capitalistic imperialistic country." He implied that enclaves and ghettos made for good "strategy" but might not make for good nationhood:

In other words we're not really handling this question at this time because we feel that for us that it is somewhat premature, that I realize the physiological value of fighting for a territory. But at this time the Black Panther Party feels that we don't want to be in an enclave type situation where we would be more isolated than we already are now. We're isolated in the ghetto areas, and we think this is a very good location as far as strategy is concerned, as far as waging a strong battle against the established order.

The Panther ideologists, if they can be called that, have thus struggled not too successfully with the "nation" that is presumably inherent in their "nationalism." The only one who has tackled the hardest question—the problem of the land—has been Eldridge Cleaver. He once tried to deal directly with "The Land Question and Black Liberation." At one point he came close to what the trouble has been: "Thus, it is not surprising that the average black man in America is schizoid on the question of his relationship to the nation as a whole, and there is a side of him that feels only the vaguest, most halting, tentative and even fleeting kinship with America. The feeling of alienation and dissociation is real and black people long ago would have readily identified themselves with another sovereignty had a viable one existed." Cleaver then went on to argue that no viable alternative sovereignty had ever existed. He had high praise for Marcus Garvey, but it turned out that Garvey "did not solve the specific question of Afro-America and its immediate relationship to the land beneath her feet. The practical prospect of Garvey's actually transporting blacks back to Africa turned most black people off because of a world situation and balance of power that made such a situation impossible." He gave Elijah Muhammad credit for knowing "that he had to deal with Afro-America's land hunger." But Cleaver considered Muhammad tactically wise enough to be "very careful never to identify any specific geographical location when he issued his call for land for Afro-

The Black Panthers 237

America." Stokely Carmichael's thesis of Black Power, Cleaver said, "does not attempt to answer the land question. It does not deny the existence of that question, but rather frankly states that at the present moment the land question cannot be dealt with, that black people must put first things first, that there are a few things that must be done before we can deal with the land question."

Yet Cleaver went on to insist: "The necessity upon Afro-America is to move, now, to begin functioning as a nation, to assume its sovereignty, to demand that that sovereignty be recognized by other nations of the world." But where? The closest Cleaver came to meeting the issue was: "Black Power must be viewed as a projection of sovereignty, an embryonic sovereignty that black people can focus on and through which they can make distinctions between themselves and others, between themselves and their enemies—in short, between the white mother country of America and the black colony dispersed throughout the continent on absentee-owned land, making Afro-America a decentralized colony. Black Power says to black people that it is possible for them to build a national organization on somebody else's land."

What is "sovereignty" without land to be sovereign of? How project "sovereignty" on "somebody else's land"? What is a "decentralized colony"? Is it made up of black ghettos in New York, Chicago, Oakland, and elsewhere, separated from each other by hundreds of miles? Is ghetto "sovereignty" a truly embryonic form of national sovereignty? It may be possible to build a national organization on somebody else's land, but how build a nation on that land?

Cleaver did not raise these questions, but he was not unaware that his notion of "embryonic sovereignty" might need some clarification. He therefore seized on what he considered to be the "parallel" between early Zionism and present-day black nationalism. The Jews, he pointed out, had also been cooped up in Eastern European ghettos. Argentina and Uganda were considered as possible sites for a Jewish homeland before the decision was finally made in favor of Palestine. The Zionists founded a virtual government in exile for a people in exile. Cleaver concluded: "They would build their organization, their government, and then later on they would get some land and set the government and the people down on the land, like placing one's hat on top of one's head. The Jews did it. It worked. So now Afro-Americans must do the same thing."

Cleaver could hardly have chosen a more unfortunate "parallel" for his cause. It is entirely based on the circumstance that the Jewish Zionists in the beginning did not have a national territorial base and were not even sure where it might be. But of one thing the Jewish Zionists were always sure—that they could not set up a national homeland in their East European ghettos. If black nationalism in the United States were prepared to get out of the American ghettos and set up a nation in Africa or elsewhere, the Zionist "parallel" might be helpful, though here again historical differences might dictate against pushing it too far. Black nationalist "Zionism" inevitably heads toward a Back-to-Africa conclusion, which Cleaver and the Black Panthers reject. The "parallel" begins promisingly but ends disastrously for American black nationalism.

In an interview with *Playboy* (October 1968) Cleaver was questioned about the plan adopted by a National Black Government Conference, which met in Detroit in April 1968 for a "Republic of New Africa" to be made up of five Southern states. "Do you think that's a viable plan?" Cleaver was asked. "I don't have any sympathy with that approach," Cleaver replied, "but the Black Panthers feel that it's a proposal black people should be polled on." From Cleaver's articles and the interview, it is hard to see just what kind of concrete, practical approach he would sympathize with.

In some ways, the Panthers have inherited the ambiguous legacy of Malcolm X. Like him, they have moved in the direction of a social rather than a purely nationalist revolution. By adding socialism to nationalism, they had to broaden their horizons to make room for whites as well as blacks, if not in their own organizations, then in some form of "alliance" and "coalition." The Panthers' position has opened them up to attacks on two sides— from those who want a pure and simple black nationalism not dependent for its ultimate success on a white social revolution and those who want a social revolution untainted by black nationalism. It has not been easy for them to maintain their uneasy equilibrium between these two camps.

[1969]

TURNING ON FOR FREEDOM

The Curious Love Affair of Sex and Socialism

by Erazim V. Kohák

My title is not a misprint. The liaison between sex and social-ism, though of long standing, has always been more an affair than a marriage. Except for occasional outbursts of passion, nei-ther partner has been particularly eager to acknowledge the rela-tionship. I am not thinking simply of minirevolutionaries whose buttons proclaim MAKE LOVE NOT WAR. They are at least half in earnest, but anyone who has ever borne arms can attest that the two activities are by no means exclusive. Not only love but death can be a great aphrodisiac.

There are other straws in the wind. Recently I came across an ad in an "underground" journal, in which a self-confessed Port-noy advertised for an "uninhibited F companion interested in *Zen, astrology, existentialism, socialism or anything mod.*" I would have passed it over with a chuckle; but in the same jour-nal the editor proclaims—quite seriously—that a silly bit of sa-distic burlesque called *Che!* is "the *Communist Manifesto* of the now revolution." God help the revolution and, for that matter, sex!

There have been sexual revolutions before, as in England under the Regency or in Germany under Weimar. Sex, it seems, is good, wholesome fun but a bit monotonous; it needs occa-sional sparkling with a Cause. Yet in the past, sex has usually come out of its excursions into Social Significance somewhat battered—though still a favorite. I am not at all sure, however, that the same can be said of social progress. Its excursions into ecstasy have been followed by Queen Victoria in one case, by Adolph Hitler in another. Historical analogies are not an argument, but our experience with *Das Kapital* suggests that it is never wise to pin social progress to any one blueprint, and it might be well to ask what the effect would be if that blueprint came from *The Amorous Drawings* of the Marquis von Bayros.

Plato included community of women among his proposals for a commune-ist society. Budding radical historians regularly supply their over-thirty-five teachers with term papers presenting Plato's *Republic* as an institutionalized sex orgy. But that is a generous misreading of the text. Plato was something of a puritan, both in his preoccupation with the passions and in his distrust of their effect on society. Like his Soviet successors, he was careful to banish all art that might arouse the passions, reserving a grudging place only for early versions of Socialist Realism and Lawrence Welk. His communal mating arrangements were certainly not designed to foster sensuous enjoyment or sexual freedom; their purpose was to protect society from passion, to restrict sex to the clinical function of assuring survival of the species. The tone is quite grim—the only thing gay about Plato was his attitude to male homosexuality. And even that was due less to any regard for sexual freedom than to his acceptance of the mores common to the Athens of his day.

Nor is Plato so unusual. In their everyday attitudes, socialist writers have regularly taken over the prevailing mores of whatever group in society was most receptive to their doctrines. In their prescriptions for the new society, however, they have usually shared Plato's distrust of passion. Marx is no exception. His Victorian contemporaries may have picked out "sexual communism" as by far the most intriguing feature of *The Communist Manifesto* and accused the Communists of having a more varied sex life than they themselves could manage but, again, the text tells a different story.

Marx, we find, does not advocate sexual communism. He accuses the bourgeoisie of having inflicted it upon the wives and daughters of the proletariat. Nor does he thank them for it as a blessing in disguise. He is indignant, and like his detractors he, too, suspects the class enemy is having far more fun in bed than is decent, seducing not only the poor working girl but each others' wives as well. A proper Victorian, Marx disapproves.

So do his followers, if they speak of the matter at all. August Bebel's *The Woman and Socialism* turns out to be anything but a ribald classic. The communes Bebel foresees are incredibly bourgeois, cooperative arrangements of proper Victorian couples, designed to bring household technology to working-class families. Accepting Marx's rather primitive version of the labor theory of value, Bebel is convinced that actual muscular exertion is the only source of value. This places a rigid upper limit on the possible increase in the productivity of labor in value terms—a man can only work so hard. Bebel concludes that *individual* workers can never create enough value to bring the marvels of modern technology within their reach. As with Plato and Marx, not individual sexual freedom but socioeconomic necessity is the basis for his commune-ism.

With the coming of the revolution, matters changed little. The puritanism of the Bolsheviks is notorious. Russian revolutionaries regarded sex as reactionary; they fitted their women into ill-shaped overalls and banned such lures of the devil as cosmetics. The U.S.S.R., Cuba, or the People's Republic of China aspire to match and surpass the capitalists in steel production, but none has the least intention of matching and surpassing even so modest a target as the *Playboy* foldout. Yet the intuitive association of sex and socialism survives all disclaimers. The relationship between sex and socialism may range from legal separation to sodomy, but it is still very much with us; and it requires explanation.

It is not particularly difficult to explain the sex phobia of some socialist theoreticians—and Communist dictators. Though willing to utilize whatever unrests are present in society, including sexual frustration, they are committed not simply to fostering change but to guiding and controlling it. They are committed to building the perfect society and, among men, perfection is never spontaneous. Society is too complex a construct for that. Perfection, as Plato already recognized, must be guided and guarded, and passions are notoriously hard to control. Philosopher kings are puritans virtually *ex officio*.

The opposite phenomenon, the common-law marriage of sex and socialism, is a converse of the Platonic considerations. Socialism and commune-ism are a response to the breakdown of community between man and man. Starting with Feuerbach's *Gesamtmensch*, radicals have sought to end the vicious isolation of individuals—caught in the productive process, joined and separated only by a cash nexus—and to establish a genuine human community. Freedom of sexual contact provides a rather facile symbol for overcoming alienation among men. Even when socialist writers and rulers chose not to use that symbol, their hearers invariably supplied it, and not without reason.

But there is a long and doubtful step between symbol and program. Against the grim background of an outdated puritanism, it may be rather easy to regard every removal of sexual restrictions as a victory for freedom, brotherhood, and enlightenment. The American Left, by and large, has yielded to this temptation. But while sexual freedom might seem an apt symbol of social freedom, it is not at all obvious that it is an adequate *program* for social action.

The sexual revolution seems to bring few of the boons promised by early pioneers who fought for progress in the darkest fifties by adopting gutter language in their classrooms. Dedicated pioneers at Berkeley or at the Grove Press may assure us that more of the same will produce something different, but their assurances grow daily less convincing. For myself, I would prefer to examine the basic premise—how valid is sex, not as personal pleasure or social symbol, but as a blueprint for progress?

I suppose we would all enjoy seeing an all-nude production of, say, Shakespeare's *Tempest*. In a fully-clad world, naked bodies do create a peculiar illusion of freedom, and it would be rather novel. But would it be progress? I doubt it. A naked *Tempest* might be fun, but an all-nude repertory theater would soon prove monotonous. Finally, skin is skin. Its initial dramatic impact might be considerable, but its dramatic possibilities would rapidly be exhausted. Costuming offers a far richer range of creative possibilities. Nudity is a possible form of costuming, and it was rather ludicrous to single it out for the Lord Chamberlain's special attention. But it is costuming which is basic and makes the richness and variety of the stage possible.

A play or, for that matter, a society may well have its roots in "nature"; but the freedom, richness, and imagination it offers its audience or its citizens are a product of art, the conventional elaboration of the natural minimum. A return to "nature" would impoverish the stage and society alike. To the extent that sexual freedom is equated with a "return to nature," it is as poverty-stricken and antihumanistic as primitivism. Freedom is a product of art, not of nature.

The appeal of nudity on stage and primitivism in society is not a function of any creative possibilities they offer, but rather of their apparent simplicity. Primitivism—the "return to nature"—in sex and society alike is an admission of inability to cope with the complexity of both society and costuming. For possibilities are always complex, and ambiguous. There is no possibility for good which does not entail the possibility of evil as well. By contrast, "nature" might offer few possibilities for genuine humanity, for freedom and imagination, but it does offer simplicity. What is natural is good, sex is natural, QED.

But how natural *is* sex? The sheer physical act of copulation may well be said to be natural, but it is also socially irrelevant. When sex becomes a symbol or is no longer a physical act but a relation between two human beings, it is no longer "natural" sex but human sexuality. As such, sex is clearly socially relevant— but it can no longer claim the innocence and simplicity of a natural phenomenon. Human sexuality, like all human activities, is highly conventional. It is socially relevant because it is a social act, and as such, it shares the ambiguity of all distinctly human acts. It can become a vehicle for *Todestrieb* as well as for *Lebenstrieb,* for the desire to dominate and destroy as well as to meet and love the other. Not by accident are love and death the two great aphrodisiacs of human sexuality.

This is the dilemma of any sexual revolution. If its program is simply sex as a physical act and its aim no more than quantitative increase in the number of individual acts of copulation per annum, then it is clear, unambiguous, but also socially irrelevant. If, on the other hand, it claims to free and foster human sexuality, it becomes socially relevant but also ethically ambiguous, a vehicle of destruction as well as of creativity.

Precisely because sex can become a vehicle of death as well as of life, we can no longer sustain the simplistic liberal illusion that drew a simple line between repression (bad) and expression (good) of the sexual impulse. Repression can, of course, become a vehicle for *Todestrieb,* for the killjoy impulse—one look at the hateful expressions in the faces of the defenders of decency is proof enough. But so can sexual expression. Not all sexual expression is necessarily the outcome of the impulse to freedom and joy. Masochism and sadism are the obvious counterinstance. In the terminology of pop revolutionism, sex can be "fascist."

I see a historical justification for this pop terminology. There was certainly nothing tepid or lifeless about the early Nazi movement. It was intense, passionate, thoroughly turned-on and existential, enough so as to satisfy Sartre's German alter ego, Martin Heidegger. The Nazi movement fairly reeked of sex. The Nazi hate sheet, *Der Stürmer,* was consummately pornographic, as crudely, openly, and inarticulately pornographic as the most underground publications of our time—and in rather the same way. The sexuality it dished out in issue after issue was of the sadistic/masochistic variety. Much as in the underground journals of our time, its aphrodisiacs were hate and death, and its pleasure was pain.

The editors of *Der Stürmer* were convinced that the orgy of destruction was justified by the nobility of the cause, an awakening, radicalizing of the German people—turning on—and that the object of its intended destruction, the German Jewry, was eminently worthy of destruction. Anyone who doubted it had sold out to the Jews. But aphrodisiacs have a way of surviving the passions they arouse. Hate remained after the sexual passions it aroused spent themselves in the Night of Long Knives, and once aroused, hate is unselective. Not only the Jews, but all of Europe, including Germany, fell victim to the sadomasochistic orgy of destruction.

The *Todestrieb*-sex of sadism and fascism does have a common basis in passion with the *Lebenstrieb*-sex of freedom and communion. But that minimal common basis does not make it any less antihumanistic, antisocial, and antisocialist. A joyless, brutal travesty like *Che!* and its journalistic counterparts have nothing to do with socialism, even though, like socialism, they are antipuritanical. They oppose puritanism with an orgy of sex as death, not with a celebration of sex as life.

The continuing hold of puritanism on American society cannot be explained simply as an arbitrary imposition on a healthy, happy society by a few vindictive puritans. The "system" sustains it, but it can sustain it only because a great many Americans choose it. Nor is their choice attributable merely to sloth or cowardice. Far more frequently, it is a rather unhappy choice of men who may not regard the tepid, lifeless propriety of bourgeois quasi sexuality as a positive good, but who still see it as a lesser evil to the death-sex orgy of *Der Stürmer* or *Che!* If the heightening of intensity in sexual passion comes to seem equivalent to a celebration of destruction, then even the choice of bourgeois propriety is not dishonorable. It may not make life free and full, but it makes it possible for the children who can laugh and play rather than die in gas chambers.

Still, the choice between not-quite-living and living-unto-death is at best a desperate choice. This is what gives an air of urgency and social significance to the quest for what, in our version of pop nomenclature, we could call "commune-ist" sex. The label has no doctrinal significance. It is at best a strained attempt to affirm the conviction that not only death but also love can be a great aphrodisiac, that intensification of sexuality does not have to mean only destruction of others, but can also mean a communion with others, a meeting of people where they live, in their bodies, a radical and free encounter.

The commune-ist sexual revolution can be found in the communes, rather reminiscent of the religious utopias, which form in the eddies of the rat race. Perhaps three or four couples, sometimes married, sometimes not, share a house, incomes, children, troubles, pleasures, bodies. Often they share a project as well, tutoring underprivileged children, housing the homeless, feeding the hungry. They are very young, though not always in years, and very earnest, and they will tell you, pleadingly, that people are never as free and together as when all clothes and inhibitions come off and that people who share common work and life share common love as well.

Theirs is a rather idyllic vision, easy to sneer at, vulnerable to ridicule. But the freedom and reality of the men and women I know who have adopted this life-style is impressive. Perhaps they have found something. They are certainly convinced of it, convinced that they are acting out the perennial dream of a Peaceable Kingdom. They are convinced they have found the freedom their contemporaries grope for, and present their love-in —or, to give it its older name, *agape*—with their ability to lock loins where most men can at best touch fingertips.

Those of us who have lived a little longer and learned how much men can cheat with their bodies, how independent the barriers among men are of their clothes, might find the symbolism apt but the hope a little naïve. Men's bodies can be naked but their souls fully clad and their daggers drawn. Yet such considerations are out of order now. Let us assume that men can in fact meet, with all barriers gone, once their clothes and sexual inhibitions are down. Let us accept for the moment the personal ideal of the commune of men completely "naked," completely open with each other. How valid is the commune-ist ideal, not as vision, but as blueprint for progress?

Oddly enough, in considering the validity of the commune-ist ideal angelology can be more useful than economics. Angelology is of little value as a descriptive science: There is a dearth of empirical evidence. But for that very reason, it has many uses as a science of pure possibilities. Since presumably neither angels nor devils exist, angelology offers a unique opportunity for projection. And since the commune-ist ideal of complete nakedness, metaphoric as well as literal, proposes nothing short of a Kingdom of Heaven on earth, angelological projection becomes singularly appropriate.

Among angels, we can say, the ideal of a complete communion, a communal existence in which all clothes and barriers to human contact are removed, would be extremely appealing. The Bible tells us that the blessed in God's presence "neither marry nor are given in marriage, but are like the angels in heaven"— presumably live in a continuous love-in, completely open, completely available, and able to meet each other without the limitations of formalized sexuality. Since by definition they are completely free, secure, and good, they need hold nothing back.

By the same token, I suppose, devils never have sex. Being totally evil, devils become incapable of sex, for sex demands a degree of mutual trust of which devils are by definition incapable.

An embrace leaves one's back exposed—and devils could not resist the opportunity. They must get their kicks by reading de Sade and by torturing each other.

Now as any angelologist can tell us, men are neither devils nor angels. They are not totally evil, and so are able to trust each other enough to lock loins and meet in love. At the same time, men are not angels, *per essentiam* and not merely *per accidens* as the Marxists would have us believe. We need not assume that they are evil, actively seeking to do harm one to another, though what we have called *Todestrieb*-sex suggests that they are also that, at least *per accidens*. But even if men are not evil, they are weak, and weakness is the *Urmutter* of cruelty. Frightened men will hurt each other, even without evil intent, simply out of fear.

Commune-ist visionaries will, to be sure, insist that their communes will change just that and produce a "new socialist man" who will be secure and free of fear. But even if, *per impossibile*, a commune were able to give its members such security that none would feel the need to strike out at the other, its members, unlike angels, would still not be omniscient. Men can hurt one another quite unwillingly, and hurt deeply. For angels, love-ins may be the *modus operandi;* for men they are at best a rather ambiguous *desideratum* precisely because in the case of men, being naked, literally and figuratively, means not only being wide open to communion but also being wide open to hurt. It takes a radical trust to be radically open, and among men there are severe limitations on trusting—not because men are unwilling to trust, but most of all because, not being omniscient, men are not unlimitedly trustworthy.

This is why, though a commune may be a symbol of a hope and even a tangible achievement of a few men and women for a very limited time, it is not an adequate model for restructuring society. Among men, clothes and inhibitions are not only barriers to communication, but also very necessary means of protection.

Not only protection against ill will, but protection against folly. Lack of omniscience survives even in Walden II or a Soviet Socialist Republic. Alienation, as Milovan Djilas pointed out recently, is not only a source of frustration, but also the barrier which protects individual freedom.

At moments, I can hear an echo of the different drummer whom my younger comrades hear in their communes. I wish them well, they are achieving something precious. I hope they keep the echo alive, and that we will not lose all ability to hear it. That deafness is what puritanism is all about, and it is death. Radical openness—commune-ism, if you wish—must remain as a perennial, insubstantial hope: the glimpse of the Kingdom. But I would hesitate to join them. Not for fear of being hurt, but for fear of hurting, because I am not all good and all wise. The ideal they are acting out is an ideal, not a blueprint for society. Man requires the protection of "clothes," barriers which not only bar but also protect.

This finally is the significance of the sexual conventions with which the young, unaware of their own capacity for hurting, are so impatient. Marriage is one such convention; so are the limitations, not imposed but formalized by society, on where, when, and with whom one can be radically open—and expect radical openness in return.

In this sense, the young are right—sex is the experimental working model for socialism. The commune-ist (and communist) vision of a society in which all "clothes" and barriers—the "bourgeois" freedoms and civil rights, the limitations of "formal" democracy—are removed and men are left entirely naked to each other is a perennial vision. Its appeal is its promise of radical commune-ion. Yet in practice the destruction of formal limitations has never created a society which could give its people bread, freedom, and justice. In every instance it has created a nightmare of men and societies broken and destroyed by well-meaning leaders who, even had they been all good, still were not omniscient. True believers may speak of these episodes as "deformations," but they are quite inevitable, a strict consequence of removing barriers which may bar men from perfect communion but also protect them from their own lack of omniscience.

Socialism for men rather than for angels, socialism with a

human face, is finally the art and the science of creating barriers between man and man which offer the maximum opportunity for communication while providing the maximum protection against human ignorance and ill will. It becomes a deeply antihumanistic nightmare when it mistakes men for angels, and sees its sole task in removing all barriers among them.

I am not a fascist because I am not a devil, and because I believe that men can communicate and meet one another. But I am not a communist because I know that men are not angels, and cannot be trusted implicitly, not even in love. I am a socialist because I believe that conventions can be replaced, that they do not have to be strained and straining relics of an irrational past but can be molded and shaped rationally, in the service of human security and human freedom. I am a socialist and a democrat because I know that a radical ideal can serve men only if it can create conventions which do this.

This, finally, applies to sexual as well as to social revolution. Radicalization, social or sexual, is not an unmitigated good. It creates opportunities, but opportunities for destruction and death as well as for love and life. If it becomes a basis for a rational restructuring of social and sexual conventions in the service of men, it offers hope. If it becomes a basis for destruction of social and sexual conventions, it no longer matters whether the ideal it invokes is love or death. The result is the same.

[1969]

ACKNOWLEDGMENTS

Many of the articles in this collection first appeared in the pages of *Dissent*. I am also grateful to the following for granting permission to reprint material:

"The Mystical Militants" by Michael Harrington. Copyright © 1966 by Harrison-Blaine of New Jersey, Inc. Reprinted by permission of *The New Republic*.

" 'Confrontation Politics' Is a Dangerous Game" by Irving Howe. First published in *The New York Times Magazine*. © 1968 by The New York Times Company. Reprinted by permission.

"Unreason and Revolution" by Richard Lowenthal. Copyright © 1969 by Encounter Ltd. Reprinted by permission.

"The New Reformation" by Paul Goodman. First published in *The New York Times Magazine*. © 1969 by The New York Times Company. Reprinted by permission.

"Black Studies: Trouble Ahead" by Eugene D. Genovese. Copyright © 1969 by The Atlantic Monthly Company, Boston, Mass. Reprinted by permission.

"The Case for Professionalism" by Robert Brustein. Copyright © 1969 by Harrison-Blaine of New Jersey, Inc. Reprinted by permission of *The New Republic*.

"The Black Panthers" by Theodore Draper was first published in somewhat different form in *Commentary*. From *The Rediscovery of Black Nationalism* by Theodore Draper. Copyright © 1969, 1970 by Theodore Draper. All rights reserved. Reprinted by permission of The Viking Press, Inc.